The Public Journalism
Movement in America

The Public Journalism Movement in America

Evangelists in the Newsroom

DON H. CORRIGAN

PRAEGER

**Westport, Connecticut
London**

Library of Congress Cataloging-in-Publication Data

Corrigan, Don H. 1951–
    The public journalism movement in America : evangelists in the
    newsroom / Don H. Corrigan.
        p.   cm.
    Includes bibliographical references and index.
    ISBN 0–275–95781–0 (alk. paper)
    1. Journalism—Social aspects.   2. Journalistic ethics.
    3. Journalism—Objectivity.   I. Title.
    PN4749.C67   1999
    302.23—dc21   98–50240

British Library Cataloguing in Publication Data is available.

Library of Congress Catalog Card Number: 98–50240
ISBN: 0–275–95781–0

First published in 1999

Praeger Publishers, 88 Post Road West, Westport, CT 06881
An imprint of Greenwood Publishing Group, Inc.
www.praeger.com

Printed in the United States of America

The paper used in this book complies with the
Permanent Paper Standard issued by the National
Information Standards Organization (Z39.48–1984).

10 9 8 7 6 5 4 3 2 1

Copyright Acknowledgments

The author and publisher gratefully acknowledge permission to use the following:

Excerpts from Davis Merrit, *Public Journalism & Public Life: Why Telling the News Isn't Enough.*
Hilldale, New Jersey: Lawrence Erlbaum Associates, 1995 (Reprinted 1998).

All tables and graphs from the *St. Louis Journalism Review*.

Excerpts from the *St. Louis Journalism Review*.

Excerpts from *Breaking the News* by James Fallows. Copyright © 1996 by James Fallows. Reprinted
by permission of Pantheon Books, a division of Random House, Inc., and reprinted by permission of
The Wendy Weil Agency, Inc. © 1996 by James Fallows.

Contents

Tables and Graphs

Preface

This book would not have been possible without my association for more than a score of years with the monthly *St. Louis Journalism Review* (*SJR*). I once heard former *St. Louis Post-Dispatch* editor William Woo paraphrase the famous "gin joint" lament of Humphrey Bogart in Casablanca with regard to the *SJR*. Woo told a journalism dinner, that "of all the towns where I could have ended up being a newspaper editor, I had to find myself in one with the *Journalism Review*." Woo had felt the sting of the *Review*'s barbs, quips, and commentary, but he was nonetheless pleased to have it around. He noted that journalism in St. Louis was the better for it.

The *St. Louis Journalism Review* is one of the few surviving, original, local-oriented journalism reviews. Every town of any size should have one. Every month, *SJR* writers from academia and the working press get together at Balaban's Restaurant in the Central West End of St. Louis to discuss the metro area's journalism scene and to plan the next issue. Review founder and publisher Charles L. Klotzer dedicated much of the July/August 1995 issue of the *SJR* to the emerging public journalism—and that helped spark my interest in writing a book about the phenomenon of public journalism.

Klotzer's editorial in the 1995 issue opposing public journalism surprised me. Klotzer had spent much of his life criticizing the news media in the *SJR* for caring too much about profits and for not caring enough about making "public life go well," as the supporters of public journalism are fond of repeating. But Klotzer's overwhelming concern about journalistic independence—the proper separations—made him reluctant to get aboard the public journalism bandwagon. As I became more involved in writing this book, Klotzer continually provided moral support and constantly sent me the latest clippings from the trade press on what was happening with the evangelists and their evolving public journalism evangel.

In 1995, Klotzer turned the *St. Louis Journalism Review* over to Webster University in St. Louis, where I had been teaching journalism for almost two decades. The presence of the *SJR* on our campus was a great impetus for this book project. The new editor, Edward Bishop, joined publisher emeritus Klotzer in sending me clips and information from the journalism trade press about public journalism. In 1996, Cole Campbell, a leading public journalism practitioner, took the reins as editor of the *St. Louis Post-Dispatch*. Within a few months, "refugees from public journalism" were showing up at the *SJR*'s monthly meetings to describe the changes being made to the *Post*'s newsroom culture under Campbell's public journalism philosophy.

Campbell's arrival in St. Louis has been fortuitous for this book. The *St. Louis Journalism Review* has followed his leadership at the *Post* closely, and I have drawn from a number of those *SJR* stories for this book. In 1997, the *SJR* and I, with the cooperation of the Webster University School of Communications, launched an extensive survey of journalism professors and daily newspaper editors around the country regarding their attitudes about public journalism. The survey project produced a number of articles for monthly issues of the *Review*. Some of the results of this project have been incorporated in Part II of this book.

The *St. Louis Journalism Review* has provided an excellent meeting ground, an agora if you will, for practicing journalists and journalism academics in St. Louis. It has been a perfect meeting ground for me, since I have worn both hats throughout my career. As a professor of journalism at Webster University, I have had the enjoyable experience of engaging in many hours of critical discussion about journalism and the communication industry with academic colleagues and students. As editor-in-chief of two weekly newspapers, the *Webster-Kirkwood Times* and the *South County Times*, with headquarters in Webster Groves in suburban St. Louis, I have had the irreplaceable experience of working every day in the field in which I teach.

There is no replacement for the practical knowledge of working in journalism for those who profess to teach it. One of the themes that becomes apparent in this book is that too much of the public journalism philosophy is theoretical and academic, and too many of the gurus of public journalism lack the experience of day-to-day journalism—experience that should be a prerequisite to launching any grandiose reform of the news industry.

Public journalism's gurus spend a lot of time talking about the need for today's journalists to connect with the public. I have to wonder how many of them have had the experience of listening to the phone calls—both ecstatic and angry— from their readers on a daily basis. I have to wonder how many of them have connected with citizens while delivering newspapers after a paper carrier has disappeared on a lark. I have to wonder how many of them have dealt with advertisers, politicians, late-breaking obits, computer crashes, and newsroom deadlines—and actually made decisions about what should make the news for their community on a regular basis.

Arguing that many public journalism advocates lack the insight and perspective provided by practical experience in the field is not simply some egoistic exercise in journalistic machismo or "the culture of toughness," to draw from the vocabulary of the public journalists. The concepts of traditional journalism—detachment, balance, editorial independence, and that elusive ideal of objectivity—are ideas that guide a real profession. They were not hatched in a foundation seminar or an academic think tank. They are concepts that grew out of everyday journalism experience over more than two centuries of reporting in America.

This book is about that journalistic concept of providing balance. Most of the tracts that have been written about public journalism have supported its arguments and the projects that have been initiated in its name. The scholarly papers presented at the Association for Education in Journalism and Mass Communication (AEJMC) have been mostly adulatory toward public journalism. The Pew Center and Kettering Foundation have put together countless brochures, manuals, and promotional videos hyping public journalism. Books that have been written about public journalism by Arthur Charity, James Fallows, and Davis "Buzz" Merritt have all been flattering of the new movement in journalism.

There is certainly a need for essays, analyses, videos, and texts that take a more critical look at public journalism. As of this writing, no foundations have stepped forward to finance critical research on public journalism. This book is a critical work, and a labor of love, for journalism, accomplished without foundation support. The premise of this book is not that today's journalism doesn't have problems. Contemporary journalism in America has plenty of failings, but they are not the failings outlined by the public journalists in their critique. In fact, the most significant weaknesses in the practice of journalism are likely to be aggravated by the adoption of the public journalism formula.

ACKNOWLEDGMENTS

As noted, this book would not have been possible without my association with the monthly *St. Louis Journalism Review* (*SJR*). In addition to Charles L. Klotzer and Edward Bishop, the *Review*'s board of editorial advisers has been most helpful. They include: Frank Absher, Safir Ahmed, Harry James Cargas, Donna Charron, David Cohen, Bonita Cornute, Irving Dilliard, Peter Downs, Eileen Duggan, Gregory Freeman, Ted Gest, David Garino, Ellen Harris, Daniel Hellinger, Dennis Judd, Roy Malone, Michael Murray, Selwyn Pepper, Steve Perron, Joe Pollack, Lou Rose, Mark Sableman, Michael Sorkin, and Sharon Stevens.

The faculty members at Webster University, too numerous to mention by name, also have been extremely supportive of this project. In 1997, Webster University President Richard Meyers and Vice President Neil George presented me with the Presidential Scholar Award and allowed me to outline my research in public journalism at a faculty dinner. I am most appreciative of their support, as well as for the encouragement of Debra Carpenter, dean of the Webster University School of Communications, and Arthur Silverblatt, a longtime media scholar and mentor who served as my department chair for almost 20 years. Ron Pennington in university research was instrumental in helping to design the survey instrument used for Part II of this book and in tabulating the information from respondents.

As a professor at Webster University, I must also thank the many students who have shown patience with my regular lectures as well as with my occasional outbursts on the topic of public journalism. I would like to especially single out the students in the newspaper production classes and those who have served on the weekly campus Journal, which I advise. Recent journal editors such as Tom Kaminski, Staci Fuemmeler, Becky Vollmer, Becky Mollenkamp, and Scott Shackford have been particularly helpful.

My colleagues at Times Newspapers in suburban St. Louis, where I have worked as an editor and reporter for more than 20 years, have shown terrific patience during the process of writing this book. My business partner, Dwight Bitikofer, who has kept the Times solvent for two decades with his dedication to hard work and honest business practices, must be singled out. My news-editorial office mates, Kevin Murphy, Marty Harris, and Ursula Ruhl, deserve mention as well. I also would like to acknowledge the support of friends in the Missouri Press Association and the Independent Free Papers of America.

Last, but certainly not least, I must acknowledge the support of my family: Christa, Brandon, and my wife, Susanne. They have granted me the time and the space at home to get this project completed. I regret the hours I missed with them in order to finish this book. Hopefully, my two youngsters will one day read this book and understand why I was so driven to complete it. My son, Brandon, already is taking an interest in journalism and the newspaper business. If I may borrow some words from public journalism philosopher Jay Rosen: May there be a "journalism worth doing" when the time comes for Brandon to join the company of the ink-stained wretches.

Introduction

My first introduction to public (or civic) journalism, both as an idea and as a movement, came in June 1995 at the annual convention of Investigative Reporters and Editors (IRE). I was a panelist at the convention on the topic of investigative reporting in the suburbs, using planning and zoning commissions as a valuable resource for looking into land deals and conflicts of interest. At the convention, I learned that the panel would consist of me and Bob Greene, the respected editor of Long Island's *Newsday* and founder of IRE.

It was certainly an honor to serve on a panel with Greene, but it was also quite intimidating. Greene talked about business tycoons of the Big Apple, Manhattan politicos, and mafioso contractors in describing his years of coverage of Long Island and the boroughs of New York City. My observations on petty corruption, slick real estate attorneys, and conflict-of-interest problems paled in comparison to Greene's war stories. But Greene was gracious and a gentleman and he found ways to weave my comments into a coherent presentation as he moderated and presented for our rather cozy panel.

After our session, I followed Greene to his next panel presentation where he talked to fledgling journalists about the nuts and bolts of city hall reporting. Unlike today's public journalists, he did not speak about deliberative conversations with quasi-official layers of the community in order to get a sense of the citizens agenda. Greene did tell the greenhorn reporters not to be in awe of the titles of government officials. He suggested they make friends with the city clerk and the mayor's secretary—"bring them a cup of coffee once in awhile"—because they could be especially helpful in getting information for stories.

When it came to the question and answer session, I was surprised to find Greene stumped by the question of a young graduate student in journalism. She simply asked him: "Mr. Greene, what do you think about public journalism?" Greene looked befuddled. After all, isn't all journalism public? What would private journalism consist of? When she asked her question again, the eyes lit up on the old warhorse of journalism. He made the observation that there are a lot of good news programs on the public television station in New York City. "They do some good stuff," noted Greene. To this day I am still more satisfied with Greene's answer than with anything I've heard from the philosophers and spokespersons for public journalism.

The young graduate student, no doubt, found a more satisfactory answer from another panel at the 1995 IRE convention, the one in which advocate Jay Rosen sparred with adversary Rosemary Armao over the efficacy of public journalism. Rosen lectured his skeptical audience and admonished them for their tired thinking. "We seize on the most fruitless cliché imaginable—objectivity—when we should be talking about things like public judgment and civic capacity. We debate whether readers should drive the agenda, when we should be discussing what makes a reader into a good citizen. We talk about what's good for journalism, what journalism is and is not, when the real issue is what communities, regions and the republic as a whole need in order to solve their problems. Public journalism puts life first. This, if anything, is what's radical about it."[1]

I took my notes from Rosen's civics lesson in Miami back to St. Louis and wrote my first story on public journalism for the July/August issue of the *St. Louis Journalism Review* (*SJR*). Charles L. Klotzer, then the publisher of the *SJR*, devoted most of the issue to public journalism with articles by Everette Dennis of the Freedom Forum, and William Woo, then-editor of the *St. Louis Post-Dispatch*. At our next editorial board meeting, a number of the *SJR* writers complained about all the coverage of public journalism. Some of the comments included: "We don't need to give any more space to public journalism." "This stuff is for a bunch of professors, it's not going to go anywhere." "I've read these articles, and I still don't know what it is."

No one at that *SJR* meeting could have predicted that in less than 18 months, William Woo would be out as editor of the *Post-Dispatch*, only to be replaced by one of the leading practitioners of public journalism, Cole Campbell. Some of the *Post-Dispatch* reporters at that 1995 *SJR* meeting, would have laughed at the suggestion that in a little more than two years, they would be in newsroom sessions on building "civic capacity," "public judgment," and "connecting" with citizens. They also had no idea that they would be losing some of their valued colleagues at the *Post* in a couple of years because of public journalism—colleagues who would leave the paper because they had no desire to conform to a new "newsroom culture" compatible with public journalism.

AN EPIPHANY

The evangelists of the public journalism philosophy are fond of writing and lecturing about their "epiphanies"—the point at which they decided to abandon traditional journalism in favor of Rosen's new brand of journalism that "puts life first." My interest in writing a book about public journalism was sparked at that 1995 IRE convention when advocate Rosen and IRE's Armao squared off over the issue of whether this reform movement was good for the news business. But my epiphany—the point at which I knew I had to write this book—came one spring day when a journalism student from a state university came into my office to interview me about how newspaper editors make decisions on news content and story structure.

The student was a junior researching a term paper assignment over spring break. When she entered my office, I asked if she was keeping a scrapbook of her published stories for job interviews upon graduation. She told me that she hadn't reported or written many stories at school, and she was more interested in communication theory and news media criticism. I was tempted to ask her how many entry-level jobs were available for journalism graduates wanting to criticize the news media—especially today when there are so many people willing to lambaste the news media for free—but I held my tongue.

We had plenty to talk about regarding news content. The city our newspaper calls home, Webster Groves, had just endured a nasty recall campaign and recall election of a controversial mayor. The mayor was accused of incompetence, trying to purge the city manager, and poorly representing the city. Her defenders portrayed her detractors as an "old guard" of "sore losers from the rich part of town," who were appalled that one of their own had lost the previous general election. The mayor won the recall election by more than a thousand votes, but she was left badly bruised and battered.

The questions from my student interrogator made it clear that she had fallen under the spell of a public journalism philosopher at her university. Our conversation went something like this:

Q. Why did your newspaper choose to run a letter that accused the mayor of being "Hitler in a skirt" and other letters that were pretty nasty on both sides of the controversy? How does this help a community make responsible public judgments?

A. We have a policy of running as many letters as possible, even the inflammatory ones. When you start editing or selecting letters for civic value or politeness, where do you draw the line? When you don't run people's letters, they suspect you have an agenda favoring one side or the other. Besides, letters can tell us a lot. The "Hitler" letter says as much about the writer as it does about the mayor.

Q. You received some letters saying all your coverage of the ugly recall campaign was giving the city a bad image. Some suggested it would keep people from moving into the city. Is there a way you could have addressed those concerns?

A. I don't think a newspaper is an extension of the local chamber of commerce. Should we not run a story about a toxic waste dump endangering residents because it will hurt real estate values? Hopefully, when things get to the point where residents begin worrying about a bad image for their city, they'll began taking some action, rather than asking the paper to quash its coverage.

Q. Why did the paper run stories with such harsh quotes from some of the most extreme spokespeople on both sides of the controversy? Couldn't you find more reasonable people to interview?

A. The people involved in these local battles, on both sides, tend to be true believers. They are going to give the most informed and interesting quotes—the kind that people will read. The extreme quotes also can be a public service. They help people in the middle make decisions about the character and legitimacy of one side or the other in a controversy.

Q. Couldn't the newspaper have taken positive actions to find some common ground for the community in all of this controversy? Did you consider holding a community forum or a public meeting on people's concerns to bring the city back together?

A. When our mayor ran for office, she listed college study and work experience in conflict resolution as one of her credentials for high office. None of our newspaper staff have credentials in conflict resolution, so it would be a little presumptuous for us to intervene. A newspaper has enough to do to try to report fairly and accurately. If we sponsored a community forum and it ended up in a free-for-all, could we cover it fairly, if at all? We would be a participant. Would people trust our coverage of such an event? Outfits like the League of Women Voters are best-suited for sponsoring community forums.

I suspect that when our conversation was completed, my student interrogator left convinced that I was a journalistic neanderthal without a clue as to my responsibility to "make public life go well." As for me, the encounter left me a little disturbed about what was being taught these days in journalism school. I also fretted about the future of this student and her plans for a career in journalism. How was she learning about journalism and preparing for a career without intensive experience in reporting and writing stories?

On a philosophical level concerning journalism, I was dismayed to find that this student was far more focused on the outcome of stories, than on the integrity of the process of gathering and presenting information. What had she been taught? A newspaper is a forum best left to the voices of the civic boosters and community peacemakers? Journalistic stories need to be tailored to enhance, or to at least protect, the image of the community? A reporter should cast around for quotes until those that are both moderate and purposeful are securely in the net?

Emphasis on the outcome of stories inevitably leads to the abandonment of any attempt at objectivity. Therein lies one of the fatal flaws of public journalism. Public journalists already have dismissed objectivity as a "fruitless cliché." Objectivity has been supplanted with a mission of "making public life go well," a totally subjective inference of duty open to all kinds of interpretation.

This author would agree that objectivity is a myth. Objectivity has never been attained and probably never will. No matter how factual, honest, and inclusive reports are, they will always be influenced by the observer's geographic location, education, personal interests, spiritual, and political beliefs. Critics on the left contend that adherence to objectivity guarantees that the news media will favor the status quo and the entrenched classes. It can be argued, of course, that we are hardly talking about objectivity if its application is so skewed.

Objectivity is an elusive ideal, such as world peace, racial harmony, universal human rights, and religious tolerance. But humankind should not abandon the search for world peace, racial harmony, universal human rights, and religious tolerance because they are elusive ideals. Journalists should not abandon the quest for objectivity because it is, admittedly, an elusive ideal. The concept of objectivity, in the context of journalism, embodies certain notions of fairness and impartiality, as well as an allegiance to neutrality, accuracy, and truth-telling. Objectivity is not a fruitless cliché, nor does it lose its potency because it is an elusive ideal. We should not be so eager to replace it with something else.

REVIEWING PUBLIC JOURNALISM

This is not an objective book. This book is not reporting in the classic sense. This project is a review of a "work in progress." As a review, it is not devoid of opinion. However, the author did take some measures to present the message and the messengers of public journalism in a fair and accurate fashion. This accounts for the extensive footnotes in the book, as well as the reliance on lengthy quotes by public journalism advocates so that their ideas and concepts can be presented in their own words.

Passing judgment on public journalism is fraught with risk. Many advocates of public journalism are ready to pounce on critics, labeling them knee-jerk, narrow-minded, and reactionary. Public journalism partisans have thrown up two great roadblocks in the way of those who would make the attempt to critique it.

The first roadblock involves the definition of public journalism. Advocates of public journalism argue that theirs is a phenomenon "in process." It is too early to know what public journalism is right now. Obviously, there is safety in ambiguity for public journalism advocates—a movement that can't be defined cannot be easily criticized. It is difficult to nail Jello to the wall. The growing legions of those who claim to be public journalists have more definitions of what this press genre is all about than Jello has flavors.

The second roadblock involves the repudiation of traditional methods of analysis. Public journalism advocates argue that their movement is a victim of "having journalism done to it." Public journalism is unfairly criticized by those who resort to the same tired methodology that they use in their outmoded approach to deciphering and reporting other issues.

These roadblocks should not stand to deter criticism of the public journalism reform movement any longer. The stakes are considerable for journalism and democratic society. One of the final chapters of this book focuses on the influence of the academic mentality on journalism. The public journalism philosophy is, in some sense, an outgrowth of a certain academic mentality that has often been called "post-modernist."

The post-modernist philosophers of academia, like the public journalists, are also tired of objectivity and the rigors of detached empirical inquiry. All truths are relative and constructs of the societies from where they originated. Whether a proposition is found to be objectively true is of less importance than whether it fits into an acceptable world view that can further certain conceptions of societal progress. This is not the sort of thinking that should influence the profession of journalism. While there is certainly room to debate this sort of thinking in the journalism classroom, it should not be taught in the classroom as the new template for doing journalism.

NOTE

1. Jay Rosen, "What Should We Be Doing?" *The IRE Journal* (November-December, 1996), p. 5.

PART I
Redeeming Journalism

Public journalism advocates grow prickly at suggestions that their leaders are gurus or that they carry their message with a religious zeal. A few advocates have protested that labeling them as gurus is a tactic by the "high priests" of traditional journalism to belittle them and their message. Journalism is often accused of having a bias toward the secular, so there's a delicious irony in this professional infighting, as the combatants hurl religious epithets at each other.

Are public journalism advocates evangelists?

In his 1988 book, *Evangelism in America*, William Packard provides a working definition of evangelism as "any type of conversionary activity that tries to effect authentic change in someone from one state of thinking and feeling to another."[1] Packard's definition is perhaps overly broad because it transcends the usual association of evangelism with religious belief, particularly fundamentalist religious belief. But there are evangelisms of all kinds and they all have one trait in common—they all attempt to convert.

Packard's definition is especially apt here because public journalism, according to its proponents, requires authentic change in the thinking and feeling of traditional journalists. Journalists who are truly converted must undergo a fundamental shift—sometimes described as a "paradigm shift"—in the way they see and interpret the world. This shift only occurs after traditional journalists take an "intellectual journey"—much as the soul-searching Govinda did in Herman Hesse's classic *Siddhartha*—to achieve enlightenment.

It is not difficult to make the case that public journalism advocates are in the business of providing enlightenment and making converts. In less than a decade of existence, leaders in the public journalism movement have sponsored hundreds of seminars, conferences, and workshops. In a virtual leap of faith, hundreds of editors, reporters, and journalism educators have entered their journalistic revival tents to hear their message and adopt at least some of the movement's tenets and practices.

These tenets and practices are now under discussion in newsrooms from the Bronx to Anaheim, from Miami to Seattle. The world of cyberspace contains more discussion for the journalistically-inclined about public journalism. The internet home page of the Washington-based Pew Center for Civic Journalism reveals a listing of dozens of public journalism projects across the country. The movement has plenty of think tanks churning out its intellectual tracts including the Pew Center, the Kettering Foundation in Dayton, Ohio, the Poynter Institute in St. Petersburg, Florida, and the Project on Public Life and the Press at New York University.

The movement also has prominent philosophers and proselytizers at the ready to catch planes for whatever journalism conference, university seminar, or newsroom affords a platform and an audience willing to hear the word. Many of those who carry the word can be found in the quarterly publication of the Pew Center with its bold nameplate "Civic Catalyst." The quarterly report promotes workshops and seminars, as well as noting deadlines for cash awards for journalism projects that put the public journalism creed into practice.

To make the case that public journalism advocates are evangelists, it's not enough to document their efforts at conversions and their energies toward changing the minds of members of an outmoded and wanting journalistic faith. There are other parallels to be drawn, parallels to the activities of those evangelists who operate in the religious sphere.

Critics of public journalism have noted that the movement is "cult-like,"[2] and that, like a religious cult, it has its own language familiar to the true believers. Public journalists talk about "deliberative conversations" with the public and "ghetto-izing" the newsroom process. They talk about "engaging citizen-readers" through "public listening" and mention the need for "quality-framing" discussions among reporters. Public journalists talk about "journalistic epiphanies," as if the move to public journalism were a religious experience.

The language of religion enters the vocabulary of public journalism advocates when they are speaking or writing about their own personal conversions. They will confess to committing the excesses and transgressions of traditional journalism before seeing the light. Public journalists, like Saul on the way to Damascus, recount the details of some dramatic incident that ultimately revealed to them their folly. This revelation inspires an epiphany—a turning point on their road to a new journalism.

The most disconcerting aspect of this evangelistic movement is the manner in which public journalism advocates dismiss or deride their critics. Religious true believers have historically shown an intolerance toward heretics with inquisitions, floggings, and public burnings. Public journalism advocates obviously do not resort to these extreme measures in reacting to critics; however, their intolerance of criticism is becoming legendary. Critics are dismissed as too ossified in traditional practice or too lethargic to make the intellectual journey to find out what public journalism is all about.

Part I of this book consists of three chapters. Chapter 1 provides a look at the evangel of public journalism and maps out the intellectual journey that many in the profession have taken on the way to conversion. Chapter 2 provides a brief look at some of the many individuals involved in the public journalism movement. This chapter is not meant to be a comprehensive survey of public journalism's many evangelists, nor is it intended to weigh the relative contributions of each contributor cited. This compendium is provided to give newcomers to public journalism a glimpse of public journalism scholars, practitioners, and intellectual fore-runners. It is a starting point for further investigation.

Chapter 3 presents some objections to the public journalism thesis. It recalls many of the premises of public journalism as explained in Chapter 1, and provides a closer examination of the validity of these premises. The chapter also touches on the confusion and contradiction that surround public journalism, as exemplified in the debate over the very name of the new movement. The movement has been referred to as "public," "civic," "communitarian," and "community" journalism, however this book has attempted to use the term "public" wherever possible in order to avoid confusion for the reader.

NOTES

1. William Packard, *Evangelism in America* (New York: Paragon House, 1988), p. 1.

2. Don Corrigan, "Does Public Journalism Serve the Public or Publishers," *St. Louis Journalism Review* (July-August, 1995), p. 9.

1
Public Journalism's Evangel

REVELATIONS, EPIPHANIES, CONVERSIONS

The word "evangel" is derived from "Ministers of the Church," those who assisted the apostles in spreading the gospel or evangel of the New Testament. Packard points out in his *Evangelism in America* that the word "evangel' is derived from the Greek word evangelion, the opening word of the Gospel of Mark that means "glad tidings."[1] The spreading of glad tidings is meant to lead to a conversion, an experience of being "born again"—a change of one's old life by putting on a new life.

The evangel or gospel of public journalism constitutes a message that is best subdivided into three parts for a cursory understanding. The first part of the gospel is an elaboration on the decline in the civic and community life of Americans as well as the unraveling of the social and political fabric. Public journalists contend that we are an alienated people—alienated from our neighbors, our larger communities, and our nation as a worthy and purposeful entity. We distrust our leaders and we find much of government to be a sham. More important, average Americans feel powerless to change this situation. The political process no longer works.

The second part of this new evangel reveals the negligence or "sins" of journalism, as it is now practiced. Traditional journalism is doing very little to counteract the declines in American life. Advocates of the new movement contend that most journalists are so immersed in a professional ethic of objectivity and detachment that they are usually content merely to chronicle the American decline. They feel no sense of responsibility to address issues in a way that could reverse disturbing trends and lead to solutions. Not only do traditional journalists fail to play a constructive role, but sometimes they add to our national difficulties with coverage that is negative and divisive.

The irony for traditional journalism, according to these critics, is that it is sowing the seeds of its own destruction. A working press that thrives on negative and divisive coverage alienates the citizenry. Citizens that are made to feel powerless and cynical have less of a reason to take an active interest in knowing about their local and national community, hence the recent declines in daily newspaper readership and in audiences for the nightly television news.

The third part of the new public journalism evangel consists of the "glad tidings." Journalists can reverse the loss of respect for their work and for their profession, as well as reverse the losses in their audiences and readership, by approaching journalism in a new way. This new approach is called public (or civic) journalism and it moves beyond the old ways of only describing what "is going wrong" in a community to imagining what "going right" would be like.[2] Journalists must begin to provide hope about public life as well as offer solutions to public problems. The new approach to journalism puts the public first—public conversation, public problem solving, and using journalism to engage people in public life.

THE GREAT DECLINES

Decline of Civic and Community Life

Advocates of public journalism are certainly not the first to lament an apparent loss of community life in late twentieth-century America. The much-mourned loss of community life in the United States has been the topic of commentary for some sociologists long before public journalists incorporated it as part of their creed. Intellectuals in the academy have been chronicling it for several decades, and generally date it as a post-World War II phenomenon that roughly corresponds with the suburbanization of America.

Beginning in the 1950s, the rise of the interstate highway system, the increasing dominance of the automobile culture, and the growth of television as the nation's dominant medium, all combined to transform the American landscape. These events after World War II led to the demise of the central city and the growth of suburban sprawl. Highways and automobiles made it possible to escape the city, and television advertised the good life beyond the urban core.

In the central city before World War II, life revolved around the activities of tight-knit neighborhood groups, the neighborhood church and political club, and the ability to walk and engage in a variety of diversions. In the new suburbs after World War II, people don't know their neighbors, television substitutes for actual human contact, and work, education, and entertainment require automobile travel to impersonal glass and steel boxes on landscaped campuses.

The loss of community is evidenced in number of ways. The spontaneous sandlot pickup games of yesteryear's city kids have been replaced by the rigid rule of organized ball leagues for suburban youth. The traditional network of owner-occupied stores, shops, and taverns along the city sidewalk has been replaced by franchise retail units amassed in malls along the interstate. The politician who showed up to shake hands and talk at the neighborhood fair or church bizarre is now an untouchable image in a box in the living room.

One of the major laments of the public journalism advocates is this loss of community, and it is their contention that this national loss has become even more pronounced and insidious in recent years. We have become a nation of cable television couch potatoes, Sega video game players, and internet nerds. We've become more isolated from public life, and as a result we have little faith in our neighbors, much less in our government, and perhaps the least in our press.

Public journalism advocates frequently cite the work of Harvard sociologist Robert Putnam, such as his essay, "Bowling Alone," to make the case that we Americans are losing touch with our communities and with each other. According to Putnam, memberships in civic groups and social clubs ranging from Rotary Clubs to bowling leagues have dropped significantly in recent years.[3] Americans are no longer joiners. It's harder and harder to find citizens to join Parent Teacher Associations, volunteer to work with boy or girl scouts, serve on town commissions, or run for local public office.

Decline of Civic and Political Life

Closely paralleling the loss of American community life and civic engagement is the attendant decline in our political life. The decline in our political life is also attributable, in part, to post-World War II changes in the American landscape. The city politics of patronage and tight-knit political precincts, where everybody knew their politicians and the political hierarchy, has given way to the suburban political clubs in which only a fraction of the populace participates. Members of these clubs often tend to be political careerists, ideologues, and one-issue voters. These club members, all too often, play an inordinately influential role during the political caucus season when candidates are selected for elections. They have also played a role in the decline of the two major political parties by alienating and driving out many ordinary citizens.

The lack of ordinary citizens' involvement in politics can be traced to the loss of the "agora." An important requirement for democracy to function, according to public journalism advocates, is a location or mechanism for deliberation to occur. In ancient Greece, this locale was the marketplace where citizens assembled to buy goods, but more importantly, to discuss the issues of the day.[4] The agora's counterpart in the United States is the town square. The town square was surrounded by the shops where citizens bought their goods, and the square itself was available for public speaking and informal meetings to discuss the issues of the day and to sort out politics.

The loss of the agora in modern-day America is best symbolized in the antiseptic and shiny-floored corridors of the shopping mall, where security personnel are on guard to prohibit the distribution of handbills or political pamphleteering that might distract citizens from the all-important mission of shopping. During the Vietnam War period, shopping centers were sometimes the object of First Amendment lawsuits by antiwar activists arrested for handing out their political pamphlets opposing the war. In the courts, the sanctity of private property prevailed over any First Amendment protection for distributing handbills in the mall.

However, a few court justices in the minority noted that shopping malls had taken the place of the town square, where American democracy had once located its agora. In usurping democracy's meeting place, these justices argued, the shopping malls had an obligation to provide some place for political discussion to take place.

To the loss of the urban political ethos and the loss of the agora, add the advent of television as a cause for the decline of our civic and political life. Television has contributed to the decline of political parties by destroying the process by which candidates move up the political hierarchy to achieve office. Those with political aspirations can bypass the old political process and go to the citizenry directly through television. Hence, the rise of Hollywood actors in high office and billionaire third-party presidential television campaigns. Television has provided a poor substitute for the agora, according to the public journalism advocates. The true agora provided face-to-face meetings and genuine discussion. Television provides powerful, if phony, symbolism, reduces issues to advertising slogans, and allows for mass manipulation funded by special interests.

These developments have contributed to the ordinary citizen's loss of interest in politics. The decline in interest in politics is reflected in recent national elections, which have drawn barely 50 percent of America's potential voters. The decline in citizen participation in the elective process has serious ramifications for the news media, according to public journalism advocates, because a major mission of the news media is to report on the nation's political life. If the citizens no longer care about their political life, then the news media lose much of their relevancy for the public.

Public journalism advocates emphasize that the nation is facing more than simply a loss of interest in politics by citizens. In fact, the citizens have come to hate politics. Public journalism advocates often draw from the work of E. J. Dionne, a *Washington Post* columnist and author of *Why Americans Hate Politics*. In Dionne's view, there are plenty of good reasons for the American populace to be disenchanted. He cites the negative campaigning of presidential campaigns as phenomena that leave the public unmoved, if not angry, impatient, and disgusted. Debate over substantive issues that concern the public gives way to Willie Horton advertising and "loyalty tests" over such ephemeral concerns as the Pledge of Allegiance in schools and burning the flag.

Dionne contends that Americans hate politics because they are tired of the terms of debate imposed by political candidates, and the "artificial polarization" defined by the contest between liberals and conservatives.[5] Dionne argues that this is the same, warmed-over "cultural wars" kind of battling that took place in the 1960s. Dionne argues further that the American public has moved past this kind of bickering, and is more interested in speaking of problems that might be solved by reasoning together.

Dionne's central thesis is that politicians are misreading the American public, that, contrary to what many believe, there is a broad consensus among the citizenry as to what the nation's problems are and the options for how they might be remedied. The failure of politicians to recognize this, and their insistence on jousting over symbolic issues that are irrelevant to most people's lives, is precisely what makes Americans hate politics.

The concluding chapter of Dionne's book has a particular ring for public journalism advocates. Dionne believes that the renewal of American politics is contingent on the creation of a new and vital center that moves away from rancor and polarization. A view is needed that "politics is not simply a grubby confrontation of competing interests but an arena in which citizens can learn from each other and discover an 'enlightened self-interest' in common."[6] According to Dionne, there must be recognition that a nation that hates politics cannot long survive as a democracy.

Decline in Public Civility

The vulgarization of American entertainment, culture, and politics has been a growing concern since the 1960s. In his 1992 study, *Carnival Culture: The Trashing of Taste in America*, James B. Twitchell chronicles contemporary examples of crassness, inanity, and sheer disregard for the idea of quality in our social, cultural, and political life. He notes that if in the beginning was the Word, in the end it will be the Image. What are the images we are facing today?

According to Twitchell, "We have seen Geraldo Rivera, *USA Today*, professional wrestling, Stephen King, *Nightmare on Elm Street*, Morton Downey Jr., Motely Crue, Jacqueline Susann, 'The Gong Show,' Harlequin romances, Andrew Dice Clay, 'Love Boat,' The Home Shopping Network, Public Enemy, *Porky's II*, a revival of comic books, *National Enquirer* headlines ('Hitler Found Alive in Florida,' and 'Son Kills Father and Eats Him'), Madonna 'vogueing' in an executive pin-striped suit with holes cut in the jacket for a torpedo brassiere, novels by most of Morton Janklow's clients (Judith Krantz, Barbara Taylor Bradford, Danielle Steel, Sidney Sheldon, Jackie Collins), Prince, Andy Capp, plastic fruit, the garbage pail kids, Roseanne Barr singing the national anthem while scratching her crotch baseball player's style, graffiti on everything, Andre Agassi in Day-Glo spandex, heavy-metal music, 'The Dating Game,' Sam Kinison, the omnipresent raised middle finger, *Conan the Barbarian*, cubic zirconium, Jimmy Swaggart, 'Teenage Mutant Ninja Turtles,' rap videos, Mick Jagger, single entendres, Eddie Murphy's concert film, *Raw*, 'Married. . . .with Children,' New Kids on the Block, 'America's Funniest Home Videos,' Freddy Krueger, soap operas, Rambo, 2 Live Crew, *Entertainment Tonight*, 'Uncle Buck'. . . ."[7]

Twitchell's list is already dated, for much of the vulgarity in American culture dies fast, but it is replaced furiously. Show business, the industry of American culture, wreaks the most havoc on American taste by pandering to the lowest common denominator. Most of the vulgarity that Twitchell catalogs in his book is part of the popular culture scene in America. But the vulgarity that is flourishing on the popular culture scene also has transformed the realm of public discourse, politics, and the news media.

Public journalism advocates decry the decline in our political discourse and the increasing absence of civility in public discussion. They lament that thoughtful and useful political discussion has been replaced by a sound-bite culture of "Where's the beef," "You're no Jack Kennedy," "There you go again," and "It's the economy, stupid." They harken back to another age, an age of lengthy and deliberative debate that produced fewer slogans and images, but more useful information both about issues and candidates. That ideal age was celebrated by the C-SPAN cable television network in the mid-1990s with its re-enactments of the historic Lincoln-Douglas debates.

According to Kathleen Hall Jamieson and David Birdsell in their study, *Presidential Debates*, the Lincoln-Douglas debates of the late 1850s are part of the national mythology because they demanded so much of both the participants and the audience. Lincoln and Douglas confined themselves to a discrete set of political concerns. Their debates advanced the issues and shed light on areas of agreement and disagreement. Their debates also required the audience to patiently follow the logic of their arguments.[8]

The Lincoln-Douglas debates were not used by the orators in an attempt to "trump" one another with a catchy phrase that might prove handy later as a political advertising slogan. The debates were not moderated by journalists intent on trapping the orators with hypothetical queries or pointed questions meant to provoke an emotional response. The debates were punctuated by citizen cheers and catcalls. They provided an opportunity for the electorate to become involved with the process of governance.

According to Jamieson and Birdsell, prebroadcast debates in America contributed to the political system by genuinely educating the electorate about the issues and personalities of the day.[9] By contrast, today's debates are often exercises in glib responses and sloganeering. As Jamieson and Birdsell point out, when President Jimmy Carter attacked candidate Ronald Reagan in the 1980 debates, he used hyperbolic language characterizing Reagan as a threat to Social Security and world peace. Reagan warded off those attacks, not by a well-reasoned and buttressed defense, but simply with the rejoinder, "There you go again."[10]

Public journalists complain that it's not simply the quality of our political debate that has deteriorated. Political discourse itself has suffered because of the antics of traditional journalists who engage each other on food-fight programs such as "The McLaughlin Group." What's worse, "The McLaughlin Group" has been cloned on local television in many cities, where hometown news celebrities strive to imitate the same style of banter and bluster—discourse that generates lots of heat, but very little light.

Public journalists also lament the rise of the radio talk show phenomenon in the United States as another example of how political conversation in this country has been sullied and soiled. Talk shows thrive on conflict as an end in itself. There is no effort made to reach a consensus. There is no effort made to mobilize an audience to work toward solutions to community problems. Real issues are given short shrift. Important issues that have real meaning are simply used for ammunition for the host's war of invective and insult. When a talk show host isn't heating up the controversy himself, he's preying upon callers whose ill-informed or outlandish views will incite others to battle on the airwaves.

The vulgarization of American political discourse in the American mass media has grave consequences for the health of democracy in this country, according to the public journalists. Conflict has become an end in itself. Important issues that have real meaning are simply used as fodder in a war of invective and insult.

Decline of Interest in News

Given the deterioration in our community and political life, as well as the trivialization of our political discourse, it should not be surprising that there is a corresponding decline in the audience for news, according to public journalists. A loss of community must certainly have a negative impact on the desire for community news. A loss of interest in political life would logically translate into a decline in the public appetite for political news, one of the staples of newspaper content. These trends make newspapers increasingly irrelevant.

In fact, the situation for daily newspapers, especially in the nation's major markets, has not been particularly healthy in the three decades since 1970. As *Washington Post* media critic Howard Kurtz notes in his book, *Media Circus: The Trouble with America's Newspapers*, the smell of death permeates the newspaper industry in recent times. "Every few months there is a repetition of the now-familiar ritual: the desperate search for a buyer, the anguished countdown, the farewell edition, the grieving in the community, the latest batch of editors and reporters tossed out on the street."[11]

As Kurtz points out, more than 150 newspapers have folded since 1970. Afternoon newspapers in St. Louis, Richmond, Nashville, Knoxville, Durham, Charleston, Tulsa, Baton Rouge, Shreveport, Louisville, Spokane, and San Diego have folded or been swallowed by morning editions. The circulations of both P.M. and A.M. newspapers have taken severe hits since 1970. The decline in the health of newspapers has led to a consolidation within the industry. More than 95 percent of American cities are now monopoly markets, and newspaper chains, which in 1960 accounted for less than half of all daily newspaper circulation, now control 80 percent of the nation's 1,580 daily newspapers.[12]

The loss of interest in newspapers and the news can be measured in any number of ways. The problem is not simply that daily newspapers have been disappearing in recent years, it's that the surviving newspapers have an audience that is also in decline. To take one measure of this decline, in a 1995 national survey, only 45 percent of Americans reported that they had read a daily newspaper the previous day, down from 71 percent in 1965 in a comparable study.[13] The decline in newspaper readership is all the more disturbing when focusing on survey demographics that show the extremely low rates of readership among the young. The loss of an audience among the young points to an even more precipitous drop in readership in the years ahead.

The bad news about readership losses has caused a virtual stampede among newspapers to change themselves into chic, with-it, relevant news products. Dailies across the country have brought in consultants to revamp layouts and redesign front pages with gimmicky index boxes, big colorful pictures, and short snappy stories. The mad quest to recover audiences has led to new type sizes, fancy headline fonts, whacky political cartooning, offbeat columns, and experimental newspaper sections. In *Media Circus*, Kurtz observes just a few of the innovations:

> There are car columns, health columns, gossip columns, advice columns, lawyers' columns, computer columns, photography columns, gardening columns, men's columns, women's columns, fishing columns, finance columns. There are parenting tips, survival tips, pet tips, dining tips, shopping tips, travel tips. There are sections called Rumpus, You, Sunday Brunch, Almost the Weekend, High Style, Home, View, Scene, Tempo, KidNews, WomenWise, Living, Life, Yo, and Yo! Info![14]

One might think that the crusade to find relevancy for newspapers and the innovations meant to recapture readers would boost the morale of the journalists working for these news organizations. However, public journalists contend that the morale in most newsrooms has never been lower. The plethora of news columns and sections and the gimmickry of howling headlines, peephole stories, big pictures, and colorful graphics are simply the telltale signs of an industry in desperation.

The degradation of news by a tabloid culture is not only further alienating audiences, it is leading to a crisis of confidence among news practitioners. There is a loss of purpose and a collapse of standards among news professionals who once strived to do their best by audiences. According to public journalists, there is a terrible confusion and "even depression that hangs over many American newsrooms as journalists contemplate their professional futures with dread."[15]

There is a way out of this morass. There is a light at the end of the tunnel. There is a road to salvation. That salvation is encompassed in the 1990s movement of public journalism, a new effort to change the nature of news so that it is more relevant to citizens and, thus, more likely to prompt citizens to take active roles in the democratic process.The journalistic reformers behind the movement contend that fewer Americans are reading or watching the news because they are isolated, alienated, and unable to see how a knowledge of the news can make any difference in their own lives. The news media exploit people's problems while neglecting to offer people any solutions to those problems.

According to the advocates of the new movement, public journalism promises to re-energize our faltering democracy. It promises to end the "disconnect" of an alienated citizenry. It promises to bring an audience back to the news, because people will at last see how knowledge of the news can lead to change that will improve their own lives. It promises to bring new respect and purpose to the much-maligned institution known as the Fourth Estate. It promises to give news practitioners a new sense of purpose.

However, before news practitioners can join the movement in good faith and practice the movement's tenets in a genuine fashion, there must be an intellectual journey. That intellectual journey must bring news practitioners to a realization of the shortcomings of traditional journalism as it has been practiced. For many news practitioners who have taken the intellectual journey, there has been an admission of sins. There has been confession and repentance.[16]

SINS OF THE NEWS MEDIA

Callous, Uncaring, and Contemptible

A great many Americans have not only lost interest in the news, they've grown to have contempt for those who bring them the news. This contempt is due to a perception that media practitioners actually cultivate a callous and uncaring attitude toward the public. That perception stems from traditional journalism's professional ethic of detachment, which insists that journalists must avoid entanglements and attachments that could compromise the reporting of a story.

James Fallows, former editor of *U.S. News & World Report* and a proponent of public journalism, makes the point that the news ethic of detachment can have a corrosive effect on the public. He challenges the traditional journalism ethic of detachment in his jeremiad, *Breaking the News*, which is subtitled, "How the Media Undermine American Democracy." In the very first chapter of his book, Fallows gives a rather extreme example of journalism detachment to illustrate why the public has become angry with the news media.

Fallows recalls a PBS program, "Ethics in America," which aired on public broadcast stations across the country in the 1980s. An episode sponsored by Montclair State College had the title "Under Orders, Under Fire," and was moderated by Charles Ogletree, a professor at Harvard Law School. In the course of the show, Ogletree brought two star television journalists, Peter Jennings of ABC's "World News Tonight" and Mike Wallace of "60 Minutes" into a hypothetical war situation in the nation of "South Kosan."

The hypothetical war situation involved U.S. troops advising South Kosanese Troops in their struggle against invaders from "North Kosan." (This scenario was obviously a hybrid of the U.S. involvement in conflicts in Korea and Vietnam.) Ogletree asked Jennings to imagine that he was employed by a network that had contact with the enemy. After difficult negotiations, the North Kosanese enemy agreed to let Jennings and his news crew travel with military units. When Jennings was asked whether he would be willing to take such an assignment, he responded in the affirmative.

Ogletree then added some new twists to the hypothetical war situation for Jennings' consideration. As Jennings and his crew are traveling with the North Kosanese military unit to visit the site of an apparent atrocity perpetrated by U.S. and South Kosanese troops, they accidentally cross the trail of a small group of American and South Kosanese soldiers. The North Kosanese troops, with Jennings and his crew in tow, set up a perfect ambush that will mean certain death for the Americans and their allies.

Ogletree then posed an ethical quandary for Jennings. Would he tell his camera crew to "Roll the tape!" as the North Kosanese opened fire on Americans and their allies? Would he make some attempt to warn the U.S. troops even though that would mean, at the very least, losing a story? Jennings' reply was that he would certainly do anything in his power to warn the Americans, even if that meant he might lose his own life.

But Jennings was brought up short by his news colleague, Mike Wallace, who expressed astonishment at Jennings' response. Wallace insisted that Jennings was a reporter and his obligation was to cover the story. At that point, Jennings backtracked in embarrassment and agreed with Wallace that his journalistic duty was to remain a detached observer of whatever might ensue in the ambush scenario.

According to Fallows, the answers by Wallace and Jennings prompted a Marine colonel on the show to express his utter contempt for the two newsmen. "Peter Jennings and Mike Wallace are just two individuals, but their reactions spoke volumes about the values of their craft," noted Fallows, "Jennings was made to feel embarrassed about his natural, decent human impulse. Wallace was completely unembarrassed about feeling no connection to the soldiers in his country's army or considering their deaths before his eyes as 'simply a story.'"[17]

What makes the Wallace performance even more contemptible, according to Fallows, was that he didn't offer the live audience for the television show any explanation or rationale for his own decision to cover the story rather than to warn the U.S. soldiers. Wallace on patrol with the North Kosanese recognized no "higher duty" to intervene in the situation and offered "no rationale beyond 'I'm with the press'—this is a nice symbol for what Americans hate about their media establishment in our age."[18]

Fallows uses this "nice symbol" to puncture the traditional journalistic ethic of detachment. He and other public journalism advocates argue that many journalists are so wedded to the ideal of detachment that they fail to feel any loyalty toward their country, their community, their cultural and religious institutions, and their fellow citizens. This ideal of detachment leads these journalists to even abandon their own natural impulses as so much unnecessary human baggage getting in the way of capturing a good story.

Fallows uses a dramatic example to show just how callous and uncaring news practitioners can be in the single-minded pursuit of a story. Fallows uses the wartime example to show how ingrained journalistic procedure and the ethic of detachment result in a failure to do the right thing. As critics of traditional journalism, public journalists regularly use less dramatic examples of situations in which those in the news business draw the contempt of the public because of their fixation on the ideal of detachment. It shows up in the crime reporter who can write stories about drive-by shootings week after week, year after year, with never a thought to writing a story demanding solutions to ending the cycle of violence. It shows up in the education reporter who can write stories about the failings of inner-city schools as a perennial assignment, with never a thought to writing a story demanding improvements in the schools and a curriculum to better the academic performance of city school students. It shows up in the political reporter who can write stories election after election focusing on polling data and who's ahead in the horse race, with never a thought about how the public might be better served with a focus on the issues which the public cares about. It shows up in the city reporter who writes regularly about the economic deterioration and population decline of his community, with never a thought about how journalism could be used to rally the community to turn its fortunes around.

According to Fallows and the public journalists, it is this attitude of aloofness in reporters that has caused the public to not only lose interest in their work, but to feel contempt for journalism. Public journalism advocates decry a system that produces journalists who are trained in a "determined detachment" that sets them apart from the consequences of their work.[19]

Elitist and Disconnected

The sin of detachment, according to public journalists, is joined by the offense of elitism. The elitism public journalists complain about is twofold. First, there is the slavish worship by journalists all over the United States for the kind of journalism that is done at *The Washington Post* and *The New York Times*. Second, because journalism has become a more respected and better paid profession in recent years, journalists no longer identify with the general populace. Instead, they are more at home with professors, lawyers, doctors, and those who govern. This change in socioeconomic status has served to distance journalists from regular people—the disconnect and detachment from regular folks inevitably results in a news product that has little relevancy for the population at large.

The first aspect of this elitist mindset of journalists may be traced to the colleges and graduate schools of journalism that train most of today's reporters. Journalism schools teach their students that newspapers such as *The Washington Post* and *The New York Times* represent the top of the heap, the very best of modern-day journalism—the model for reporters and writers aspiring to the best. As a result, journalists all over the country adopt a set of attitudes and ethics, as well as an approach to journalism, that may be appropriate to New York or Washington, D.C., but which are totally out of sync for Sandusky, Ohio, Wichita, Kansas, or Idaho Springs, Idaho.

Public journalists argue that elite publications such as *The Washington Post*, *The Wall Street Journal* or *The New York Times* can afford to take a sanctimonious approach to journalism, paying homage to the ideal of detachment and taking a fierce stance of independence from those institutions and individuals which they cover. These publications can posture in this way because they serve an elite niche and are not dependent on general circulation support like many daily newspapers.

Most daily newspapers, by contrast, especially in the new climate of increased competition from other media, cannot afford to be so aloof and independent. They are ill-served by reporters who adopt the elitist approach of *The Times* and *The Post*. They are better served by reporters who adopt a public journalism philosophy of connecting with a community, who acknowledge that they have a stake in the success or failure of community institutions and individuals. The elitist attitudes of the scribes at *The New York Times* or *The Washington Post* constitute an extravagance. According to public journalists, the rest of newspaperdom would be wise to identify such extravagance and banish it from their news operations.

A corresponding sin of elitism which afflicts conventional journalism, according to the public journalists, stems from the improvement of the economic status of journalists. Before World War II, reporting was a working-class occupation and few of those working for newspapers had college degrees. The upside of this lamentable economic condition was that reporters had living standards that made them kin to most Americans. They were in touch with the majority of the populace and could write from that perspective. Hence, the popularity of most newspapers with the country's working stiffs.

In the 1950s and 1960s, journalism began to change with the advent of profitable television broadcasting and the consolidation in the newspaper industry, which resulted in fewer, but more profitable, daily newspapers. Newspaper jobs began attracting better educated people and college degrees gradually came to be a requirement for reporting positions. Reporters have now lost touch with the lifestyle and living standards of the majority of the populace. As public journalism advocate Fallows writes: "The status revolution in big-time journalism has given many reporters a strong if unconscious bias in favor of 'haves' rather than 'have-nots.'"[20]

Fallows devotes a lengthy chapter of his book, *Breaking the News*, to the transformation in income status of journalists, which distances them from the plight of average Americans. He argues that the situation is exacerbated by new celebrityhood of those at the top of the income scale in journalism. These journalists have become TV stars who pontificate on news hours, do battle with each other on talk shows, and collect huge fees on speaking engagements with organizations that may seek to influence their reporting.

Fallows goes after the pundits who populate such shows as "The McLaughlin Group," "Crossfire," the "Capital Hill Gang," and more in a chapter entitled, "The Gravy Train." These journalists have become bigger names in the eyes of the public than the people they cover, Fallows complains. They have reduced the practice of journalism to entertainment and their strident, pugnacious behavior gives all journalists a bad name.

The move to elitist status and celebrityhood has further distanced journalists from average Americans and had a negative impact on the credibility of the profession. In his chapter, "The Gravy Train," Fallows lets Fred Wertheimer, former president of Common Cause, have the last word. Wertheimer notes that journalists have always been disliked, but increasingly they also are losing respect and credibility.

"If I am an average Joe, what is a 'journalist' to me? It is somebody who shows up on TV a lot, yells and shouts, gives me all his opinions, and makes sharp-edged remarks. He is ideological and is attacking other journalists," declares Wertheimer. "If the people who do this are journalists, isn't it a logical conclusion

for me to believe that this is what journalists are? That's all I see. The whole pun-
ditry world of TV has done a very serious job of eroding the concept of credible
journalism in the public's mind."[21]

Negative Nabobs of Negativism

To the sins of detachment and elitism, add the offense of a negative attitude.
Traditional journalists have often subscribed to a press ethic of "comforting the
afflicted and afflicting the comfortable." They place a premium on the watchdog
role of sniffing out government malfeasance, political corruption, and general
wrongdoing. As a result, failures and shortcomings are favored as good copy. Negative stories often dominate the headlines.

The Watergate reporting of Bob Woodward and Carl Bernstein is often credited with ushering in a new era of negative, muckraking journalism. The success
of Woodward and Bernstein in helping to bring down a corrupt presidential
administration, and the fame and fortune that followed, was the inspiration for
burgeoning journalism school enrollments.

In his *Public Journalism & Public Life*, Davis Merritt describes all of this as
the "post-Watergate syndrome," and contends that what should have been a
shining moment in journalism, quickly deteriorated into an era just as threatening
to public life as had been the election of Richard M. Nixon and his gang of corrupt cronies. Journalists suddenly saw themselves as folk heroes, catching crooks
and cleaning up public life.

"Seeing Richard Nixon as a prototype rather than anomaly, journalists
began treating all political figures at any level as suspects in the next Whatever-
Gate," observes Merritt. "The sewer commissioner who drives his county-owned
car to the grocery store at night isn't G. Gordon Liddy but, hey, we do the best we
can with what's at hand."[22]

Merritt argues that the democratic process, superbly served by the actual
Watergate reporting of Woodward and Bernstein, came to be devalued by the constant harping of self-indulgent reporters. The harm was compounded by journalists' propensity to hand themselves award, plaques, and citations for every scalp
taken in the fevered atmosphere of muckraking reporting—from that of the sewer
commissioner to that of the city dog catcher. And gradually the trend moved from
catching crooks in government "to superficial exploration of everything that was
a problem—that is, everything negative—about society, from AIDS to zebra
extinction."[23]

All this raking of muck has served to alienate American citizens not only
from their government, but from their press as well. Public journalists are united
in their contention that there has been too much emphasis on the negative in conventional journalism. It encourages what one adherent describes as "learned helplessness." According to Ed Fouhy, former executive director of the Pew Center for
Civic Journalism, it promotes the feeling that a problem is "so big, so complicated
that the viewer or reader is left with a sense that it is beyond the capacity of ordinary men and women."[24]

Conflict-oriented, Episodic, Extremist

To the sins of detachment, elitism, and negativity, add the insatiable appetite for conflict as another of the mortal offenses of traditional journalism. The news value of "conflict" has for years been taught in journalism textbooks as a primary criterion for deciding what makes an event newsworthy. When two aldermen square off over how to get drug dealers off the street—that's news. When two state legislators square off over passage of a concealed weapons bill—that's news. When members of a pro-life group get into a shouting match with members of a pro-choice group at a civic center demonstration—that's news.

Public journalists eschew this conflict-oriented coverage. In their view, journalists must end all this rancorous reporting and begin providing hope about public life, as well as solutions to community problems. In their view, the gravitation toward conflict reporting in itself constitutes a bias and also undermines the traditional journalists' insistence on a stance of detachment. In choosing to cover issues in a manner that puts a premium on conflict, the traditional journalist has opted to stir up the pot, inflame emotions, and raise the volume of the debate. This is hardly a detached stance, argue public journalists. The traditional journalist becomes an actor in the mix of community interests and, in the conflict mode of reporting, chooses to aggravate a problem rather than to seek a solution to it.

Nowhere has this been more true, according to public journalism advocate Fallows, than in the public policy area. In covering the 1993 debate over a national health care policy, for example, Fallows contends that journalists had little interest in actually explaining the Clinton plan and other proposals offered. Journalists only became energized over the issue when it became politicized, and Republicans and Democrats began attacking each other's positions. In all of the coverage devoted to the fighting, the public was never offered a clear picture of what the health care proposals actually entailed, according to Fallows.[25]

The disposition of traditional journalists toward conflict-oriented reporting carries with it a requirement for giving vent to both sides in any dispute. This requirement is known as providing balance to a story, of paying deference to the idea of objectivity. If both sides are heard, then neither side can protest about being left out of the discussion.

Public journalists argue that the reporting profession's obsession with providing balance is actually a disservice to the public. This is because there are some instances in which it is quite clear that there are not two legitimate sides to an issue. This is also because in the mania to achieve balance, the profession also has a marked tendency to seek out the polar extremes, according to public journalists. In a pool of opinions which run from A to Z, typical journalists will choose to run the opinions of A and Z. In a pool of opinions which run from 1 to 10, typical journalists are likely to run the opinions of 1 and 10.

"Journalists keep trying to find people who are 1 and at 9 on a scale of 1 to 10, rather than people at 3 and 7 where most people actually are," declares public journalism advocate Cole Campbell, editor of the *St. Louis Post-Dispatch*. "Journalism should say that the people from 3 to 7 are just as newsworthy as those at either end of the spectrum lobbing bombs toward the middle."[26]

Framing issues at the extremes not only makes it unlikely that the public will receive a fair and accurate picture of reality, contend public journalists, it also makes it unlikely that the public will be able to relate to what the issue is all about. The majority of the American populace gravitates toward the middle of the spectrum, rather than at the polar ends. If most of this populace is convinced that the news media is not reflecting their viewpoints, then they may very well decide that they have no stake in what is under the lens of the news media. Consequently, there is a further erosion of readers and audience.

Covering stories only when there is conflict has other drawbacks—it guarantees that most issues are going to be covered in an episodic manner. The issue of racial divisions in this country and how to heal those divisions is a prime example. Coverage of the racial divide inevitably arises when there is social disorder or urban riots. The issue then gets lost when times are more placid. Covering issues in this episodic manner also insures that a problem is never followed through to a solution, and without the news media spotlight upon them, the major players in these conflicts are under less pressure to follow problems through to a solution.

A PATH TO REDEMPTION

The evangel or gospel of public journalism constitutes a scripture in tripartite, and candidates for conversion to this new evangel can only be disturbed and demoralized by the revelations in the initial two segments of this intellectual journey. First to be acknowledged are the revelations on the great declines, ranging from the loss of community to the unraveling of the political process. Among the most depressing realizations to emerge in the examination of these declines in our public life is that they have come to jeopardize the very need for news information and the news practitioner, according to the public journalists.

Even more distressing is the subsequent revelation that journalism, as it is now practiced, is doing pitifully little to address the loss of community, the decline in civility, and the crisis of confidence in the democratic process. In fact, traditional journalism simply exacerbates these public problems. And so comes the next preachment to be absorbed in the intellectual journey, which ideally prompts a cathartic recognition of the serious offenses of "detachment," "elitism," "negativity," and "conflict orientation" that are endemic to traditional or conventional journalism. While there are certainly many more venial offenses to catalog in the failings of journalism as it is now practiced, these are most often heralded as the Four Horsemen of the journalistic apocalypse.

Candidates for conversion to the new evangel may well be despairing at this point in the intellectual journey, but it is precisely at this juncture that the glad tidings appear on the horizon. Public journalism arrives to offer converts a new set of values to supercede, if not supplant, the older verities of journalism. Public journalism offers converts a host of new ways to connect with the public and to revive civic life. Public journalism offers converts a new wholistic approach to craft and a bolstered confidence that 10 or 20 years down the road they will be engaged in a journalism worth doing.

In Search of Core Values

Traditional journalists often contend that they deal in facts and not in values. Value judgments are to be confined to the editorial page, while the news is to be reported dispassionately on the front page. Public journalists like Davis Merritt insist that traditional journalists are fooling themselves, because they are expressing certain core values in the very act of selecting what stories they will write about for front page news. Journalists who write stories about a senator who steals or a company that dumps chemicals are expressing values.[27]

Public journalists argue that everything journalists do involves values, and the values that have come to most alienate the public involve the procedural values of journalism. These values are apparent on television news when shouting reporters push microphones in the faces of the bereaved in the aftermath of tragedy. These values are apparent when newspapers rush faulty information into the morning edition to scoop the competition on the latest scandal's details. These values are apparent when a story accuses a government official of malfeasance and it includes the proviso, "attempts to reach Mr. So-And-So for comment were unsuccessful."

These values are apparent, according to public journalism advocates such as James Fallows, when a high profile reporter such as Mike Wallace of CBS professes that he would rather get a behind-the-lines battle story in a wartime situation than warn U.S. troops that they are about to walk into an ambush. These are the values that leave the public thinking that journalists are callous, uncaring, and, at times, contemptible.

In the ever-growing volume of literature on public journalism, two concepts can be separated out as primary in the new set of core values public journalism would bring to the profession. In the new mindset of public journalism, a reporter should continually ask whether the information about to be disseminated has the capacity to help "public life go well." In the new mindset of public journalism, a reporter also should continually ask whether he or she is performing as "a fair-minded participant" on the stage of public life. What do these concepts mean?

According to James Fallows, the phrase—"public life going well"—is drawn from the philosophical writings of Harvard philosopher Michael Sandel.[28] The phrase crops up again and again in the writings of public journalism advocates Jay Rosen and Davis Merritt. Fallows defines it as "a shared sense by citizens that they have some connection to and control over the institutions that make the big decisions, and therefore that they need the information journalism provided about public life."[29]

For public journalists, the obligation to help public life go well is a civic responsibility that can be translated in any number of activities that go beyond traditional reporting, such as a newspaper operation promoting a voter registration drive to bring more people into the process; a newspaper, radio, and television outlet teaming up to sponsor citizen workshops and forums on how to allocate the state budget—and reporting on their results and how state legislators react to those results; a newspaper teaming up with civil rights organizations to encourage citizens to sign a public pledge to work for racial understanding and harmony.

Obviously, these activities go beyond the passive act of reporting the news, of simply being a conduit for quotes from various parties interested in a particular issue. These activities require news practitioners to be "fair-minded participants" in public life. They require journalists to connect with the public and to engage the public, rather than to simply inform the public. To be a fair-minded participant in public life, journalists must have "a knowledge of the rules—how the public has decided a democracy should work—and the ability and willingness to provide relevant information and a place for that information to be discussed and turned into democratic consent."[30]

In the new world of public journalism values, a reporter can no longer simply stand along the side of the wall at the meeting in the city council chambers furiously jotting down quotes of the city officials for a story. If a citizen or council member gets up from a chair and tugs on that reporter's sleeve and asks—"What are you doing?"—the reporter can no longer simply answer, "I'm with the press."

Reconnecting: Reviving Public Life

Traditionally, public life has been viewed as the province of those who become politicians and elected officials. Politicians and elected officials are said to have entered public life. According to public journalists, the news media must scrap this limiting definition of what makes public life. "Public life is everything that pulls people out of their private worlds and puts them in touch with common concerns—everything from nightlife, bowling leagues, union meetings, and town hall debates. It is also the habits of mind and heart that permit people to understand each other, discuss their views, and get along despite their differences."[31]

The public journalist leaves the newsroom and gets down in the trenches with folks at the tractor pull, bowling competition, union meetings, and town hall debates. If those bowling league meets, union meetings, and town hall debates are few and far between in the public journalist's particular locale, then it behooves the public journalist and the news operation to create the needed public spaces. This might entail sponsorship of a town hall meeting on the topic of the future of the community. It might entail a series of focus groups in which ordinary citizens are invited to the newspaper offices to explain what is on their minds. It might require the newspaper operation to sponsor citywide block parties, with free pizza, where neighbors could discuss what's right and wrong about their communities— with the open ears of the press nearby.

In some sense, this is all about the public journalism mission of re-engaging the public. Public journalism advocate Jay Rosen is fond of borrowing a term from communication scholar Michael Schudson, who refers to the journalist's "capacity to include."[32] The most important function of journalism, according to public journalists, is to include the public and thus to re-engage them in public life and the democratic process. For Rosen, journalism has no choice but to include the public and to re-engage the citizenry in public life. "Public journalism is about forming as much as informing a public, for the assumption that the public exists always and for all time is, in fact, a complacent one."[33]

While traditional journalists see their job as one of passively providing a news product for public consumption, public journalists see their job as re-engaging the public in civic life so that they will want to be informed. Jay Rosen has described "an index of leading civic indicators" that public journalists should used to monitor and promote the revival of civic life. Journalists should examine such indicators or measures as "citizen participation, cooperative problem-solving, coalition-building, inclusiveness, setting a common agenda, planning for the future, etc."[34]

Building Civic Capital

A civic catalyst is anything that acts to improve the decision-making process in a community and that moves it to find solutions to its problems. A newspaper, radio, or television news organization can build civic capital through efforts to re-engage citizens and to reverse civic disintegration. Traditional journalism, all too often, has been part of the problem, rather than the solution. Traditional journalism has simply become a factor in the process of civic disintegration in communities that are suffering breakdown. This is because of conventional journalism's predilection for covering the negative—failures and shortcomings.

A newspaper that engages in public journalism in a community suffering breakdown will not simply hammer away with stories about crime, dysfunctional schools, and renegade politicians. Ideally, it will perform as a civic catalyst in such a community and go about the work of identifying civic capital. "Capital" is clas-sically defined by economists in connection with productivity. Arthur Charity, author of *Doing Public Journalism*, describes civic capital as "anything that improves the productivity of a community—that is, its ability to meet crisis, solve problems, live connectedly."[35]

A newspaper operation that practices public journalism in a community suf-fering breakdown will look beyond the negative happenings and seek out civic capital. Civic capital might consist of cultural groups, block clubs, citizen associ-ations, and neighborhood leaders. All of these entities can provide positive role models and counter the images of failure and corruption.

Public journalism's intellectual journey to redemption ultimately leads to a journalism that is redeeming. It involves making a break from passively chroni-cling demise, to actively encouraging a search for civic renewal and the re-engagement citizenry. Whereas, in the past, newspeople often just pointed to prob-lems and walked away, with public journalism they are now trying to find what works. In the past, journalists often wrote about social maladies and then let other institutions, such as government, worry about the solutions. Public journalism gives news practitioners a dispensation from the old rules of detachment and watching from the sidelines and gives them the new charge to make public life go well.

A Prescription: "Wholistic Journalism"

Jay Rosen of the public journalism movement credits Gene Patterson of the *St. Petersburg Times* with the concept of whole journalism. "A whole journalism would not stop at exposing the ills and ailments; it would also focus on creating a healthy public climate. A whole journalism would not equate politics with 'government' and its misdeeds; it would see public problem-solving as the best definition of the political sphere, and it would ask how this sphere could be made to work better."[36]

Rosen compares the fledgling public journalism movement to the early days of the holistic medicine movement in the health profession. According to Rosen, medical providers in the late 1970s began to ask if they had defined their mission wrong. Instead of seeing a doctor's job or a nurse's job as that of treating the sick and curing diseases, the early advocates of holistic medicine began to redefine their mission as keeping people healthy, to practice preventive medicine.

In carrying out this analogy even further, Rosen assures new converts to the public journalism movement that they should not be disheartened if at times they feel unsure as to just what exactly they are doing. After all, in the early days of holistic medicine, the ideas associated with it were more of a premise and a hypothesis than a primary concern of medicine. The new public journalists must not be afraid to experiment.

Today, holistic medicine has had a major impact on medicine and is part of a philosophy of health care involving an emphasis on nutrition and diet, attention to exercise and stress reduction, and an overall goal of finding healthier ways to live. Public journalism can have much the same evolution, according to Rosen. Public journalism is still very much in an experimental stage and involves a set of premises. "Like holistic medicine, public journalism wants to begin in a different place," declares Rosen. "Rather than starting with the ruptures and breakdowns that make for news, it asks about the conditions that allow for a healthy public life. Public journalism rejects as too limiting a disease model of community life, in which things become interesting only when they begin to break down."[37]

Whole journalism involves a dream and a quest that may never succeed. Rosen, like all good prophets, advises new converts that the road will be long and the naysayers along the way will be many. The busy environment of American newsrooms will not easily give pause to examine such ideas as "civic participation, deliberative dialogue, cooperative problem-solving, taking responsibility for the place you live, making democracy work."[38] What's more, the prospects for a new whole journalism dim when looking at the modern phenomena of fragmenting media audiences and an ever-expanding array of media channels and voices. Nevertheless, Rosen insists the stakes are too high for the health of democracy and the future of journalism to not make the attempt to bring the wholistic dream to reality.

Rosen also advises new converts that creating a new vocabulary and a new mission for journalism is only the beginning. The actual practice of public journalism is fraught with peril and requires much vision and energy. Anyone who has tried it will readily concede that it's much harder than conventional journalism, according to Rosen, because public journalists must find the citizens, seek out their agenda, and reflect their concerns fairly and accurately in news coverage. This is a much more involved process than simply consulting the Rolodex and latching onto the pronouncements of the experts and officials.

In order to attain the dream of a wholistic journalism and to persevere in the day-to-day work of committing public journalism in locales across the country, the new converts need a prayer, a mantra, an apostles' creed. This became apparent at one of the first newspapers in the country to begin experimentation under the news premises of public journalism. *The Virginian-Pilot* of Norfolk, Virginia, whose editor was public journalism advocate Cole Campbell (now at the *St. Louis Post-Dispatch*), initiated some of the early projects under the wholistic journalism formula. There, a group of reporters and an editor designated as the "public life team" devised a message and took the pledge:

We will revitalize a democracy that has grown sick with disenchantment. We will lead the community to discover itself and act on what it has learned. We will show how the community works or could work, whether that means exposing corruption, telling citizens how to make their voices heard, holding up a fresh perspective or spotlighting people who do their jobs well. We will portray democracy in the fullest sense of the word, whether in a council chamber or cul-de-sac. We do this knowing that a lively, informed, and most of all, engaged public is essential to a healthy community and to the health of these newspapers.[39]

—Mission statement of Virginian-Pilot Public life team

This creed for the apostles of public journalism is refreshing, according to Rosen and other public journalists, because there is marginal lip service given to the self-important professional norms and conventions of traditional journalism. This missionary creed also lacks the breast-beating of journalistic preambles that concentrate on the serious work that must be carried out under the First Amendment protections. This is a creed that redefines what makes news according to its utility in promoting a healthy political climate, a healthy and lively community that in turn can play a role in keeping journalism healthy.

Traditionally, news has been defined by a set of criteria that have less to do with the ordinary citizen and a healthy community, and more to do with the unusual citizen and aberrations in the community. Consider the criteria for what makes news in the standard college journalism textbook:

Impact. When an event or idea is thought to seriously affect a large number of people, it is important as news.

Proximity. An event or happening is bigger news if it happens in the news circulation area, rather than 1,000 miles away.

Timeliness. When an event or idea is especially relevant to an audience today, it is important to tell it as soon as you can.

Prominence. Well-known people and institutions are likely to be more interesting to an audience.

Novelty. The unusual and the bizarre attract the interest of audiences. A nineteenth century editor once contended: "When a dog bites a man, that is not news, because it happens so often. But if a man bites a dog, that is news."

Conflict. Whether it is politics, war, crime, or sports—conflict is an important factor in what attracts the attention of an audience.[40]

The traditional criteria for news provide benchmarks that are admittedly more "objective" and less academic than the indicators for news used under public journalism. However, the emphasis on timeliness, novelty, prominence, and conflict often is destructive to the democratic process, according to the public journalists. The emphasis on timeliness often means that faulty information is rushed into print in the mania to beat a deadline. The emphasis on novelty and prominence give the ordinary citizen a skewed view of the world and sometimes serves to belittle that citizen's own voice and place in the world. The emphasis on conflict means that there is less concern for efforts at arriving at solutions and making public life go well.

Under the new mission of public journalism carried out by news organization's public life teams, the new criteria for news might well be:

Revitalization. When an idea or event can quash cynicism and renew faith in democracy, it is especially newsworthy.

Self-discovery. When an idea or event will help a community understand itself and take stock of strengths and weaknesses, it becomes newsworthy.

Self-actualization. Information that can help ordinary citizens make their voices heard and that can improve their community should be told.

Perspective. Corruption needs exposure and is part of what makes news, but this should be put in perspective with the good news spotlighting people who do their jobs well.

Self-governance. Democracy at work is a fitting subject for exposition, whether it be found in a council chamber, PTA, or a crime block party.

Engagement. When an idea or event can show a lively, informed, and most of all, engaged public—that idea or event merits journalistic coverage and citizen attention.

As Davis Merritt insists in the title of his book on public journalism, "telling the news is not enough." It is certainly not enough for the prospective converts to public journalism who have made the intellectual journey through the great declines, through the sins of the news media, and through to the evangel's redemptory message that unveils a wholistic journalism.

NOTES

1. William Packard, *Evangelism in America* (New York: Paragon House, 1988), p. 2.

2. Davis Merritt, *Public Journalism & Public Life: Why Telling the News Isn't Enough* (Hilldale, New Jersey: Lawrence Erlbaum Associates, 1995), p. 113.

3. Robert Putnam, "Bowling Alone: America's Declining Social Capital," *Journal of Democracy* (January, 1995), pp. 65–70.

4. Merritt, op. cit., p. 9.

5. E. J. Dionne Jr., *Why Americans Hate Politics* (New York: Touchstone, 1991), pp. 24–38.

6. Dionne, op. cit., pp. 237–255.

7. James B. Twitchell, *Carnival Culture: The Trashing of Taste in America* (New York: Columbia University Press,1992), p. 3.

8. Kathleen Hall Jamieson, and David Birdsell, *Presidential Debates* (New York: Oxford University Press, 1988), pp. 49–56.

9. Ibid., pp. 17–37.

10. Ibid., pp. 170–171.

11. Howard Kurtz, *Media Circus: The Trouble with America's Newspapers* (New York: Times Books, 1993), pp. 329–330.

12. Ibid., pp. 329–330.

13. Jay Rosen, "What Should We Be Doing?" *The IRE Journal* (November-December, 1996), p. 6.

14. Kurtz, op. cit., pp. 355–356.

15. Rosen, op. cit., p. 6.

16. Stan Cloud, "Confessions of a Sinner," *Civic Catalyst* (April, 1996), p. 3.

17. James Fallows, *Breaking the News* (New York: Vintage Books, 1996), p. 15.

18. Merritt, op. cit., pp. 42–43.

19. Ibid., p. 42.

20. Fallows, op. cit., pp. 77–78.

21. Ibid., pp. 127–128.

22. Merritt, op. cit., p. 58.

23. Ibid., p. 58

24. *Civic Journalism: A Video Study Guide*. Washington, D.C.: Pew Center for Civic Journalism, 1995, pp. 2–3.

25. Fallows, op. cit., pp. 224–226.

26. Ibid., p. 246.

27. Merritt, op. cit., pp. 93–97.

28. Michael Sandel, *Liberalism and the Limits of Justice* (New York: Cambridge University Press, 1982), p. 183.

29. Fallows, op. cit., p. 250.

30. Merritt, op. cit., pp. 94–95.

31. Rosen, op. cit., p. 7.

32. Jay Rosen, "Public Journalism as a Democratic Art." Pamphlet adapted from a presentation at the American Press Institute, Reston, Virginia, November 11, 1994, p. 11.

33. Jay Rosen, "What Should We Be Doing?" *The IRE Journal* (November-December, 1996), p. 7.

34. Ibid., p. 7.

35. Arthur Charity, *Doing Public Journalism* (New York: Guilford Press, 1995), p.11.

36. Jay Rosen, "Public Journalism as a Democratic Art." Pamphlet adapted from a presentation at the American Press Institute, Reston, Virginia, November 11, 1994, p. 4.

37. Ibid., p. 3.

38. Ibid., p. 4.

39. Ibid., p. 7.

40. The Missouri Group, *News Reporting and Writing* (New York: St. Martin's Press, 1988), pp. 4–6.

2
The Evangelists

More than a few journalism educators, newspaper editors, reporters, and radio talk show hosts have dismissed public journalism as a fad. Their attitude is summed up in the words of one talk radio personality: "This is something that will go away if we don't talk about it too much."[1] Most of these media personalities, educators, and news practitioners underestimate the zeal, energy, and loquaciousness of those attracted to the evangel of public journalism. Public journalism is a passion for its converts within the news media, many who have grown to loathe what they see as the inadequacies and the excesses of their profession.

This passion is sometimes the only cement that holds advocates of public journalism together, for the proponents can be a very diverse group. In their diversity, they can often bring vastly different interpretations to the meaning of public journalism. This has been referred to as "the definition problem" of public journalism. For example, the journalism professor whose academic compass points toward the social sciences tends to view public journalism as a justification for a brand of reporting that is advocacy-oriented. This reporting addresses social inequities and the uneven distribution of income in society. In contrast, the journalism professor whose academic compass points toward business and economics is likely to view public journalism as a justification for reporting that is more market-oriented. This reporting provides news fare tailored to fit public taste as determined by surveys and focus groups. Ideally, this tailoring will help recapture lost audiences and boost the bottom line for news businesses.

The differing interpretations of public journalism become obvious in even the most cursory examination of the many spokespersons for the movement. For example, journalist and educator Chuck Stone subscribes to a public journalism that is advocacy-oriented and which campaigns on issues on a newspaper's front page. In contrast, Davis "Buzz" Merritt cautions against the view that public journalism is advocacy journalism. Declares Merritt, "It does not mean trying to determine outcomes, but it does mean accepting the obligation to help the process of public life determine the outcomes."[2]

This chapter's alphabetical listing of public journalism's evangelists includes theorists and practitioners, but the categories for those associated with public journalism can be refined to an even greater extent to include philosophical forerunners, foundation supporters, scholars, and educators. Some of these proponents cannot be summarily categorized as in one camp or another. For example, Davis "Buzz" Merritt is clearly one of the major theorists of public journalism with his book, *Public Journalism & Public Life: Why Telling the News Isn't Enough*, which attempts to explain the philosophy that fuels the practice. Nevertheless, Merritt also has to be recognized as a public journalism practitioner with his early experiments in reporting with the new approach as editor of *The Wichita Eagle*. Cole Campbell is another public journalism proponent who could easily merit a designation as theorist and practitioner.

Philosophical forerunners include John Dewey, Neil Postman, Robert Putnam, Michael Sandel, Michael Schudson, and Daniel Yankelovitch. Public journalism's philosophical forerunners have authored works from which the movement's ideas and key tenets have been drawn. Advocates have likewise drawn from the work of Robert Putnam who argues that Americans are more isolated from public life and less connected with their communities. Advocates have drawn from the work of Postman because his analysis of the shortcomings of the conventional news media is consistent with their own indictment. Schudson's scholarship has been important because of its work in exposing the unspoken power of journalists in their capacity to frame stories in particular ways.

Examining the philosophical precursors of public journalism, John Dewey would have to be singled out for special attention. Dewey's observations on the press and democracy figure heavily in the many manuscripts authored by Jay Rosen, who is often referred to as the guru of public journalism. Rosen's contention is that the "last great exchange" on the subject of the press and its role in democracy was between Dewey and Walter Lippmann in the 1920s.[3] Rosen clearly comes down on the side of Dewey whom he feels was much more sensitive to the role of an informed public in the decision-making of a democracy.

Theorists include James Carey, Cole Campbell, James Fallows, Philip Meyer, Davis Merritt, and Jay Rosen. Some journalism researchers might take issue with the inclusion of Campbell, Fallows, and Meyer as theoreticians for public journalism. Campbell and Fallows are practitioners whose daily lives continue to be absorbed in the process of doing journalism on a regular basis. Nevertheless, Campbell and Fallows have both written thoughtful pieces that have been incorporated into the public journalism philosophy. Meyers is most noted for his work in journalistic survey work and precision journalism; however, he also has contributed discourse as a friend of public journalism on its need to better define and defend itself.

While Rosen frequently laments his designation as the guru of public journalism, there is no question that he has become the oracle that is ultimately sought out for comment in any exposition on public journalism. For that reason alone he has to be singled out as the most noted theoretician for the reform movement. His close ally, James Carey, has written some remarkable pieces on democracy and the press, the impact of the new technologies, and the adversarial style of the press. In Carey's most recent collection, *James Carey: A Critical Reader*, the noted media scholar and cultural historian endorses public journalism as "an experiment whose end is in doubt, but whose purpose is not: it is nothing less than the re-creation of a participant, speaking public, ritually formed for democratic purposes, brought to life via conversation between citizen journalists and journalist citizens."[4]

Practitioners include Dale Allen, Jennie Buckner, Frank Denton, Randy Hammer, Alex Marshall, and Steve Smith. Hundreds of newspapers have experimented with public journalism in some form; therefore, it is beyond the purview of this work to list all of the many practitioners who have engaged in projects or story series works that are consistent with the new approach to news media. Some of these practitioners have been singled out because they have been vocal on the topic of public journalism or they have been recognized for excellence in its execution.

Smith, editor of the *Colorado Springs Gazette-Telegraph*, is a frequent seminar speaker and conference panelist who defends public journalism from its critics, whom he dismisses as elitists. Allen is the editor of the *Akron Beacon-Journal*, which won the 1994 Pulitzer Prize for public service for the excellence of its series, "A Question of Color," which was aimed at improving race relations in the Akron, Ohio area.

Scholars include Jay Black, Carolyn Click, Clifford Christians, Renita Coleman, and Bob Steele. Black, who holds the Poynter-Jamison chair in media ethics at the University of South Florida, has put together a useful collection of perspectives on public journalism with his book, *Mixed News: The Public/Civic/ Communitarian Journalism Debate*. Black includes in his collection an article by Poynter Institute ethicist, Bob Steele, who wrestles with the issues of detachment, journalistic independence, and public journalism.

Clifford Christians is a communication scholar who emerges from the communitarian tradition. Christians is the author of *Good News: Social Ethics & the Press* along with John P. Ferré and P. Mark Fackler. Christians and his colleagues argue for a fundamental change in the news media's worldview that would allow journalists to incorporate certain common moral norms in framing stories. Christians and other communitarians are attracted to public journalism as consistent with the communitarian philosophy.[5]

Some of the individuals in this compendium have been selected as scholars for the papers they have presented on public journalism at academic conferences, such as the annual conventions of the Association for Education in Journalism and Mass Communication (AEJMC). Coleman's paper, "The Intellectual Antecedents of Public Journalism," contends that the reform movement in journalism has its intellectual origins with the 1947 Hutchins Commission and the emergence of social responsibility theory.[6]

Foundation Supporters include Ed Fouhy, David Mathews, Cy Porter, Rebecca Rimel, and Jan Schaeffer. Ed Fouhy and Jan Schaeffer, early leaders of the Pew Center for Civic Journalism, have been at the forefront of efforts to foster public journalism projects at newspapers around the country. Newspapers and other interested parties, such as journalism schools and civic organizations, are invited to apply for funding from Pew for specific projects. A number of practitioners included in this compendium have been involved in the Pew Center's Project Reconnect initiatives. Rebecca Rimel is president of the Pew Charitable Trusts, which allocates $180 million of foundation money annually.

There are any number of other foundations that have been part of the public journalism movement, either as funders or as part of specific public journalism projects. Cy Porter has served as community journalism director for the Radio And Television News Directors Foundation (RTNDF) and has authored a management reference guide entitled, *Community Journalism: Getting Started*. David Mathews is author of *Politics for People* and is president of the Dayton, Ohio Kettering Foundation, which has been involved in newspaper consulting work and has assisted many dailies with their public journalism projects.

Educators include Arthur Charity, Cheryl Gibbs, Mark Haab, and Ed Lambeth. Haab merits note as a proponent of incorporating public journalism techniques into high school level journalism, an idea that is destined to spread beyond his home state of Indiana. College journalism professor Gibbs insists that with the publication of Charity's, *Doing Public Journalism*, Merritt's *Public Journalism & Public Life*, and the many monographs of Rosen, there is now a sufficient body of scholarship and available texts to teach public journalism at the university level.

Lambeth, a professor at the University of Missouri School of Journalism and founder of the public journalism interest group of the Association for Education in Journalism and Mass Communication, is one of those university instructors on the cutting edge. He is teaching public journalism methodology, as are a number of other professors across the country. Charity's book, *Doing Public Journalism*, is the first text for college use and includes a teacher's guide with public journalism exercises for students.

This is an incomplete listing of public journalism's many advocates. Also a few sentences on each individual's observations can hardly do justice to the thinking that each has committed to the idea of public journalism. Additionally, not all of the public journalism evangelists listed are equal in their contributions to the evangel. Obviously, theorists such as Rosen, Carey, and Merritt have created a more extensive body of work than others. This compendium is simply offered as a starting point for those interested in making "the intellectual journey" advocates insist is required for any understanding or commitment to doing public journalism.

PUBLIC JOURNALISM'S PHILOSOPHERS, THEORISTS, AND MORE

Dale Allen

Dale Allen is editor of the *Akron Beacon-Journal*, which won the 1994 Pulitzer Prize for public service for the excellence of its series, "A Question of Color." The project was aimed at improving race relations in the Akron, Ohio area.

The series identified barriers to better race relations between blacks and whites in the community, and enlisted different organizations to help with projects to bring blacks and whites together.

In December 1993, the paper ended the series by asking residents to mail in a coupon with a New Year's pledge to work at improving race relations in 1994. More than 22,000 residents returned the coupons. The paper also had 10,000 T-shirts, pins, and caps made bearing the logo, "Coming Together," which celebrated the collaboration on efforts to encourage diversity and better race relations.[7] The *Akron Beacon-Journal* project has been hailed by some public journalists as a classic example of how public journalism works, while other public journalists contend that this is not a good example of the philosophy in action.

Rob Anderson

Professor Rob Anderson of St. Louis University has collaborated with professors Robert Dardenne of the University of South Florida and George Killenberg, also of South Florida, to write, "The Conversation of Journalism: Communication, Community, and News." Anderson argues that journalism is broken and that something must be done before newspapers become superfluous in public life. Anderson and his colleagues advocate "a particular kind of public journalism that is faithful to one of our oldest social structures, the commons. Instead of a bundle of news reports, the newspaper becomes—like a town commons—a site for public dialogue shared by all citizens and accessible to all citizens.[8]

Lisa Austin

Lisa Austin, a research director for the Project on Public Life and the Press, contends that journalists have played a role in the deterioration of public life. They have done this by failing to see story subjects as citizens. A new, alternative coverage is required. "Alternative coverage begins to encompass new sources, group interviews, or a broad source base such as an interview pool of poll respondents," declares Austin. "Instead of seeing a citizen they are interviewing as merely a 'good quote,' 'a reader,' or 'some idiot,' it is possible for a journalist to recognize times when sources step out of themselves and weigh their own interests against the needs of the community."[9]

Peter Bhatia

Peter Bhatia of *The Oregonian* and John Russial of the University of Oregon's School of Journalism and Communication have engaged in a public journalism project addressing the disconnect of environmental protection groups and environmental businesses and industry. This is by far one of the most difficult areas in which to bring opposing parties to common ground.

The Oregonian is conducting the effort to find common ground among opposing environmental interests under the Pew-funded Project Reconnect programs. The program seeks to end different types of disconnect and to give news organizations an opportunity to explore "coverage that rings more 'true' to that [disconnected] public without abrogating journalistic values and responsibility for objectivity and fairness."[10]

James Batten

James Batten, long-time chairman and chief executive of Knight-Ridder Inc., was a hard-nosed traditional journalist who came to see public journalism as a way to revive interest in newspapers. In his later years, Batten encouraged newspapers in the Knight-Ridder group to experiment and to find ways to connect with their communities. Now deceased, Batten is cited as one of the early believers in public journalism.

An annual award for excellence in civic or public journalism is now given in honor of James K. Batten and carries his name. The award of $25,000, funded through the Pew Charitable Trusts, is meant to foster Batten's commitment to journalism that encourages citizen participation as well as informed citizens. According to Pew officials, this can be demonstrated by "work that helps residents identify problems, promotes true and careful deliberation, of possible solutions, illuminates the common ground on difficult issues and advances participatory democracy in other ways."[11]

Jay Black

Jay Black has spoken favorably on the impact of the public journalism movement at the annual convention panel sessions of the Association for Education in Journalism and Mass Communication (AEJMC). Black has put together a useful collection of perspectives on public journalism with his book, *Mixed News: The Public/Civic/Communitarian Journalism Debate.*

Black, who holds the Poynter-Jamison chair in media ethics at the University of South Florida, offers an extended annotated bibliography of books, monographs, and academic and trade articles on public journalism at the conclusion of his book.[12]

Judy Bolch

Judy Bolch of *The Raleigh News & Observer* and the University of North Carolina's School of Journalism have been cooperating on a public journalism project addressing the disconnect of news reporters and coverage of blue-collar neighborhoods. As newspaper staffs become populated with college graduates and journalists who've attained master's degrees, there is concern that the news organizations are less in touch with the blue-collar segment of their communities.

The Raleigh News & Observer is one of six newspapers doing public journalism under Pew-funded Project Reconnect programs. Among the approaches being used by the six newspapers to reach out to disaffected audiences are focus groups, community forums, moderated discussions with opinion leaders, one-on-

one interviews with citizens and community leaders, surveys, and techniques of public listening.[13]

David Broder

David Broder, a highly-respected political reporter and columnist for *The Washington Post*, is credited with implicitly endorsing the approach of public journalism based on his speeches and writings about the work of political reporting. In a speech at the University of California at Riverside, Broder criticized much political reporting as cynical and an insiders' game. He said that too many political reporters are more closely aligned with the candidates and the consultants, rather than to the public whom they are supposed to serve.[14]

In an article in the *St. Petersburg Times* in 1996, Broder is critical of the lack of civility in our public and political conversations, and he argues for initiatives that increase civic involvement. He declares that the movement of promoting civic life is gaining support on a number of fronts.[15]

Jennie Buckner

Jennie Buckner, the executive editor of *The Charlotte Observer*, has helped spearhead the public journalism projects at the North Carolina newspaper along with editor Rich Oppel, reporter Rick Thames, and with the cooperation of publisher Rolfe Neill. Buckner and her colleagues have probably pioneered more public journalism projects than any other newspaper.[16]

After depressing crime statistics about Charlotte were released in 1994, the newspaper decided to try something different. Buckner says traditional crime reporting leaves residents frightened and depressed about the future of their community. After amassing some grant money from the Pew Center for Civic Journalism and several media and charitable partners, the *Observer* launched the series, "Taking Back Our Neighborhoods," an 18-month project that focused Charlotte's attention on ten target areas in an effort to reduce crime.[17]

Cole Campbell

Cole Campbell, editor of the *St. Louis Post-Dispatch*, has often been cited as one of the key practitioners of public journalism, primarily because of his previous work at the (Norfolk) *Virginian-Pilot*. Campbell often takes aim at two criteria of what makes news under traditional journalism: novelty and conflict.

"For too long our standard of news has been novelty; what's new or different or unusual or deviant, and not, in fact, information that helps people solve problems," insists Campbell. "We need to help people take the information that they already have access to, and fertilize it, and develop it so they can begin to really pick some bouquets, and pick some things that they can eat; help people understand the meaning of what's happening in the world rather than simply telling them: 'Here's the latest bulletin.'"[18]

James Carey

James Carey, author and professor in the graduate school of journalism at Columbia University, has written much about the ideal of public life. He notes that public life can be described as vital and viable when citizens are involved with their communities, when citizens are engaged in public conversation about improving their communities, and when citizens share a hopefulness that they can make a difference in the direction their communities take.

The role of journalists, according to Carey, is to see that public life goes well. "The god term of journalism—the be-all and end-all, the term without which the entire enterprise fails to make sense—is the public," declares Carey. "Insofar as journalism has a client, the client is the public. The press justifies itself in the name of the public: It exists—or so it is regularly said—to inform the public, to serve as the extended eyes and ears of the public, to protect the public's right to know, to serve the public interest."[19]

Hodding Carter III

Hodding Carter III holds the Knight Chair in journalism at the University of Maryland College of Journalism and is an ardent proponent of public journalism. Carter believes that traditional journalism is full of purveyors of cynicism and despair. Only the dramatic reform of public journalism will improve the outlook for the news media.

"We are now in the middle of real change because, despite ourselves, we know that, if we don't, we are as dead as every other institution that refused to change in the middle of change," Carter tells his colleagues in journalism.[20]

Arthur Charity

Arthur Charity is the author of *Doing Public Journalism*, which has been adopted for college journalism classes that teach the public journalism approach. Charity talks about the need for public journalists to locate and develop civic capital. Philosophers and practitioners of public journalism have begun to speak about civic capital as something that improves a community and its democratic process.

Charity describes civic capital as "anything that improves the productivity of a community—that is its ability to meet crises, solve problems, live connectedly." A newspaper should become a locus of civic capital rather than simply a conduit of information.[21]

Clifford Christians

Clifford Christians is a University of Illinois professor who believes in a journalism grounded in community instead of individualism. Christians sees many parallels between public journalism and his own conception of communitarian journalism. He believes public journalism at its best is communitarian journalism.

What exactly is communitarian journalism? Professor John C. Merrill of the University of Missouri School of Journalism says it is journalism that "should solidify the community, not fractionalize it; absolutist ethics needed for social harmony and cohesion; reluctance to publish stories that might fractionalize society; desire to bring social harmony through 'positive' journalism; de-emphasizing older Enlightenment liberalism and journalistic autonomy."[22]

Carolyn Click

Carolyn Click of *The State* in Columbia, South Carolina, and Ernest L. Wiggins of the College of Journalism and Mass Communications at the University of South Carolina have been involved in a public journalism project to address the disconnect with conservative Christians and people of religious faith. This particular "disconnect" has come under increasing scrutiny as conservative Christians view newspapers as a largely secular and hostile culture.

Under the Pew-funded Project Reconnect programs, "Newsroom staffs will be involved in discussions and briefings that focus on how [each] paper currently frames stories of particular interest to its disconnected public and how it might provide coverage that rings more 'true' to that public without abrogating journalistic values and responsibility for objectivity and fairness."[23]

Renita Coleman

Renita Coleman, an academic and scholar at the University of Missouri-Columbia, has analyzed public journalism from a number of perspectives. Her 1996 paper given at the convention of the Association for Education in Journalism and Mass Communication (AEJMC), argues that the definitions of the movement articulated thus far are inadequate for the development of an explicitly theoretical foundation upon which to do research. She further argues that public journalism's link with various theories of communitarian philosophy should be studied as an aid to defining its place in journalism's history.

Her 1997 paper given at the annual convention of AEJMC examined treatment of public journalism in the *Columbia Journalism Review* (*CJR*), the *American Journalism Review* (*AJR*), and the Nieman Reports. In reviewing 45 articles, Coleman said the treatment has, in most cases, matured from "name calling and black-and-white reporting" to more reflective pieces on public journalism.[24]

Frank Denton

Frank Denton is editor of the *Wisconsin State-Journal* in Madison, Wisconsin, which is credited with some of the most original experiments of the 1990s in public journalism. Denton contends that ordinary citizens can be pulled into town hall meetings, candidate debates, and citizenship training by a news media that commits to caring about their concerns. In its experiments, the Madison newspaper teamed up with radio and television outlets for a collaborative effort.

"We the People," is the name associated with Denton and the public journalism experiments that were conducted by the *State Journal*. Started as a one-time presidential election project, it soon evolved into an ongoing exploration of the manner in which politics and public policy affect ordinary people. Subsequent projects involved town hall meetings on the federal deficit, property tax relief, health care reform, and more.[25]

John Dewey

John Dewey, educator, philosopher, and author in the early twentieth century, is championed by many public journalists as a prophet on the need for the public to be engaged in policy decisions. Dewey appears frequently in the writings of public journalism advocate Jay Rosen as well as in the work of James Fallows in his critique of the press. Dewey's views are often contrasted with those of journalist and philosopher Walter Lippmann. Fallows maintains that the philosophical argument between Dewey and Lippmann about the roles of government and the press echo the arguments today between public journalists and their critics.

Dewey is credited with arguing that a healthy process of democratic decision-making is every bit as important as the efficacy of the result. If citizens are not involved in the big decisions made by a society, then those decisions would be undermined by the alienation and unhappiness of the bypassed citizens. In contrast, public journalists insist that Lippmann believed society in the twentieth century had become too technologically advanced and intricate for the old-style democracy of town hall meetings and plebiscites. The only option for effective modern-day governance lay in the creation of an expert class that would manage the country's communication as well as its governmental affairs. Under this modern-day arrangement, communicators and journalists would help lead public opinion to the right decisions in an increasingly complex society.[26]

E. J. Dionne

E. J. Dionne is a newspaper columnist for *The Washington Post* and the author of *Why Americans Hate Politics*. Public journalism proponents frequently draw from his work in putting together their critique of political and public life in America. Dionne targets a lack of imagination in political argumentation, which he feels is still rooted in the culture wars of the 1960s. Dionne insist that most Americans are tired of ideology and more interested in pragmatism in solving society's problems.

Dionne is convinced that the renewal of American politics will happen with the creation of a new and vital center that moves away from acrimony and partisanship. What is needed is a view that "politics is not some grubby confrontation of competing interests but an arena in which citizens can learn from each other and deliver an 'enlightened self-interest' in common."[27]

James Engelhardt

James Engelhardt of the University of Oregon has applied Steven Lukes' multidimensional conception of power to the public journalism movement. Engelhardt argues that there is a difference between civic journalism and public journalism. This is an interesting approach to the subject because much of the literature in the field assumes that "public" and "civic" journalism are one and the same thing.

Civic journalism is more scientific and based on polls and collecting data, according to Engelhardt's study presented at the 1997 convention of AEJMC. In contrast, public journalism is based more on citizen input and citizen forums, Engelhardt insists. He does give credence to the advocates' cause by maintaining that both public and civic journalism consist of more than just good journalism.[28]

James Ettema

James Ettema is a professor at Northwestern University and a public journalism advocate. Ettema says that underprivileged communities have not fared well under traditional journalism approaches.

Traditional journalism has given American society a view of these communities as little more than "needy and problematic and deficient neighborhoods populated by needy and problematic and deficient people," according to Ettema. He argues that journalism should focus on community assets in underprivileged areas to give a more positive rendering of these communities. Public journalism is a way to focus on cultural groups, block clubs, citizen associations, and neighborhood leaders, that is, community assets, as a way to break out of the confining negative coverage of underprivileged areas.[29]

Amitai Etzioni

Amitai Etzioni, chairman of the Communitarian Network in Washington, D.C., is considered one of the spiritual and philosophical forerunners of public journalism. Author of the manifesto, *The Spirit of Community: Rights, Responsibilities, and the Communitarian Agenda*, Etzioni has attempted to chart a centrist position in American politics that is wed to neither liberal nor conservative ideologies as expressed among the fringe elements in U.S. political parties.[30]

Communitarians find a vindication of much of what they've been saying for decades in the arrival of the public journalism movement of the 1990s. Communitarians have long denounced the negativity of the news media and the conflict model that has been used by reporters to frame stories on national and international issues.

Ed Fouhy

One of the major influences on journalism in the West in this century has been the Cold War, which has divided the world into "us" and "them." This has resulted in an "us" and "them" approach as a convenient template for many journalistic stories, especially in foreign affairs.

Public journalist Ed Fouhy, past director of the Pew Center for Civic Journalism, argues that the breakdown of the old bipolar world, with the fall of the Berlin Wall and Soviet communism, should also be an impetus for ending an outdated bipolar journalistic approach to news coverage.[31]

James Fallows

James Fallows is a former editor for *The Atlantic* and the former editor of *U.S. News & World Report.* He is the author of *Breaking the News: How the Media Undermines American Democracy.* Fallows insists that journalists, especially political reporters, like to report as insiders providing coverage for other insiders.

Fallows contends that the reporters who cover politics in this country put too much energy into covering the wrong kinds of stories. They concentrate on the horse race aspect of elections and "gotcha' stories" instead of concentrating on issues. A gotcha' story can involve reporters catching a candidate making a statement that contradicts something the candidate said earlier, and focusing excessively on what might simply be an honest gaffe.[32]

James Fishkin

James Fishkin, a professor in the department of government at the University of Texas at Austin, is often credited as the inventor of the deliberative opinion poll, which has struck a chord with many in the public journalism movement. According to this concept, a representative sample of Americans gathers in one place for several days to meet candidates in an election, to judge them face-to-face, and to deliberate and discuss issues with candidates.[33]

Fishkin's book, *Democracy and Deliberation: New Directions for Democratic Reform*, is highly recommended by public journalism advocates as a key to understanding the concept of deliberative democracy. Fishkin says he believes survey research can be used much more constructively than it has in the past when used by a news media committed to improving public life. He also says the "considered judgments of a nationally representative microcosm should have a certain authority, a kind of recommending force."[34]

Chris Gates

Chris Gates is a leader of the National Civic League, an organization known for its "All America Cities Awards." In recent years, the league has been involved in efforts for national civic renewal in cooperation with foundations, chambers of commerce, and other civic groups.

Gates argues that old-style journalism is failing to document the stories of civic renewal emerging across the country. According to Gates, old-style journalism concentrates on covering a handful of people in a given community—the people who matter and who make most of the decisions. Gates argues that journalism now has to adjust to new circumstances because community activism is bringing more people into decision-making who merit news coverage. Gates further argues that news practitioners must increasingly make the work of a community their work as well.[35]

Cheryl Gibbs

Cheryl Gibbs is one of an increasing number of journalism professors across the country teaching public journalism in university courses. Gibbs argues that with the publication of Arthur Charity's *Doing Public Journalism*, Davis Merritt's *Public Journalism & Public Life*, and the many monographs of Jay Rosen, there is now a sufficient body of scholarship and available texts to teach public journalism practice as a way to do journalism.

In her 1995 research into university teaching of public journalism, Gibbs examined how techniques were being incorporated into college journalism coursework at Indiana University, Ithaca College, University of Missouri, University of South Florida, Wichita State University, and more. At Indiana University, Dave Boeyink had his students examine five ways of thinking about journalists' relationships to their community: as entertainers, objective conduits, watchdogs, advocates, and public journalists. The class was divided into teams to develop a news coverage plan that fit each one of the philosophies.[36]

Theodore Glasser

Theodore Glasser, professor at Stanford University, suggests that public journalism makes a citizen into a participant and not simply a spectator. He argues that "a publicly told story engages others not by informing them but by inviting them to share in the discovery of a world in which they can recognize themselves."[37]

Glasser contends the stance of the traditional press as "detached observer" results in its failure to see itself as a public institution that is bound by the same standards and accountability as is expected of other public institutions.

Mark Haab

Mark Haab is the publications director and *Owl* newspaper adviser at Warren Central High School In Indianapolis, Indiana, and a leading proponent of public journalism at the high school level. Haab became excited about public journalism after a meeting with Dennis Cripe, executive director of the Indiana High Press Association, who explained to him the growing professional trend of public journalism in reporting.

Among the possible elements of public journalism that can be brought to high school publications, according to Haab, are: previewing a story idea with reader response, focusing on success stories, and holding town hall meetings for the whole school community. "Having this idea of civic journalism proves to your administration that you're not out in every story just to tear the school down—to dig for that little piece of dirt."[38]

Randy Hammer

Randy Hammer, executive editor of the *Huntington Herald-Dispatch* in West Virginia, began looking for ways to address the region's economic problems in 1993. The area had been hit heavily in the last decade by a loss of manufacturing and coal mining jobs. After convening a meeting with local leaders and sending out reporters to interview hundreds of citizens about their vision of the region's economic future, the newspaper ran a special section entitled, "Our Jobs, Our Children, Our Future."

As with most public journalism projects, Hammer was eager to get citizen involvement in the project. A major item in the project was a clip-out coupon which asked: "What one thing should be done to bring jobs to the area?" The coupons came back to the newspaper with plenty of ideas and the paper followed with a coupon asking for volunteers to help with projects and town hall meetings on the economic future of Huntington.[39]

Dennis Hartig

Dennis Hartig is a practitioner of public journalism and the managing editor of *The* (Norfolk) *Virginian-Pilot*. Hartig subscribes to a view that news organizations should have "well-defined public purposes that serve as boundaries for story assignments and news judgments."[40]

These purposes include framing politics as a community problem-solving process and not simply as a contest between competing interest groups. Hartig worked with Cole Campbell, past editor of the Virginia paper, on some of the first public journalism projects.

Richard Harwood

Richard Harwood, president of The Harwood Group and author of *Meaningful Chaos*, has been involved in newspaper consulting work and has assisted many dailies with their public journalism initiatives. In 1992, he was tapped by public journalism advocate Cole Campbell, then editor of *The Virginian-Pilot*, to train the paper's public life team in public listening and to consult with them about how they might use their work with citizens.

Harwood tells reporters that they must reconsider their conventional journalistic habit of telling people about bad news—the environment is on the skids, the schools are in ruin, criminals are running free and creating mayhem. "It's not that people don't want bad news, it's that they want it in the context of the 'whole story,' which includes what can be done."[41]

Janice Hume

Janice Hume was one of a team of academics at the University of Missouri who authored a study using q-methodology to explain how news practitioners view public journalism. The study found that a sizeable number of journalists are struggling to find new ways to practice journalism, with a new emphasis on involving citizens in shaping media content.

The study came up with four typologies in the examination: civic journalism supporters, concerned traditionalists, neutral observers, and the responsible liberals. Responsible liberals make up the largest type of journalists from the two dailies examined in the study. "What separates the responsible liberals from civic journalists is their belief in the need for a change," the study reported. "Responsible liberals don't think journalists have failed in their responsibilities and don't see a need for basic changes in journalism, while civic journalists see a need for a new press system."[42]

Max Jennings

Max Jennings is a practitioner of public journalism and the managing editor of the *Dayton Daily News*. Public journalism is a movement whose time has come as we shift from a system of representative democracy to a new era of participatory democracy, according to Jennings.

"We older white men for decades have framed the nation's news coverage in the same old ways, through the same personal filters, using much the same type of reporter methodology," confesses Jennings. He says it's time for a change.[43]

George Killenberg

George Killenberg of the University of Southern Florida has collaborated with professors Robert Dardenne, also of the University of South Florida, and Rob Anderson of St. Louis University, to write "The Conversation of Journalism: Communication, Community, and News." Killenberg's gravitation to public journalism is apparent in a number of his essays as well as in another textbook he has written, *Public Affairs Reporting*.

Killenberg believes traditional journalism has put too much focus on official viewpoints, an emphasis that appears to be endemic with the conventional beat system. Stationed as they are at police headquarters or the courthouse, reporters naturally learn to rely on "reliable sources." Killenberg applauds public journalism for its philosophy of moving reporters out of their small circles and into the larger arena of public life.[44]

Ed Lambeth

Ed Lambeth is the founder of the civic (public) journalism interest group of journalism professors (AEJMC) and the author of *Committed Journalism*. Lambeth has held seminars on how to incorporate public journalism into college classroom teaching.

Lambeth takes particular aim at the adversarial stance of the traditional news media—the watchdog role that the press plays in reporting on the rich, the powerful, and those elected to positions of power. "There is a sense in which an adversarial posture becomes an ideology that prevents the sensitive interpretation and application of the principles of humaneness, truth telling, justice, freedom/ independence, and the stewardship of free expression," declares Lambeth, a journalism professor from the University of Missouri-Columbia.[45]

Alex Marshall

Alex Marshall is an urban affairs reporter whose newspaper, *The Virginian-Pilot* of Norfolk, Virginia, is credited with some of the first experiments in public journalism. Marshall describes public journalism as not simply a technique, but a philosophy. He advocates a new kind of investigative reporting that moves toward uncovering the failures and successes of government and society, rather than revealing the misdeeds of minor public officials.

Marshall's philosophy is reflected in one of his favorite sayings, "Journalism focuses too much on the rotten apple and not enough on the rotten barrel." Public journalism encourages more attention on the health of the barrel, whether it's rotten or sound.[46]

David Mathews

David Mathews is author of *Politics for People* and president of the Kettering Foundation, which has been involved in newspaper consulting work and has assisted many dailies with their public journalism projects. The Kettering Foundation, located in Dayton, Ohio, assisted the *Dayton Daily News* with its public journalism project on juvenile violence. Kettering consultants completed a National Issues Forum (NIF) Guide that was useful for *Dayton Daily News'* editors as they planned out their "Kids in Chaos" project.

Mathews says he believes citizens are disenchanted with systems in this country because they no longer solve problems. Not the political system, the judicial system, or the educational system in the United States seems capable of solving problems in many citizens' eyes. Mathews believe journalists should consult less with the professionals in these systems and more with the disenchanted citizens. "I think that what should happen with newspapers is that stories are presented in public terms, in terms of what is valuable to the public, which is different in most cases from what is valuable to the experts or the professionals.[47]

Davis "Buzz" Merritt

Davis "Buzz" Merritt is a former editor of *The Wichita Eagle* and author of one of the leading texts on public journalism. Merritt challenges many of the fundamental tenets of traditional journalism and calls for a paradigm shift in thinking among reporters and editors. This involves the shift to public journalism.

Reporters and editors must do more than simply engage in projects that are inspired by the public journalism creed. Broad mental shifts must occur, according to Merritt, that bring about a journalism that moves "beyond only describing what 'is going wrong' [in a community] to also describing what 'going right' would be like. By describing realistic possibilities that lie beyond immediate solutions, it informs people of their potential choices for the future."[48]

Philip Meyer

Philip Meyer is well known for his books on polling and the use of statistics in journalism. He is the Knight Professor at the University of North Carolina at Chapel Hill. Meyer has been both a critic and an advocate of public journalism. He contends that much of the criticism of public journalism must rest on the shoulders of its early promoters who have been reluctant to give it a definition or anything more than some vague theoretical underpinnings.

Meyer has sorted out six attributes of public journalism which he feels are important to its definition and its defense. Those attributes include a desire to rebuild a community's sense of itself, an insistence on a longer attention span by the news media when it covers a problem or issue, a willingness to delve more deeply into the systems that direct our lives, more attention to the rational middle ground on public issues and less attention to the bizarre extremes, a preference for covering substance over tactics in reporting on political issues, and a desire to foster deliberation so that a community may talk with itself to work through a problem to a solution.[49]

Christine Newby-Fiebich

Christine Newby-Fiebich is a scholar who has studied the agenda-setting function and related influences of the news media. Among mass communication scholars, the importance of agenda-setting studies is immense. These analyses examine the power of the news media and how the issues journalists select, or do not select, to report affect the everyday lives of ordinary people.

Newby-Fiebich examined the "agenda-setting function of local and national media" on the Wichita, Kansas area, where *The Wichita Eagle* practices public journalism. Newby-Fiebich found that local television has the biggest impact on setting the agenda for citizens, while the daily newspaper appeared to have an impact on the way citizens rank concerns. Consequently, the public journalism practice of *The Wichita Eagle* may have had an impact on the beliefs of the public regarding the significance of various issues.[50]

John Pauly

John Pauly is a professor and chair of the communication department at St. Louis University. An advocate of public journalism, Pauly has written a number of scholarly essays on the public journalism philosophy and its execution. Pauly argues that public journalism can only work well at a newspaper when it becomes part of the philosophy of the news operation or part of a transformation of the traditional newsroom culture.

Pauly says that the critique of traditional journalism that is found in public journalism has been around for at least 15 years, and actually supersedes the 1990s movement of public journalism. This critique holds that traditional journalism is too conflict-oriented, treats readers as news consumers rather than as citizens, and that reporters are too often fixated on ideals of objectivity and detachment. "Journalists have taken this critique seriously only in recent years because of the declines in readership and economic difficulties at papers," says Pauly. "That's why public is more than just a fad, because I think there are deep structural problems with newspapers, such as readership decline, that are not going to go away."[51]

Robert Paynter

Robert Paynter is a reporter with the *Akron Beacon-Journal*, which won the 1994 Pulitzer Prize for public service for the excellence of its series, "A Question of Color." Paynter led a team of 28 reporters, artists, and photographers in the public journalism project that looked at prejudice in the general populace of Akron, both black and white. Reporters teamed up with civic organizations and initiated programs to support dialogue between blacks and whites, and to bring people back to some "middle ground."

According to Paynter, more than 140 organizations in the greater Akron area responded to the call to act as staging grounds for deliberative dialogue between blacks and whites. The paper published a model New Year's resolution, urging readers to make this pledge: "My New Year's resolution is to do everything I can in 1994 to improve race relations."[52]

Glenn Ritt

Glenn Ritt is a news executive with *The Record* in Hackensack, New Jersey, which has been involved in several forays into public journalism, particularly in the area of political coverage. Ritt believes that news practitioners have to move beyond a parochial concern with product, and to a larger concern about culture and process. In that spirit, Ritt has initiated a number of ventures, including use of the internet to help diverse audiences connect with *The Record* newsroom.[53]

Ritt concedes that not all experiments in public or civic journalism are going to work. A 1996 public journalism experiment at *The Record* to boost citizen interest in election races had dismal results. The conclusion from the experience is that public journalism alone cannot overcome the negativity of political advertising in election campaigns, a negativity that corrupts the democratic process and alienates potential voters.[54]

Neal R. Peirce

Neal R. Peirce is an urban affairs writer who has been contacted to do a number of research studies on individual American cities. His reports are often published as a series in the city daily and form the centerpiece of a public journalism project to revitalize a downtown area or a region. Many of his reports attribute the decline of urban cores to poor schools, racism and white flight, and urban sprawl.[55]

Peirce, a nationally-syndicated columnist, considers himself to be a public journalist. He argues that newspapers should not feel reticent about crossing a troubling line in an effort to motivate the community to improve itself. He contends there is a vacuum of leadership in many U.S. cities and no other group is in a position to do the job.

Cy Porter

Cy Porter has served as community journalism director for the Radio And Television News Directors Foundation (RTNDF). In that capacity, he has authored a management reference guide entitled *Community Journalism: Getting Started.*

Porter is an advocate of so-called collaborative projects that partner print and broadcast media together in a public journalism initiative.

"Partners are encouraged to make frequent contacts with residents through polls, small surveys, interviews, telephone groups or even focus groups or town meetings," declares Porter. "It is important that the project hinge on one issue and that the issue be set by a thorough understanding, via research, of top priority community concerns."[56]

Neil Postman

Neil Postman is a professor at New York University and a scholar who has written numerous books on the shortcomings of the news media, including *Amusing Ourselves to Death,* and *How to Watch TV News.* Postman believes that too much of what is classified as news, particularly on television, is entertainment fodder that does little to inform citizens.[57]

Postman also believes that Americans are suffering from an information glut that has prompted them to turn off and tune out. The detached style of news practitioners prevents news from being put into context in a way that citizens could use it and act on it. Postman's critique is quite popular with public journalists who also are critical of the traditional journalism's definition and presentation of news.

Robert Putnam

Robert Putnam is another primary intellectual source for the philosophical underpinnings of public journalism's critique of American society. Putnam is associated with the concept of civic or social capital that is so widely used in the lexicon of public journalism. An essay of Putnam's that struck a chord with public journalists is his "Bowling Alone: America's Declining Social Capital," which argued that Americans are more and more disaffected and withdrawn from public life.[58]

Public journalists have latched onto the idea of civic capital and believe that news organizations can play a role in identifying or building civic capital. For example, town hall meetings, as cooperative ventures among civic organizations and the news media, can bring people together to deliberate on issues. This, in turn, can play a major role in the revitalization of public life and the political process.

Rebecca Rimel

Rebecca Rimel is the president of the Pew Charitable Trusts, which allocates more than $180 million of foundation money annually. The Pew family is heir to a fortune that can be traced to the Sun Oil Co. When Times-Mirror was about to close its doors to its Center for the People & the Press earlier in this decade, Pew foundation money came to the rescue.

Since that time, the Pew Charitable Trusts have provided millions of dollars to support public journalism projects. Many of these journalism projects are collaborative ventures which partner a newspaper, a broadcast outlet, and a university or public relations firm. Rimel says the foundation is funding the best ideas that will put the country back on course and that will reinvent our communities.

"Many people feel helpless to make a difference," says Rimel in the July 1996 issue of *Civic Catalyst*, a publication of the Pew Center for Civic Journalism. "And unfortunately that's leading to a great deal of hopelessness. This we all feel is a formula for disaster. What we really need to do is be about re-engaging the public, and, we often say, renewing our democratic heart."[59]

Jay Rosen

Jay Rosen is a professor at New York University and the director of the Project on Public Life and the Press. His monographs and articles on public journalism have made him the intellectual guru of the public journalism movement. Rosen's call for this reform movement is based on the premise that we are witnessing civic disintegration in America.

A community is suffering civic disintegration when its citizens are alienated from the political process and when they feel that their participation in the process no longer makes a difference. In a community suffering civic disintegration, citizens feel alienated, powerless, and are unlikely to make the effort to be involved in elective politics. Civic disintegration can be brought about by a number of factors, including economic setbacks and job dislocation as well as by poor political leadership.

The news media's job is to make citizens feel connected again, to help empower them to make a difference. Public journalists have created and eagerly embraced the adjective, "connectedness," to describe the degree to which citizens are engaged in the life of their communities.

Rosen describes this concern in his essay, "Community Connectedness"— something which he says is in serious decline and which results in a concurrent erosion in the news media audience. "At its core is the concern that millions of Americans are somehow withdrawing from public life, at both the local and national levels. Along with this creeping trend toward disengagement has come, of course, the steady decline in newspaper readership."[60]

Michael Sandel

Michael Sandel, Harvard University professor, scholar, and writer, is given credit for the phrase—"public life going well"—which is the rallying point of so much of public journalism's efforts. As Davis Merritt of *The Wichita Eagle* is fond of saying, telling the news is not enough, journalists also have an obligation to make public life go well.

"When politics goes well," declares Sandel, "we can know a good in common that we cannot know alone." This is a frequent theme of public journalism advocate Jay Rosen, who believes that the writings of Sandel offer a prescription for the malaise of conventional journalism. When journalism takes on the mission of making public and political life go well, then there will be relief from the grim spiral of public cynicism and hope for a restoration of the authority of the press as an institution.[61]

Jan Schaffer

Jan Schaffer succeeded Ed Fouhy as director of the Pew Center for Civic Journalism, one of the major funders and driving forces behind public journalism projects. Schaffer contends that public journalism has had wide acceptance in American communities, but she is mystified at some of the resistance she still sees among reporters in many newsrooms.

As a major promoter for putting public journalism into practice, Schaffer has a number of tips for changing the culture of newsrooms and getting newsrooms to connect with the community. Among other suggestions: bring in outside thinkers to challenge your staff, remove fear of failure and of experimentation, invite members of the community into the newsroom to sit in on meetings, and use formal and informal survey methods to find out what is on people's minds.[62]

Michael Schudson

Michael Schudson is a professor and journalism scholar who takes the view that the elite press traditions in this country, which are adopted by so much of the media outside the confines of New York and Washington, D.C., ill serve the majority of Americans. People dislike news as it is now packaged because it is not reader-friendly and it is not placed in a context that has meaning for the average citizen.

In his book, *The Power of News*, Schudson contends that the obligation of journalism to place information into context for citizens is only going to increase with the exponential growth of the channels of communication in the years ahead. People are going to want more help, not less, in interpreting and explaining the onslaught of information. "It is hard to picture the contemporary world, even in the face of a technology that makes each of us potentially equal senders and receivers of information, without a specialized institution of journalism."[63]

Steve Smith

Steve Smith is a practitioner of public journalism and editor of the *Colorado Springs Gazette Telegraph*. He is a frequent speaker and panelist at seminars on putting together public journalism projects. Smith defends public journalism from its critics, whom he dismisses as elitists. He describes public journalism as populist, "born in the heartland, nurtured in the South and Midwest and growing out of the hopes, fears, and dreams of journalists like me—editors of small and mid-size newspapers struggling to reconnect with their communities in meaningful ways."[64]

Among Smith's public journalism efforts is a project to address the disconnect between his paper and the merchant community over business coverage. Smith says business groups in Colorado Springs once looked at his paper as "dedicated to negativity" in its coverage of commerce. Smith says that it was true that his paper was "once libertarian and dedicated to total disconnect." However, Smith says the paper is now more interested in being a partner in a boom town community. He notes that hiring interns to work in covering the business community has helped to reconnect the newspaper with a vital constituency in Colorado Springs.[65]

Bob Steele

Bob Steele is a specialist in ethics at the Poynter Institute for Media Studies, an advanced school and research facility for both print and broadcast journalists in St. Petersburg, Florida. Steele believes there are significant ethical questions in the debate over the legitimacy of public journalism, a debate that he says often gets bogged down into polarized positions.

Steele argues in a June 1995 position paper that public (or civic) journalism cannot ignore the critics' concerns about detachment and independence. Civic journalists must be aware of the dangers as they move from detached observers to agenda setters, from independent reporters to community convenors. Traditional journalists must acknowledge that they share a goal with public journalists in the quest to serve citizens and society. "The differences [between traditional journalists and civic journalists] are not as great as they are sometimes painted," declares Steele. "There is considerable common ground."[66]

Martha Steffens

Martha Steffens was the metro editor of the *Dayton Daily News* who worked with editor Max Jennings to put together a project aimed at reducing juvenile crime in the greater Dayton area. Steffens and her reporting team put together a project that included giving free pizza to any group that would agree to talk about teen violence and juvenile crime and send comments back to the paper. According to Steffens, 300 groups and 2,000 citizens responded and the project, "Kids In Chaos," got fully underway.

Stories followed about children who had been perpetrators of crime or victims of crime. Civic groups and experts became involved in holding forums to address juvenile crime problems. The paper ran laundry lists of suggested actions to curb crime by young people with ideas coming from parents, police, and even elementary schoolchildren.[67]

Chuck Stone

Chuck Stone is the Walter Spearman professor in the University of North Carolina School of Journalism and Mass Communications. He is the author of three books and founding president of the National Association of Black Journalists. He has been editor of three newspapers. He was involved in a public journalism effort at the *St. Louis Post-Dispatch* in 1997, when he was asked by editor Cole Campbell to do a stint as readers' advocate and public ombudsman during a heated mayoral election contest.

In his essay, "Heroes and Inspirations: The Making of a Civic Journalist," Stone contends that the first lesson in civic or public journalism is "to listen to your readers and their main concerns. Editors must be journalistic messiahs, but readers can also be apostles." Stone argues that he did one of his first successful public journalism exercises in 1961 in the District of Columbia when he campaigned as editor of the local paper against road construction trucks being routed by a high school. Stone ran a five-column blank space in the newspaper with a cutline below that read: "This space reserved for the first student to be killed by one of the trucks being rerouted through the neighborhood." Stone said his journalistic effort was denounced as irresponsible, but shortly thereafter the trucks were rerouted.[68]

Jack Swift

Jack Swift, now deceased, is often credited with initiating the first public journalism project at his *Columbus Ledger-Enquirer* in Georgia. Public journalists find inspiration in studying the genesis of their movement in this small daily's initial foray.

When "Columbus Beyond 2000: Agenda for Progress" ran in the paper with little community response, editor Swift initiated and directed a 1990 community task force that sponsored town hall meetings and backyard barbecues to engage citizens to become participants in directing their community's future. Thus, the 1990s phenomenon of public journalism was born.[69]

Rick Thames

Rick Thames is a public life editor of *The Charlotte Observer*, a daily in North Carolina that has been one of the most active newspapers in the public journalism movement. One of Thames' specialties has been to conceptualize the public journalism approach to covering politics.

Thames' number one rule for covering elections is to find out what matters to voters and to play to those issues. Finding out what's on voters' minds can involve conducting issues polls, holding focus groups, and consulting with citizen respondents throughout a campaign.

"Somehow, the news business has drifted from the important role we journalists play as public servants," writes Thames in an October, 1995 *Civic Catalyst*. "We've tended to align ourselves with power brokers, government insiders, and political analysts, instead of with citizens. Some go so far as to dismiss average people as a naive bunch who need to be saved from themselves. That view is very wrong."[70]

Gil Thelen

Gil Thelen, former executive editor of *The State* in Columbia, South Carolina, is a public journalism advocate who contends that its techniques energize residents. After putting those techniques to use in Columbia, he was chosen to be executive editor of the *Tampa Tribune* in Florida. He explains that newspapers have an obligation to create "public spaces" where citizens can wrestle with tough issues and come to "public judgment."

"What's really hurting this [public journalism] is the way the elite press is smashing around anything that smacks of experimentation," notes Thelen in a 1997 *Quill* article. He argues that elite publications such as *The New York Times* and *Washington Post* have been able to set the standards, framework, and values of journalism for too long.

"And a lot of the people in my newsroom want to work for them," adds a disappointed Thelen. "Everybody defers to them. Maybe that's the source of resistance [to public journalism]."[71]

Daniel Yankelovitch

Daniel Yankelovitch, author of *Coming to Public Judgment: Making Democracy Work in a Complex World*, must be counted among the primary intellectual sources for public journalism's solution-oriented approach to societal problems. According to Yankelovitch, as a nation we have become quite sophisticated about techniques of measuring public opinion, but we are quite deficient in how to improve it.[72]

Yankelovitch believes there are "laws" that can be isolated to describe the evolution of public opinion from mass opinion to public judgment through three stages of development. Many public journalists believe that they have an important role in presenting news in a manner so that it helps citizens come to public judgment—the most advanced form of public opinion.

NOTES

1. Statement made by radio talk show host Kevin Horrigan to Don Corrigan on radio station KTRS-AM afternoon talk show, June, 1997.

2. Davis Merritt, *Public Journalism & Public Life: Why Telling the News Isn't Enough* (Hilldale, New Jersey: Lawrence Erlbaum Associates, 1995), p. 116.

3. Davis Merritt, and Jay Rosen, *Imagining Public Journalism: An Editor and Scholar Reflect on the Birth of an Idea* (Bloomington, Indiana: Roy Howard Monograph, 1995), p. 17.

4. Eve Munson, and Catherine Warren, *James Carey: A Critical Reader* (Minneapolis: University of Minnesota Press, 1997), p. 338.

5. Clifford Christians, Mark Fackler, and John Ferré, *Good News—Social Ethics & the Press* (New York: Oxford University Press, 1993), p. 90.

6. Renita Coleman, "The Intellectual Antecedents of Public Journalism." Paper presented at AEJMC Convention in Anaheim, California, August, 1996, p. 10.

7. Arthur Charity, *Doing Public Journalism* (New York: Guilford Press, 1995), p. 140.

8. Jay Black, editor, *Mixed News: The Public/Civic/Communitarian Journalism Debate* (New Jersey: Lawrence Erlbaum Associates,1997), pp. 96–114.

9. Lisa Austin, Davis Merritt, and Jay Rosen, *Public Journalism Theory & Practice* (Dayton, Ohio: Kettering, 1997), p. 40.

10. Don Corrigan, "Public Journalists Suffer Setback," *St. Louis Journalism Review* (September, 1997), p. 13.

11. Black, op. cit.

12. Corrigan, op. cit., p. 13.

13. Arthur Charity, *Doing Public Journalism, A Teacher's Guide* (New York: Guilford Press, 1995), p. 1.

14. James Fallows, *Breaking the News* (New York: Vintage Books, 1996), p. 25.

15. Black, op. cit., p. 236.

16. Edward Miller, *The Charlotte Project* (St. Petersburg, Florida: The Poynter Papers, No. 4, 1994), pp. 75–85.

17. Charity, op. cit., pp. 134–135.

18. Cole Campbell, "The Challenge Is to Reclaim Our Moral Authority" from *News Breaks: Can Journalists Fix It?* (Washington, D.C.: Pew Center, 1997), pp. 4–5.

19. James Carey, "The Press and the Public Discourse," *Kettering Review* (Winter, 1992), p. 11.

20. Hodding Carter, III, "1997 Batten Symposium: News Breaks: Can Journalists Fix It," *Civic Catalyst* (Summer, 1997), p. 4.

21. Charity, op. cit., p. 11.

22. John Merrill, *Legacy of Wisdom* (Ames: Iowa State University, 1994), p. 181.

23. Corrigan, op. cit., p. 13.

24. Ibid., p. 13.

25. Staci Kramer, *Civic Journalism: Six Case Studies* (Washington, D.C.: Pew Center for Civic Journalism, 1995), pp. 12–21.

26. Fallows, op. cit., p. 238.

27. E. J. Dionne Jr., *Why Americans Hate Politics* (New York: Touchstone, 1991), p. 354.

28. Corrigan, op. cit., p. 13.

29. James Ettema, and Limor Peer, "Good News from a Bad Neighborhood: Civic Journalism as a Vocabulary of Community Assets." Paper presented in Chicago at the annual conference of the International Communication Association (ICA), May, 1996, p. 5.

30. Charity, op. cit., p. 166.

31. Remarks made by Ed Fouhy at a seminar panel at the Association for Education in Journalism and Mass Communication (AEJMC) in Anaheim, California, August 10, 1996.

32. Fallows, op. cit., pp. 165–169.

33. Charity, op. cit., p. 167.

34. Cheryl Gibbs, *Speaking of Public Journalism* (Dayton, Ohio: Kettering Foundation, 1997), pp. 44–45.

35. Chris Gates, "The Old vs. a New Model of Journalism, *Civic Catalyst* (Fall, 1997), p. 7.

36. Cheryl Gibbs, "Teaching Civic Journalism," *Civic Catalyst* (January, 1997), p. 8.

37. Black, op. cit., p. 242.

38. Tim Cleland, "A Lesson in Civic Journalism," *J•Communique*, Ball State University (October, 1997), pp. 6–7.

39. Charity, op.cit., pp. 141–142.

40. Dennis Hartig, "Changing the Personality of Local News Pages," *Civic Catalyst* (Fall, 1997), pp. 8–9.

41. Cheryl Gibbs, *Speaking of Public Journalism* (Dayton, Ohio: Kettering Foundation, 1997), pp. 51–60.

42. Janice Hume, et al., "Civic Journalism: The Practitioner's Perspective." Paper presented at the AEJMC Convention, Chicago, August, 1997, p. 18.

43. Max Jennings, "Today's Journalism: An Assessment," *Civic Catalyst* (Fall, 1997), p.12.

44. George Killenberg, *Public Affairs Reporting* (New York: St. Martin's Press, 1992), p. 28.

45. Ed Lambeth, "Committed Journalism" (Bloomington: Indiana University Press, 1986), p. 99.

46. Alex Marshall, "Focusing on the Rotten Barrel," *The IRE Journal* (November-December, 1996), pp. 8–9.

47. Gibbs, op. cit., pp. 11–19.

48. Davis Merritt, *Public Journalism & Public Life: Why Telling the News Isn't Enough* (Hilldale, New Jersey: Lawrence Erlbaum Associates, 1995), p. 113.

49. Philip Meyer, "Discourse Leading to Solutions," *The IRE Journal* (November-December, 1996), pp. 3–5.

50. Christine Newby-Fiebich, "Issues and Agendas: The Case of Witchita, Kansas Revisited." Paper presented at the AEJMC Convention, Chicago, August, 1997, pp. 22–26.

51. Don Corrigan, "Public Journalism Must Progress Slowly," *St. Louis Journalism Review* (March, 1998), p. 11.

52. Don Corrigan, "St. Louis Native Wins Pulitzer for Racial Study," *St. Louis Journalism Review* (May, 1994), p. 9.

53. Glenn Ritt, "We Need to Do It or They'll Do It Themselves," *Civic Catalyst* (Summer, 1997) p. 5.

54. Glenn Ritt, "Public Journalism Can't Do It All," Pew Center for Civic Journalism Press Release, May 12, 1997.

55. Anne Peterson, "Peirce Report Offered No Unique Solutions," *St. Louis Journalism Review* (October, 1997), p. 1.

56. Cy Porter, *Community Journalism Getting Started* (New York: Radio and Television News Directors Foundation, 1996), pp. 2–3.

57. Neil Postman, and Steve Powers, *How to Watch TV News* (New York: Penguin Books, 1992), pp. 11–25.

58. Robert Putnam, "Bowling Alone: America's Declining Social Capital," *Journal of Democracy* (January, 1995), pp. 65–70.

59. Rebecca Rimel "Investing in Risk: Re-engaging the Public," *Civic Catalyst* (July, 1996), p. 10.

60. Jay Rosen, "Community Connectedness: Passwords for Public Journalism" (St. Petersburg, Florida: Poynter Institute, 1993), p. 4.

61. Michael Sandel, *Liberalism and the Limits of Justice* (New York: Cambridge University Press, 1982), p. 183.

62. Jan Schaffer, "The Best or Worst?" *The Quill* (May, 1997), pp. 25–27.

63. James Fallows, op. cit., p. 301.

64. Steve Smith, "Getting Down and Dirty with the Critics," *Civic Catalyst* (January,1997), p. 3.

65. Don Corrigan, "Public Journalists Suffer Setback," *St. Louis Journalism Review* (September, 1997), p. 13.

66. Robert M. Steele, *The Ethics of Civic Journalism: Independence as the Guide* (St. Petersburg, Florida: Poynter Institute Paper, June, 1995), pp. 1–7.

67. Charity, op. cit., pp. 64–65.

68. Chuck Stone, "Heroes and Inspirations: The Making of a Civic Journalist." Honors lecture given to the scholastic journalism division of the AEJMC convention, Chicago, 1997.

69. Fallows, op. cit., pp. 250–251.

70. Rick Thames, "Covering Politics Civic Journalism Style," *Civic Catalyst* (October, 1995), pp. 1, 3 ,15.

71. Jan Schaffer, "The Best or Worst?" *The Quill* (May, 1997), p. 26.

72. Daniel Yankelovitch, *Coming to Public Judgment: Making Democracy Work in a Complex World* (Syracuse: Syracuse University Press, 1991), pp. 1–11.

3
Dissenters: Doubting the Doctrine

GOING TO EXTREMES

Public journalism has become one of the hottest ideas—and one of the most heated controversies—in the news business. Public journalism has divided newsrooms, it has divided the journalism academic community, and in some instances, it has divided news management against working reporters. It has sparked debates about the nature and function of news that rival those of the 1960s, a decade when the country was torn by the strife of the civil rights era and, the Vietnam War. The controversy and polarization of that time prompted some in the news business to discard the ideal of objectivity and to experiment with advocacy journalism.

Public journalists are the great news experimenters of the 1990s. Public journalism's many supporters and converts publicly eschew divisiveness and discord, but their evangel inevitably invites the dissent of those who are not ready to jettison the tenets of traditional journalism. Public journalism's evangelists continually denounce conflict-oriented reportage; however, they openly concede that a part of their agenda has been to create a storm within the news business.

"The movement has actually generated controversy within the profession of journalism," declares Jay Rosen, the outspoken philosopher of public journalism. "That, in fact, was part of the goal—to get journalists talking."[1]

Public journalism advocates have found their way onto the radar screens of the news business in a major way and in a relatively short period of time. Supporters contend that as many as 600 daily newspapers have engaged in public journalism projects.[2] Proponents have expounded on the public journalism philosophy at news media think tanks such as the Poynter Institute in St. Petersburg, Florida, and the American Press Institute in Reston, Virginia, as well as at national conventions of the Society of Professional Journalists, the Investigative Reporters and Editors, the International Communication Association, and more. They have found their way into the lecture halls at schools of journalism from coast to coast, from Columbia University in New York to Stanford University in Palo Alto.

The irony is that public journalism advocates have only found their way onto the media radar screen by creating controversy and by adopting some of the same rhetorical methods for which they condemn traditional journalists. In their efforts to put down today's news media, public journalists often resort to painting bizarre caricatures of journalists and their behavior, portrayals that might be better placed in exaggerated Hollywood movies or television dramas, but which have little to do with the day-to-day life of the average reporter in the business. Public journalists denounce the conventional news media for framing issues in the extreme, yet employ the most extreme examples of press performance in their own crusade to indict the conventional news media for failing the American public.

This is most apparent in the writings of public journalism champion James Fallows. Fallows accuses traditional journalists of being elitist and out of touch with the average American, primarily because a few celebrity journalists like Diane Sawyer and Sam Donaldson pull down million-dollar salaries. Fallows condemns traditional journalists for being shallow and combative, based primarily on the behavior exhibited on radio talk shows and a few Sunday morning TV news roundtable programs where pundits square off. Perhaps the most extreme example of press perfidy exploited by Fallows is in the first chapter of his book, "Breaking The News."

In that chapter, Fallows recalls the PBS program, "Ethics in America." As noted previously in this study, one episode of that 1980's ethics program had the title of "Under Orders, Under Fire," and was moderated by Harvard Law professor Charles Ogletree. It's useful to look at the details of that episode, which were such a revelation for Fallows, once again. In the course of the PBS show, Ogletree brought two star TV journalists, Peter Jennings and Mike Wallace into a hypothetical war situation in the nation of "South Kosan."

Under moderator Ogletree's hypothetical war situation, U.S. troops were advising South Kosanese troops in their struggle against "North Kosanese" invaders. Ogletree asked Jennings to imagine that he was employed by a network that had successfully contacted the enemy. The North Kosanese enemy agreed to let Jennings and his news crew travel with its military units after some tough negotiations. Jennings said he would certainly be amenable to taking on such an assignment.

Several new twists to the Kosanese War situation were added by Ogletree for Jennings' consideration. As Jennings and his crew are traveling with the North Kosanese military unit to visit the site of an alleged atrocity perpetrated by U.S. and South Kosanese troops, they accidentally cross the trail of a contingent of American and South Kosanese soldiers. With Jennings and his crew in tow, the North Kosanese troops set up a horrific ambush that will mean certain destruction for the Americans and their South Kosanese allies.

Jennings was then confronted with an ethical dilemma. Would he tell his camera crew to "Roll the tape!" as the North Kosanese cut the Americans and their allies to shreds? Or would he make some attempt to warn the U.S. troops even though that would mean, at the very least, losing a sensational story? Jennings' replied that he would put his life in jeopardy to warn the Americans of the enemy ambush.

But, as Fallows notes in his book, Jennings was brought up short by his news colleague from CBS. Wallace expressed exasperation with Jennings' response. Wallace insisted that Jennings was a reporter and his first obligation was to cover the story. At that point, Jennings backtracked in embarrassment and agreed with Wallace that his journalistic duty was to remain a detached observer of whatever might ensue and to cover it for his network.

"Peter Jennings and Mike Wallace are just two individuals, but their reactions spoke volumes about the values of their craft," stressed Fallows. "Jennings was made to feel embarrassed about his natural decent human impulse. Wallace was completely unembarrassed about feeling no connection to the soldiers in his country's army or considering their deaths before his eyes as 'simply a story.' "[3]

Clearly, the use of this story should be objectionable, especially to public journalists, because it represents framing an issue in the extreme. Is it fair to make generalizations about an entire profession based on the reaction of two individuals to an extraordinary set of hypothetical circumstances? How representative are Mike Wallace and Peter Jennings of rank-and-file news practitioners in America? How many reporters go behind enemy lines to confront life-and-death, ethical quandaries during their journalistic careers? How typical is the hypothetical wartime reporting situation in North Kosan as described by Ogletree to Wallace and Jennings?

Fallows' use of this story to illustrate the attitudes and ethical standards of today's reporters brings to mind the presidential debates of 1988, when Governor George Dukakis was asked by a reporter how he would react to a hypothetical rape and deadly attack perpetrated against his wife. The question was clearly intended to bait Dukakis because of his opposition to capital punishment. The reasoned and unemotional reply by Dukakis did not sit well with many Americans who felt that the candidate should have shown some outrage. Public journalists have argued that the question was unfair and outrageous and, in any event, shed little light on the candidate's ability to be a good president. Can it not be similarly argued that the hypothetical Kosan War situation sheds little real light on the ethics and attitudes of today's average reporter? Yet, Fallows builds much of his opening book chapter, "Why we Hate the Media," on the hypothetical Kosan War situation.

The use of this story by Fallows to shed light on the attitudes and ethical standards of today's reporters is also deplorable because it opens old wounds and exploits resentments against the news media still lingering from the Vietnam War period (the Kosan scenario was obviously a hybrid of the U.S. involvement in conflicts in Korea and Vietnam). The American news media are still accused of "losing" the Vietnam War because of a perceived "disloyalty" and failure to support U.S. servicemen and their mission in Southeast Asia in the 1960s and 1970s.[4] Fallows knows full well that this historical view of the news media's role in the Vietnam conflict is pernicious, as well as simply wrong, and should be debunked at every opportunity. Fallows' use of the Kosan War situation only serves to perpetuate a dangerous myth that American reporters have no loyalty to cause or

country, that their behavior leads to the loss of American lives, and, perhaps, even
to the loss of wars.

In his attempt to unmask today's reporters as sinisterly detached, what is the
implication of Fallows' use of the hypothetical Kosan War situation? Is the conclusion to be drawn that American reporters don't belong reporting behind enemy
lines, but instead belong on the military's bandwagon, supporting U.S. interven-
tionism wherever it occurs? Fallows' use of the Kosan War parable certainly feeds
into the belief system of those who define patriotism as "my country right or
wrong," and who believe the American press should adopt a similar stance when
reporting U.S. actions abroad. The folly of this perspective is apparent in the
many examples throughout U.S. history when the American people have been ill-
served by a jingoistic press—a press that has avoided the labor and risk of dispassionate analysis, and instead simply rubber-stamped American governmental
policy.

Fallows' use of the hypothetical Kosan War situation actually speaks volumes about the methodology employed by public journalism advocates in cri-
tiquing today's conventional journalism practice. The problem is not simply Fallows' selection of this ill-advised parable to make his point. The problem is the
transparent hypocrisy in using such an extreme example, when public journalists
are constantly hammering away at traditional journalists for just such infractions—framing issues at the extremes. Public journalism advocate Fallows per-
sists in this methodology throughout his jeremiad against traditional journalism
practice.

For example, Fallows and other public journalists are convinced that far too
many of today's journalists are out of touch—that they identify with politicians,
lawyers, and consultants, rather than with average citizens. Today's journalists are
college-educated, elitist, and making big money. In the chapter of his book on the
press entitled, "The Gravy Train," Fallows seems to lament the passing of the days
when reporting was largely a working-class activity.[5] In those days, reporters
knew the pulse of the people because they themselves were regular people.

In the "Gravy Train" chapter, Fallows concedes that there are still a lot of
journalists today who are underpaid and who lead fairly ordinary lives, but he then
launches into page after page of anecdotes about celebrity journalists with multi-
million dollar salaries, scads of money for television appearances, and agents
booking $35,000 lecture gigs around the country. All of this pampering and
largesse, according to Fallows, shows journalism's loss of connection with the
public and a need for some mechanism to put reporters back in connection with
regular folks—and that mechanism is the public journalism approach.

The flaw in the analysis by Fallows is that once again he is using the most
extreme examples to make his point that today's journalists are out of touch. The
hypocrisy is all too apparent when Fallows and other public journalists are continually nagging at traditional journalists for just such infractions—those of
framing issues at the extremes. In fact, Fallows' use of these celebrity profiles is
an insult to the thousands of journalists who can barely afford the basic amenities
of life. Many younger journalists survive on their passion to be a part of this pro-

fession, and not much else. Fallows' profiles certainly run contrary to the research findings of two Indiana University professors, David H. Weaver and G. Cleveland Wilhoit, in their study entitled, "The American Journalist of the 1990s."

According to Weaver and Wilhoit, the average American journalist is a 36-year-old, married, white, Protestant male earning an annual income of about $31,000 a year. Only about one percent of American journalists make more than $100,000 a year, and most journalists obtained their degrees from public universities. Fifty-nine percent of journalists are married, compared to 62 percent of the general adult population. About 40 percent of journalists have at least one child living at home, compared to 49 percent of other Americans.[6]

In her essay, "Whither the Civic Journalism Bandwagon," *St. Louis Post-Dispatch* reporter Charlotte Grimes expresses her exasperation with advocates of public journalism and their harping about the elitism of traditional journalists. In fact, Grimes turns the tables on Fallows and other public journalists by pointing out that many of their ilk fit the profile of elitist, whether by education, income, or highly paid stops on the lecture circuit. Journalism may have a problem with its handful of celebrities such as Cokie Roberts, Sam Donaldson, Michael Kinsley, and the regulars of "The McLaughlin Group" or "The Capitol Hill Gang," but they are hardly typical of the profession. The typical journalist, "the one who works at the majority of newspapers and television stations covering the local school board, the mayor, and the fire down the street—is another creature entirely," writes Grimes. "More than likely, this journalist has a mortgage, parents needing Medicare and children needing an education, and nightmares about losing health insurance and paycheck if the media mogul decides to downsize."[7]

PUBLIC JOURNALISM'S FALSE PREMISES

A major thesis of the public journalism evangel is the reciprocal nature between the health of a community's civic or public life and the health of journalism as a vital profession. If a community suffers from a decline in civic engagement, from a loss of interest in its political life, from a loss in the quality of its public discourse, then there should be no surprise if there is a corresponding loss of interest in its "community conversation," which is known as journalism. The corollary of this proposition is that if a journalistic enterprise wants to reverse its declining fortunes, then it would be wise for it to take an active role in encouraging civic engagement. It also would be wise for a floundering journalistic enterprise to reach out to revive interest in the political process and to elevate the level of political discourse. Such measures would presumably improve the situation for journalism.

The problem with this premise is that it seems to be based on the intuitive feelings and the intellectual wanderings of its evangelists, rather than on any painstaking empirical research by a range of sociologists and political scientists. The major tenets of the evangel—that civic engagement is in decline, that political life is in decline, that public discourse is in decline—are all premises that may very well be false. At the very least, they are questionable.

Civic Life in Decline?

Public journalists maintain that Americans are no longer joining service clubs, civic and social groups, or community organizations. They are "bowling alone."[8] They are turning their backs on the PTA, the church auxiliary, and the Rotary Club. They have moved from tight-knit city neighborhoods to sprawling suburbs where they have lost any sense of connection. This contention that civic and community engagement is on the wane, that more and more Americans are alienated, insular, and isolated, is disconcerting for a democratic society, but it is also a contention open to challenge.

Americans were joiners when Alexis de Tocqueville made his famous trip to America to study democracy in the 1830s. The French scholar could not avoid noting this amiable aspect of national character. "Americans of all ages, all conditions, and all dispositions are forever forming associations," observed de Tocqueville. "There are not only commercial and manufacturing companies . . . but associations of a thousand other kinds—religious, moral, serious, futile, restricted."[9]

There is plenty of evidence that Americans are still joiners. According to statistics compiled by the editors of the Encyclopedia of Associations, more than 80 percent of Americans have a membership with some organization.[10] This statistic does not even include the colossal membership rolls of groups such as local chambers of commerce, labor union affiliates, or the American Association of Retired Persons, the men of the 1995 Million Man March or the 1997 Promise Keepers convergence on Washington, or the 2,500 members of the American Gourd Society. This country boasts literally millions of organizations, and, while Americans like their individuality, they like it even more when they can express it with a group of like-minded people. Messies Anonymous sports some 3,000 members who are self-confessed chronically disorganized people. The Society for the Eradication of Television has almost 1,000 members who would love to make prime-time television a distant memory and who advocate throwing television sets out living room windows. The 15,000 Mikes of Mikes of America, the 1,500 Jim Smiths of the Jim Smith Society, and the 500 Bobs of Bobs International celebrate the commonality of a name.[11]

Men are joining the Male Liberation Foundation, the National Organization for Changing Men, Men International, Men's Rights, and the Men's Rights Association. Women are joining Women in the Wind, Women on Wheels, Emily's List, as well as the National Organization of Women. Senior citizens are joining groups such as Grandmothers for Peace, Grandparents Anonymous, and the Grey Panthers. There are collectors groups advocating the collection of pencils, locks, spoons, marbles, political campaign buttons, Barbie dolls, hand fans, antique door knobs, milk bottles, vacuum tube radios, fishing lures, bumper stickers, and more.[12]

Everett C. Ladd of the Roper Center for Public Opinion Research, author of *Silent Revolution: The Rebirth of American Civil Life and What It Means for All of Us*, insists that all the noise about the unraveling of America's social fabric is bunk. We are still joiners; we are just joiners of different things. We are members of collectors groups, ballroom dancing clubs, soccer leagues, grass-roots political movements, and even Ross Perot's Reform Party. According to Ladd, civic life is thriving in America no matter how frustrated we may be with our political system and our politicians. "Individualist America in its post-industrial era, as Ladd puts it, "is a vigorously civic America."[13]

The movement of many Americans from urban centers to the suburbs in the post-World War II period, and the subsequent loosening of community ties, is another piece of the public journalism lament over civic disintegration. Public journalists find suburbanites to be disengaged and accuse them of turning their backs on the problems of inner-city crime, quality of city schools, deterioration of urban cores, and regional economic health. Indeed, this may be one of the reasons why so many public journalism projects at big city newspapers take aim at urban sprawl and seek to sensitize suburbanites about their "obligations" to an entire metropolitan region, rather than to simply their own backyards.[14]

Public journalists make a mistake in labeling so many of the citizens of suburbia as disengaged and uncaring. The late Massachusetts Senator and U.S. House Speaker Tip O'Neill was fond of observing that, "All politics is local." That piece of wisdom is particularly true in the suburbs, where many citizens are extremely engaged in local issues ranging from land use to mass transit to quality of schools. Suburbanites aren't always disengaged; they're simply focused on issues that are closer to home and less intractable. The public journalists' unhappiness with the suburban mentality mimics the obligatory distaste for suburbia harbored by many intellectuals in academia. Sociologist Alan Wolfe in his 1998 study, *One Nation, After All*, found that "the intellectuals' disdain for suburbia—that they label as smug, narrow-minded and indifferent—is in itself a poorly-informed and outdated perspective."[15]

Political Life in Decline?

There is no question that Americans are increasingly vociferous, if not always eloquent, regarding their disgust for politicians and their frustration with the political party system. The populace is not easily mobilized on complicated issues such as campaign funding reform; however, polls show that many Americans believe that political corruption is widespread. They believe that politicians in Congress are heavily influenced by campaign contributions and that these legislators support unwarranted pork barrel projects that drive up taxes and budget deficits. At the same time, polls show that Americans do not always extend these unflattering beliefs to the legislators who represent their own political jurisdictions.

There are many contradictions in the views exhibited by the American populace on politicians and the political system, and this has been especially apparent through the late 1990s when citizens have held an American president in low regard for moral integrity and character, but in high regard for performance and leadership. These contradictions underline the perils when public journalists attempt to make broad generalizations about the deterioration of political life in the United States, based on recent election turnouts or the latest public opinion polls.

Public journalists contend that there is a great decline in political participation and a precipitous loss of interest in politics. Ultimately, public journalists have rallied around the analysis of E. J. Dionne who says that Americans hate their politics.[16] But there is a contradiction here—hatred is not apathy, ennui, or indifference. In fact, today's hatred of politics is spurring more citizens to political action. Witness the recent rise of Libertarian Party candidates and Ross Perot's Reform Party. Witness the rise of national movements to reduce taxes, to balance the budget, and to save programs such as Social Security and Medicare. Witness the rise of state propositions and other ballot measures that supersede the authority of state legislators.

Public journalists' belief that there is less participation in politics today is disputed by any number of experts. These experts also will note that today's participation is much more inclusive as compared to decades as recent as the 1950s and 1960s. Kathleen Hall Jamieson is one scholar of the American political scene who insists that today's participation in the American political process is far preferable to that of earlier decades when involvement by women, blacks, gays, and other minorities was barely visible or non-existent.[17]

Public Civility in Decline?

Certainly most educated Americans can share the public journalism movement's unhappiness with the level of public discourse in America, whether that discourse involves political discussion at a neighborhood cocktail party or merely family conversation at the dinner table. However, the decline in the level of public discourse in America has much more to do with Bart and Homer Simpson, Beavis and Butthead, Jay Leno's "Tonight Show," and the media antics of Jerry Springer and Howard Stern, than it does with any general malaise created by the failures of American politicians or errant journalists.

The despair of intellectuals generally over the atrophy of high culture, the dominance of low culture, and a decline in public discourse has resulted in all kinds of apocalyptic visions—visions that are much more frightening than even those of the public journalists. After all, public journalism's evangelists predict only the slide of democracy and the demise of the news business. Intellectuals such as Francis Fukuyama are pronouncing "The End of History." Fukuyama says "the ineluctable spread of consumerist Western culture" may well mean "not just the end of the Cold War, or the passing of a particular period of postwar history, but the end of history as such: that is, the end point of mankind's ideological evolution."[18]

Regardless of whether the lament over the decline of public discourse comes from public journalists or other apocalyptic intellectuals, this fact must be faced: the trashing of taste, culture, and public discourse in America represents a triumph of the popular will. "Old-style intellectuals may not like what is published, projected, and broadcast, but it is far closer to what most people want most of the time than at any other period of modern history," declares James Twitchell in his *Carnival Culture: The Trashing of Taste in America.*[19]

In describing the decline of public civility and public discourse, the public journalists most often point to the "news as spectacle" coverage of such phenomena as the O. J. Simpson murder trial and President Bill Clinton's infamous sexual indiscretions. The news media have obsessed over these events, according to the public journalists, at the expense of more substantive issues such as health care reform and the survival of Social Security. Public journalists also take aim at the explosive growth of talk radio shows and television news programs, such as "The McLaughlin Group" or the "Capitol Hill Gang."

James Fallows in his *Breaking the News* lambastes these television programs for treating politics as something trivial, as something to be viewed in much the same light as a sports contest. Fallows vents particular ire against "The McLaughlin Group." He is exasperated with each of the participants' political predictions, which punctuate the end of each show, complaining that the prognostications "allow the reporters to act as if they possess inside knowledge, and there is no consequence for being wrong."[20]

Fallows chases after "The McLaughlin Group" again and again in his book. He decries, in one chapter, how host John McLaughlin has reduced the quality of political discussion "by shoehorning every public issue into a scale of '1 to 10' ranking."[21] He blasts away further at McLaughlin for boiling all judgments about politicians down into a roundtable of "guesstimates" as to whether it was a "good week" or a "bad week" for the politico in question.[22] In another chapter, Fallows delights in quoting from an online discussion group titled "Pundicide" in which one participant says, "I'd like to dip 'The McLaughlin Group' in cajun-style batter and deep fry them all so I could sell them as Pundit McNuggets. . . . Low on nutrition, but they taste great cuz there's such high fat content."[23]

The comment about "Pundit McNuggets" is telling. The news shows that Fallows and other public journalists attack may not present political discussion on the level one might expect in a political science classroom at Stanford, Harvard, or the University of Illinois. Nevertheless, there is a place for "Crossfire," "The McLaughlin Group," and the "Capitol Hill Gang." They present politics as a sports package or as fast food nuggets, and with these pedestrian approaches they have actually served to popularize politics. They have brought more everyday people into the process. It can even be argued that they have "democratized" political discussion, making it accessible and fun for folks who would otherwise switch the television channel to a Sunday sports preview.

What has been sacrificed because of these shows? Does any informed observer really believe that political sophisticates have abandoned an Ivy League approach to political discussion for "The McLaughlin Group"? "The McLaughlin Group" may be an interesting sideshow for political sophisticates and news junkies, but it can be safely assumed that they still seek real nourishment elsewhere. Meanwhile, the antics of McLaughlin and others have served to bring more regular folks into the process. "The McLaughlin Group" has also resulted in a number of political discussion clones at television stations across the country, providing "Pundit McNuggets" for the local hoi polloi on issues in any number of locales, further popularizing and "democratizing" politics and the news.

It may be harder to argue with the public journalists regarding their objections over the massive news media coverage of the O. J. Simpson murder trial and President Clinton's sexcapades and indiscretions. There may well be more substantive issues, such as health care reform and the survival of Social Security, that should take precedence. But in the marketplace of news, and in the audience ratings of television, O. J. Simpson and Kato Kaelin, Bill Clinton, and Monica Lewinsky have won hands down. The public's media appetite has been served, and who is to say that the obsessive coverage has yielded nothing for the public but thick batter and oily fat.

In the case of the omnipresent coverage of the Clinton-Lewinsky scandal, the public learned about the impeachment process and modern interpretations of the term, "high crimes and misdemeanors." It also can be argued that the public learned about actual commitment to family values in Congress, the range of political hypocrisy in high places, and Congress's preference for partisan political strife over work on substantive issues. The most salacious details of the scandal were not generated by mercenary news operations, but handed to the news media by the office of the special prosecutor. While the Clinton-Lewinsky scandal was certainly exploited for "news as spectacle," the coverage, nevertheless, provided plenty of public education.

In the case of the continual O. J. Simpson coverage on the nightly news, cable news networks, radio talk shows, and more, the public learned much about the judicial system, more than anyone could have anticipated. The public learned about the roles of prosecutors, defense lawyers, and judges, and the role that money can play in purchasing an effective team of defense attorneys. On the day of that now infamous O. J. Simpson verdict, the public learned in dramatic fashion about the extent of the racial divide in this country. No academic report could have brought the point home more effectively.

The irony of the public journalism advocates' anguish over the "news as spectacle" and "The McLaughlin Group" phenomena is that their complaints seem rather antidemocratic on closer examination. The evangelists of public journalism make much of the need to connect with the disenchanted public, but when that public connects in the marketplace of news with coverage of O. J. Simpson, the reformers can get quite preachy. The evangelists take care not to protest the public's taste in these matters too much, but instead aim their barbs at the traditional news media for the terrible venality in serving up these fatty, batter-covered morsels to a helpless and dysfunctional public.

A footnote to this is the performance of Fallows as editor of the weekly news magazine *U.S. News & World Report*, a job he settled into after writing his critique of the conventional news media. There is evidence that Fallows tried to implement a public journalism approach at *U.S. News* with some of the unpredictable cover stories the weekly ran under his reign, but even Fallows was unable to resist the demands of the marketplace. Throughout Fallows' short tenure as editor, *U.S. News* had its share of Clinton scandal covers, with Monica Lewinsky and Paula Jones as backdrops to tease readers into dining on fatty, non-nutritional fare.

News Business in Decline?

Public journalists argue that the news business is in decline because of a decline in civic engagement, a loss of interest in political life, and a deterioration in the quality of public discourse. Public journalists hope to fix these "problems areas" in our public life, and consequently revive the news business. But, as we have seen, there is every indication that public journalists have misread these problem areas, as well as misinterpreted their impact on the health of journalism and the news business.

What's more, as public journalists go about the work of addressing these perceived problem areas, their remedies for what ails the news business are much more likely to drive increasing numbers of the public away from the news media. Does anybody really believe public journalists will attract more newspaper readers by involving suburbanites in solution-oriented coverage of distressed urban cores—places they fled years, if not decades, ago? Does anybody really believe public journalists will attract more newspaper readers by separating issues from personalities in politics? Will they garner more readers by abandoning "horse-race" election coverage in favor of more serious analysis? Does anybody really believe public journalists will attract more newspaper readers by turning up their noses at political scandal stories? Will they do better focusing instead on the viability of Social Security in the year 2015?

If public journalists are so wrong about so much, how can we be sure that they're on target with their assertions that newspapers and the news media are in decline? This question certainly merits examination.

The setbacks endured by the daily newspaper industry in this country in recent decades do not necessarily indicate an alienated and disenchanted public, a public that has lost its appetite for news, as public journalists are wont to claim. In fact, the public's appetite for news remains quite healthy, it is simply being satisfied in a variety of other venues. In all of the literature of public journalism, there is precious little mention of the thousands of weekly newspapers that dwarf the number of dailies. Many of these weeklies have had their genesis in recent years; they serve the needs of the majority of the American populace that now lives in suburbs.

The surviving major city daily is ringed by dozens of suburban weeklies in just about every major metropolitan area in the United States. These weeklies provide the suburban dweller with much of the news about the immediate area involving schools, public safety, city government, and nearby business development. The old city dailies are simply not up to the task. "There is a dirty little secret about local news," says William Woo in regard to the plight of dailies. "You can't cover it comprehensively . . . and it's time to be honest about it."[24]

In making the point before a 1997 meeting of editors, Woo gave details about the *St. Louis Post-Dispatch* operation, which he formerly managed as the daily's editor. Woo noted that when he left the paper in 1996 it had about 50 reporters dedicated to covering local news—one reporter for about every 50,000 residents in a metropolitan area of 2.5 million people.[25] Woo told editors that newspapers like the *Post* were in the unhappy position of trying to determine where to put precious resources to make sure that priority stories would be covered.

Suburban weeklies are in a much better position to cover local news than downtown dailies—even dailies that struggle to keep up with satellite news bureaus. Weeklies are focused and don't waste pages and pages of news that has little relevance for much of the readership. For better or for worse, suburban dwellers are often content to rely on their community weekly for local news while turning to television for news about what's going on downtown and in the region generally.

City magazines and alternative weeklies in major metropolitan areas also have siphoned off entertainment advertising dollars from the dailies, as well as younger readers who are especially interested in the entertainment reviews written by their peers in the alternative weeklies. The rise of business weeklies in metropolitan areas also has hurt the big city newspapers, because they bring a focus to that specialty coverage few dailies can match.

Ask the veterans of the daily newspaper business, many who are being replaced by reporters filled with the new ideas of public journalism, about why the papers have been in decline. They are likely to smirk at the suggestion that daily newspapers are floundering because of a "disconnect with the citizenry." They are likely to laugh at the hypothesis that newspapers are adrift because they are too aloof or uncaring about public life. They will tell you instead that dailies are suffering because readers can get their sports around the clock on ESPN and other sports channels, their stock quotes and business news instantaneously on the internet, and their news from the local city hall in the suburban newspaper that arrives on the front lawn every week free of charge.[26]

The decline of the major daily newspaper market in the United States is not a mystery, it's an inevitability that has been brought on by changes in the country's demographics as well as by revolutions in information technology. There is more mystery in projecting what daily newspapers will look like one or two decades into the next century. Will they be smaller, but more costly, products, serving a more elite market? Will they put more emphasis on interpretation and opinion-shaping, or will they stand by their traditional role as "a paper of record" providing an account of the day's major activities? Will they still be on newsprint, or will they be served up on home computer screens or as one of the 500 cable channels on digitalized television screens? Will they be niche, electronic products on the internet?

The information age has only been made possible, in part, by a voracious public appetite for more and more news. Public journalists miss the big picture when they cling to their contention that the public's interest in news is evaporating based on the circulation declines of major dailies and the fluctuations in the audiences for the nightly television news. These indices focus on only a small portion of the growing information outlets—and they do not constitute in themselves an accurate gauge for measuring the public's desire for news. Public journalists may have put their finger on a few factors in a multitude that have led to circulation declines for dailies, but they have hardly isolated the most important causal explanations for those declines. The veterans of the daily newspaper business offer a far more reliable source for the causal explanations.

FORGIVE US OUR PRESS PASSES

Public journalism's evangelists frequently express shock and dismay at the angry response they get from many others in the field of journalism. After all, we are only trying to show the way to recovery and revival, they cry out. We are simply trying to bring back news audiences and readers and, in the process, to make journalism worth doing again, they insist. James Fallows, in his keynote speech at the 1996 James K. Batten Symposium on Excellence in Civic Journalism, denounced the "in-house criticism" public journalists have endured from editors and reporters at some of the leading newspapers in the business.

"I had expected many of them to receive the public journalism concept as I did—as a source of varied, potentially valuable suggestions for rejuvenating our craft," Fallows told his sympathetic audience. "You can imagine my surprise to find that this sort of puff adder's nest of modern journalism, where you stick your hand in and the puff adders come out from all corners of the swamp."[27]

Fallows describes the hostility as characteristic of a reflex action, rather than a reasoned counter-argument. Jay Rosen, Ed Fouhy, Jan Schaeffer, Davis "Buzz" Merritt, and other vocal supporters of public journalism have also dismissed critics as reflexive and reactionary; and they, too, have expressed surprise and amazement at the range and intensity of the attacks on their doctrines. Merritt, one of the better-known proselytizers for public journalism, complained bitterly in an *Editor & Publisher* magazine "Shop Talk" piece that the reformation press concept "has had journalism done to it."[28]

Perhaps it's a symptom of what occurs to a journalist when objectivity and detachment are jettisoned, but it seems odd indeed that public journalists are so surprised when their colleagues take exception to their wide-ranging critique of traditional journalistic practices and values. If public journalists reflected on their message in a less partisan manner, they might better understand the intensity of the reaction. The evangelists of public journalism catalog the sins of conventional journalism as those of being callous and uncaring, elitist and disconnected, cynical and negative, and contentious and conflict-oriented.

When the "sinners" protest this catalog of charges heaped on them, it's a marvel that the public journalists then recoil and feign surprise at the reaction. It takes a certain messianic mindset for public journalists like Fallows to summarily dismiss critics as reactionary and reflexive. Or, for that matter, to liken them to puff adders—venomous, hog-nosed snakes. Of course, from the perspective of the new reformers, perhaps the ultimate insult to be thrown at critics is to simply accuse them of "doing journalism."[29]

Aloof and Uncaring?

Traditional journalists still strive after an elusive ideal of objectivity or, at least, fairness. The ideal of objectivity has been valued in the past for some very important reasons. When newspapers moved from the party press period in post-Colonial America to the age of the penny press or mass circulation press in the Civil War period and afterward, great changes were inevitable. Publishers needed to move away from politicized and opinionated coverage in an attempt to appeal to the new mass audience. Publishers also needed to move partisan blunderbuss off the front page so as not to offend advertisers. This does not mean that opinions disappeared from the newspaper; they simply found a new place in the paper now known as an editorial or commentary section.

Ironically, newspapers that appeared to be the most credible because of their objective front-page news sections consequently attained a certain power and credibility in their opinions that appeared in the editorial pages. Henry J. Raymond, one of the founders of the early-day *New York Times*, was an ardent subscriber to the idea of objectivity. He wanted to make his publication a "paper of record," a dependable and accurate journal of the events and issues of the day.[30] As the excesses of sensationalism and Yellow Journalism faded after 1900, more and more big city dailies fashioned themselves as papers of record with news sections of objective reporting and a commentary section for analysis and opinion.

There are additional explanations for the ascendancy of objectivity and its incorporation as a foundation of American journalism. Some historians trace its rise to an effort to elevate the journalistic art into a science. The emerging scientific viewpoint in the West put a premium on the distanced observer as being the most accurate and foolproof. Science found that the mere act of observing can impact the natural order of events, hence the methodology of a distanced, empirical observer became most valued in the field of discovery. These ideas heavily influenced the philosophy of the "discoverers" in journalism.

In recent years, there has been a decreasing reverence for the idea of objectivity. The social and political turmoil of the 1960s spawned the advocacy journalism of underground newspapers. These were unabashedly biased in favor of the civil rights movement and against the continuation of the war in Vietnam. Many weekly newspapers, which continue to practice advocacy journalism, survive and, indeed, thrive today. Relativism, in all its various forms, has been embraced in the West, and even science has increasingly argued against the idea that there is anything approaching absolute objectivity.

Today, many traditional journalists concede that there can be a place for advocacy journalism—though not in publications that would be papers of record—in the mix of modern-day reportorial genres. Most traditional journalists would also concede that there is no such thing as absolute objectivity. Journalistic perspectives are inevitably affected by economic status, religious upbringing, cultural influences, and ethnic origin, to name only a few factors. Nevertheless, traditional journalists are not ready to throw up their hands and abandon the effort to strive for objectivity.

Public journalists insist that the traditional journalistic concern for objectivity, balance, and detachment is bad public relations. Public journalists argue that reporters who simply report the facts of crime, without offering solutions to crime in their chronicles, appear cold and aloof. Public journalists argue that reporters who simply report the economic decline of their communities, without incorporating solutions to reverse deteriorating conditions, appear indifferent or disloyal.

Merritt writes that traditional journalists feel compelled to "maintain a pristine distance, a contrived indifference to outcomes, else the news product be contaminated." According to Merritt, traditional journalists "insist that they cannot care what happens, or at least must not be caught caring." How then, Merritt argues, "can people who profess to not care what happens be trusted to inform us?"[31]

Traditional journalists can often counter that many of them got in to the profession, and sacrificed more lucrative career options, because they care about people. Traditional journalists can also counter that there are editorial pages to argue the cause of the public. Editorial pages provide an ample forum for content to combat any public perception that a journalistic enterprise is aloof or uncaring, distant or disloyal; but advocacy does not belong on the front page dressed up as news.

Traditional journalists also take exception to the sloganeering of public journalism's evangelists that "telling the news is not enough."[32] Telling the news is a formidable challenge in itself—and an art that has yet to be perfected, and, when telling the news may not be enough, there are always the editorial pages and column inches that can be devoted to insightful investigative reporting. However, the news product itself should be impartial and tamper-proof.

Traditional journalists regularly get an earful from the public even without the deliberative listening techniques, focus groups, polling, and all the other paraphernalia of public journalism. They will tell you that the public may occasionally gripe about aloof and uncaring reporters, but the public's number one complaint against reporters and journalism involves perceptions of press bias, slanted news, and hidden agendas. Discarding the elusive ideal of objectivity in favor of a missionary creed of "making public life go well" will hardly address the public's overriding complaint with the news media.

Elitist and Disconnected?

Public journalists are quick to accuse traditional journalists of being self-important, elitist, and arrogant. They are self-important, according to public journalists, because they often can command the attention of the most important people in town—whether that town be the nation's capitol or Missoula, Montana. They are elitist, according to the public journalists, because they are usually financially secure and have college degrees that bolster their conviction that they know what information best serves the public. They are arrogant, according to public journalists, because they are intransigent and unwilling to experiment with new ideas and new approaches to news that would better serve the needs of the public.

Traditional journalists have little problem defending themselves against these epithets hurled their way by the evangelists of public journalism. Fallows and other public journalists like to hold up a handful of overpaid, celebrity journalists in Washington and New York, as indicative of the self-importance and elitism that is tainting the profession. In fact, most journalists tend to be solidly middle class and they work at medium-sized and smaller news organizations. If they have the opportunity to interview the most important people in town during the work week, it is still highly unlikely that they're mixing it up with the same folks on the golf course or at the country club on the weekends.

The complaints about too many post-Watergate journalists having college degrees and being "too white collar" has been around since President Gerald Ford declared an end to our long national nightmare of Watergate. The complaints about too much education and financial security for journalists seem rather odd. Simply argued: Was journalism better off when reporters were paid poorly and the profession was viewed as a stepping stone to employment with the business and political bosses whom they covered? Would journalism be better off if publishers quit hiring people with college degrees?

College degrees or not, public journalists argue that today's reporters are too isolated and disconnected from the common man. They argue that those who work in today's news media have an obligation to hang up on their important sources, put their phones down, get out of their office chairs, and get out on the street to find out what the public is saying. This sort of thinking has inspired the creation of the Journalism Values Institute (JVI), sponsored by the American Society of Newspaper Editors, the Harwood Group, and the McCormick Tribune Foundation. Public journalism critic William Woo has taken aim at JVI and speaks for a lot of traditional journalists.

"I agree with JVI that in sourcing stories, journalists should look beyond the usual suspects and authorities," Woo told an audience of California editors. "But I am cautious about the assumption that . . . the opinions of the man or woman on the street will shed as much light on a complicated issue as those of a politician, a college professor, or bureaucrat—people who have spent a career focused on the issue. There is a dangerous anti-intellectualism in the assumption and I think we need to recognize it."[33] Woo added that the values newspapers ought to consider for adoption include a disrespect for bigotry, ignorance, orthodoxy, pretense and being "profoundly ordinary."

The sort of thinking, which Woo criticizes, also is responsible for the newspaper trend of polling the common man and the common woman in order to find out what kind of news fare should appear in the daily paper. It doesn't take a soothsayer to predict that many of these polls will reveal a demand for more news about sports and what's happening down at the shopping mall, at the expense of international news and political commentary. Should a newspaper abdicate its important role in being a public educator on the basis of such polls? Should a newspaper abdicate its role of providing international news and commentary for those who care about such things and devote all its product to the larger audience with more pedestrian tastes?

Biased Toward the Negative?

Traditional journalists are often viewed in the same dim light as lawyers who are sometimes characterized as "ambulance chasers." Many times conventional journalists are actually a couple of lengths ahead of the attorneys in the chase to catch up with those ambulances; and while the attorneys are simply holding up a business card and asking if they can be of service to accident victims, the journalists are sticking a microphone in the bloodied faces of the injured and shouting, "How did it feel to get run over by that truck?"

Members of the press, the bar, the medical field, and every other human endeavor occasionally behave badly at crisis events and in stressful situations. The solution to this dilemma is hardly one of advising lawyers, doctors, and the press to steer clear of disaster scenes. The press plays an important public education role when it covers crime scenes, natural disasters, and human tragedy. The press also has an important watchdog function in the coverage of calamities and life's tragedies. The glare of the news media is an impetus for the officials in charge to make sure that planes don't fall out of the sky, trains don't jump the tracks, and cars don't explode on impact.

Nevertheless, public journalists contend that traditional journalism concentrates on plane crashes, train wrecks, exploding cars, and public malfeasance. All of this negative fare takes its toll on confidence in public life and weakens the conviction among the public that there is anything citizens can do to address the problems. This "learned hopelessness" among members of the public is one of the more insidious side effects of traditional journalism's bias toward the negative, and only guarantees that things will get worse.

In *Public Journalism & Public Life*, Merritt scolds today's journalists for their negativity and presents the hypothetical headline, "25,890 Airplanes Land Safely; One Crashes in NYC."[34] Merritt, like Rosen and others, believes that journalism must put more energy into showing where public life is going well, rather than simply focusing on the worst in society. He believes the emphasis on the negative is driving readers and audiences away from the news media as well as doing irreparable harm to public life.

But the manner in which a society copes with disaster can be extremely useful in identifying broader social and economic patterns. "For it is in response to disaster that a community's mechanisms for protection, self-renewal, mourning, consensus, and generosity are most severely tested," report K. S. Coates and W. R. Morrison in their analysis, "Towards a Methodology of Disasters." Morrison and Coates note that "it is in the aftermath of disaster, as a town, region or nation attempts to rebuild for the future that one finds, perhaps, the clearest evidence of a social, economic, and political agenda . . . or the absence of such an agenda."[35]

The point is that the news media's preoccupation with disasters is not simply to fulfill a prurient or voyeuristic need. The news media's obsession with the man-made disasters of political life also serve purposes that go beyond the the prurient and the voyeuristic. They also give us insight into the political community's mechanisms for protection, self-policing, self-renewal, mourning, consensus, and gen-

erosity. If we are continually disappointed by the failures of the political community's mechanisms in these important areas, that's hardly a justification for cutting
back on muckraking coverage of the wrecks and crashes in political life. If we are
disappointed by the public's slowness to react to every revelation with outrage,
that still is not a justification for pulling back.

Anyone who has studied the history of muckraking journalism in this
country is aware that its popularity with the public is cyclical. At times, it has been
embraced by the public; it has mobilized citizens to call for change and the public
clamor has moved the citizens' elected representatives to act. For some media
scholars, this process has been called the "mobilization model" of investigative
reporting, wherein media exposés lead to public policy reforms by first changing
public opinion.[36] The mobilization model is integral to the democratic tradition
and the news media's role is key.

Nevertheless, journalism's muckraking function is not effective at every
time and in every place. At times, the journalism of reform is merely tolerated or
ignored by the public. The public's threshold for outrage fluctuates, and at times
that threshold has been raised because of citizen exhaustion, a period of cynicism,
or an economic prosperity that leaves the public relatively content. This is a natural condition of democracy and it is not an alarm signaling the need for some vast
overhaul of journalism.

Public journalists are presently alarmed that the public does not seem to be
as enthralled with journalism, particularly print journalism, in the current milieu,
and so they complain that too many of today's reporters are adversarial—that
these reporters have found their inspiration in the muckraking mythology of
Woodward and Bernstein. The public journalists conclude that now is time to call
off the "junkyard dogs" of the profession. Now is the time for a kindlier and gen-
tler journalism. Now is the time to closet the watchdog and to reach an accord with
those who would be watched.

At this juncture, it might be useful to recall the platform of the *St. Louis
Post-Dispatch*, written by Joseph Pulitzer in 1907, upon his retirement. This was
at a high point in the cycle of muckraking's favor with the public. Pulitzer said his
leaving the newspaper would make no difference in its cardinal principles, "that it
will always fight for progress and reform, never tolerate injustice or corruption,
always fight demagogues of all parties, never belong to any party, always oppose
privileged classes and public plunderers, never lack sympathy with the poor,
always remain devoted to the public welfare, never be satisfied with merely
printing news, always be drastically independent, never be afraid to attack wrong,
whether by predatory plutocracy or predatory poverty."[37]

Notice Pulitzer's use of those two most absolute words, "never" and
"always." Pulitzer did not say: "always oppose public plunderers, unless focus
groups show the public is bored with these kinds of stories." Pulitzer did not say:
"always be drastically independent, unless it's time to show citizens that we are
stakeholders in the community." Pulitzer did not say: "always attack wrong,
whether by predatory plutocracy or predatory poverty, unless such attacks demor-
alize the public into a state of learned hopelessness."

Contentious and Conflict-Oriented?

Public journalists would have us believe that there has never been such a contentious news media—a press so oblivious to the carnage and wreckage it leaves in its wake as it reports every hint of scandal, corruption, and sexual indiscretion in public life. It is unquestionably true that there have never been so many technological outlets for communication of such news; however, the news product itself is not substantially different than it has been throughout the American democratic experiment.

As seasoned journalist Shelley Ross has written in her excellent book, *Fall From Grace*, a history of sex, scandal, and corruption in American politics from 1702 to the present, the American press has always been busy uncovering scandals and the foibles of leaders. Political misdeeds are older than the republic, and throughout U.S. history an aggressive news media has consistently exposed irregularities and illegalities on all sides of the political fence.

George Washington was called a liar in the press of his time. Upon his retirement from the presidency, there were those who called for public rejoicing in the newspapers. Ross reports in her book that while the first president was actually above reproach, press accounts of the iniquities of the first cabinet were closer to the mark. The first cabinet found itself knee-deep in scandals, ranging from financial misconduct to torrid tales of sexual blackmail—most of it focused on the office of Treasury Secretary Alexander Hamilton.[38]

Thomas Jefferson had a soft-spot for married women that was ridiculed in the New York newspapers. They pronounced him a "scandal" and a "scourge." The presidency of Zachary Taylor was rife with corruption and duly noted in the press of his time. Hillary Clinton has nothing on Mary Todd Lincoln when it comes to ill treatment at the hands of the press. Mrs. Lincoln, nicknamed "The Hellcat," was unpopular in the North because she was from a prominent Southern family of slaveholders, while the South hated her because she deserted their cause. Grover Cleveland was elected president despite the scandal of an illegitimate child and the newspaper cartoons showing a baby crying: "Ma! Ma! Where's my pa?"[39]

Thomas Jefferson railed against the personal attacks and negativity of the press of his own time, but in the end concluded "were it left to me to decide whether we should have government without newspapers or newspapers without government, I should not hesitate to prefer the latter."[40] Alexander Hamilton, likewise, denounced the press of his time for its spirit of abuse and calumny, yet acknowledged that the press should be unbridled in its privilege to criticize both public measures and the men who author them.

Two European visitors to early America, Charles Dickens and Alexis de Tocqueville, were horrified by the excesses of the press in this new and untamed land. Journalists in their own countries would face the wrath of the law in making such charges against the authorities, and the mention of such charges in the press in their countries might well have created an immediate crisis in governance.

England's Dickens was inspired to write satire about U.S. papers, tagging them with nameplates like, "The Sewer," "The Family Spy," "The Stabber," and

"The Peeper." In his account of newspapers in America, Dickens captures the
sales pitch of a newsboy hawking "The Sewer," as he shouts: "Here's The Sewer's
exposure of the Wall Street Gang, and the Sewer's exposure of the Washington
Gang, and the Sewer's exclusive account of a flagrant act of dishonesty committed
by the Secretary of State when he was eight years old; now communicated, at a
great expense, by his own nurse. Here's The Sewer."[41]

The brilliant French chronicler de Tocqueville marveled that America was
the one country in the world with "the fewest germs of revolution," while having
a press that was destructive without just cause for its indignation. Despite their fas-
cination and frequent horror with the American press, both de Tocqueville and
Dickens left America with an admiration for its unruly press. As the French author
observed, the American press "constitutes a singular power, so strangely mixed of
good and evil, that it is at the same time indispensible to the existence of freedom,
and nearly incompatible with maintaining public order."[42]

In the face of the public journalists' attacks on today's journalism for its con-
tentiousness and natural disposition toward conflict, traditional journalists need
only offer a history lesson. The tradition of a rough and tumble press runs deep. It
has been a part of American life since the days of George Washington, but the
republic has survived, and public life has continued. The right to criticize those in
public life is a right that was primarily on the minds of those who fought to separate from the rule of the English monarchy, and those minds were fully aware that
such a guarantee might one day boomerang to besmirch their own reputations and
peace of mind.

A PROBLEMATIC REDEMPTION

The evangel of public journalism is a gospel in tripartite. It is a gospel that
rests on several articles of faith. First, that public life is suffering a great decline.
Second, that journalism is not only suffering because of this decline, but that traditional journalism is contributing to the decline because of its detachment,
elitism, negativity, and conflict-orientation. The third article of the gospel is that
it is within the power of journalists to change and to heal their profession. This can
be accomplished through the conversion to a public journalism philosophy, which
can also reverse the declines in public life.

Although the evangelists of public journalism offer a panoply of survey
results and assessments by social scientists supporting the premise that public life
is in decline, these offerings are selective and can be contradicted without too
much difficulty. Much of their critique of public life and its decline is based on
anecdotal evidence and short-term trends, rather than a long-range view of the
American scene. For example, how can public journalists really argue that Americans are more disconnected and isolated than ever before, when most Americans
lived in a predominantly rural, agrarian environment less than a century ago? Iso-
lation was much more of a fact of life in the past. Public journalists may be able
to make a better case that participation in political life has been less than ideal
based on recent voter turnouts, but these election statistics are hardly irrefutable
evidence that democracy is in crisis.

The second article of faith among the evangelists of public journalism—that today's journalism could serve the public far better—has more credibility. Public journalists occasionally provide some useful insights on the conventional news media in this regard. However, as deficient as contemporary journalism may be, in many respects, yesterday's journalism was far worse at serving the public. Much of the energy of journalism throughout U.S. history has been focused on the trivial, the sensational, the scandalous—and the news business today is not profoundly different. What is different today is that the public has many more choices and channels for news information—and many of them offer more useful and accurate information than was available even a generation ago. The article of faith that the quality of journalism is in decline, with the result that the public is losing interest in journalism, is based largely on the performance of major dailies and the old networks' nightly news broadcasts.

The third article of faith among the evangelists—that it is within the power of journalists to change their profession and reverse declines in public life through a public journalism philosophy—is easily the least credible and most outrageous portion of their sermonizing. In the vast majority of news media organizations, journalists have pitifully little power, and in those news organizations that have opted to experiment with the public journalism philosophy, it has only been done at the behest, or with the blessing, of top news executives, publishers, and corporate owners. In many news organizations, where public journalism has found favor, it has been executed from the top down, and skeptical reporters have fallen into disfavor or been nudged out the door.

The issue of whether reporters have the power to make a revolution is really beside the point. Of overriding significance is that public journalists can only make the case for a dramatic departure from traditional journalism if there are, in fact, crisis situations in the quality of public life and in the health of today's news business. There must be real upheaval in the profession and in the quality of public life to call for a reform movement that would replace, or diminish, the influence of some of the time-honored values of the traditional news process. A real upheaval has not arrived, and most journalists are not ready to make this revolution, even if it were within their power.

Still, it can be argued, if the philosophy and practice of the new public journalism have so much to offer, it shouldn't really matter if the first two articles of faith in the public journalism gospel are found wanting. The potential contributions and possibilities of this new public journalism should be examined on their own merit. The problem is that there is a wide array of opinion on just what constitutes a public journalism concept or a public journalism reporting project. Surveys of newspaper editors and journalism professors (conducted as a part of this study) confirm that much confusion exists about public journalism, both in the abstract and in its actual execution.

The confusion is not really surprising. Many academics and practitioners purport to speak for public journalism; their messages are often muddled, if not contradictory. Some public journalists say that the new movement's best practices simply constitute old-fashioned, good journalism. Other public journalists become angry at this suggestion. They argue that it is much more than good jour-

nalism, it is a reformation, and contend that attempts to label it as "just good journalism" are part of a strategy to dismiss public journalism as inconsequential.

A number of vocal academics express affection for public journalism
because they proclaim that at long last the pretense of objectivity can be dropped,
and journalists can crusade for a more equitable distribution of income in society,
for social justice, and for an end to capitalism's excess. They view it as a new version of advocacy journalism, which is informed by the wisdom of the academy.

A number of anxious news executives are attracted to public journalism,
because they proclaim that at long last the pretense of separation between advertising and editorial can be dropped, and front pages can be put in the service of
commerce.

The confusion and contradiction that exists about public journalism is
exemplified in the debate over the very name of the new movement. Proponents
cannot agree on what the movement is called. Is it public journalism or is it civic
journalism? Staci D. Kramer, a St. Louis free-lance journalist who did much of the
writing for the Pew Center's publication, *Civic Journalism: Six Case Studies*, has
her own theory for why there are two names for the phenomenon. According to
Kramer, "public journalism" is the name used primarily by academics in mass
communication and refers to the theory behind the movement. "Civic journalism"
is the name used primarily by the practitioners and refers to the reporting projects
that fall under the rubric of the movement.[43]

James Engelhardt of the University of Oregon argues that there is a difference between civic journalism and public journalism, which has nothing to do
with a split between academics and practitioners. According to Engelhardt, civic
journalism is more scientific and based on polls and collecting data. In contrast,
public journalism is based more on citizen input and citizen forums. Engelhardt,
nevertheless, contends that both public and civic journalism consist of more than
just good journalism practice.[44]

At a 1996 conference of the International Communication Association
(ICA) in Chicago, Rosen had another explanation for why there are two names for
the movement. Rosen said there are two terms because there are two foundations
heavily involved in funding the phenomenon. "No foundation wants to fund the
same kind of project," Rosen told ICA. "But the names don't really matter. I don't
see any real difference between the two. I don't see any camps dividing on one
side or the other."[45]

If names don't matter and definitions don't matter, what are we left with?
Apparently, we are left with something akin to baroque music, a Southern accent,
or an Impressionist painting. We are left with something so subtle, and yet so revolutionary, that it defies description. We are left with something that will never be
fully appreciated or understood by impatient critics or "just the facts, ma'am"
journalists. We are left with a vague evangel.

Public journalists argue that their movement is for real, that it will change
the way reporters do their jobs, that it will give the tired and demoralized institution of journalism a dramatically new edifice, that it will revitalize the flagging
democracy. Given all this, are observers of this new movement asking for too

much when they seek a definition of public journalism from its proponents? Should curious observers and the incredulous be satisfied simply to know that public journalism is an elusive phenomenon but, nonetheless, real?

NOTES

1. Jay Rosen, comments made at public journalism roundtable at the 1996 International Communication Association (ICA) meeting, Chicago, May, 1996.

2. Scott Sherman, "The Public Defender," *Linguafranca* (April, 1998), pp. 49–56.

3. James Fallows, *Breaking the News* (New York: Vintage Books, 1996), p. 15.

4. Peter Braestrup, *Big Story* (New Haven: Yale University Press, 1983).

5. Fallows, op. cit., pp. 74–77.

6. David H. Weaver, and Cleveland G. Wilhoit, *The American Journalist in the 1990s* (Mahwah, New Jersey: Lawrence Erlbaum Associates, 1996), pp. 1–26.

7. Charlotte Grimes, "Whither the Civic Journalism Bandwagon." Position paper presented at S.I. Newhouse School of Communication (Syracuse, New York, 1997), pp. 126–127.

8. Robert Putnam, "Bowling Alone: America's Declining Social Capital," *Journal of Democracy* (January, 1995), pp. 65–70.

9. Deborah Burek, and Martin Connors, *Organized Obsessions* (Detroit: Visible Ink Press, 1992), p. v of introduction.

10. Ibid., p. v.

11. Ibid., p. v.

12. Ibid., p. v–vi.

13. Grimes, op. cit., p. 128. See also Everett C. Ladd, *Silent Revolution: The Rebirth of American Civil Life and What It Means for All of Us* (New York: Free Press, 1999).

14. Anne Peterson, "Peirce Report Offered No Unique Solutions," *St. Louis Journalism Review* (October, 1997), p. 1.

15. Allen Wolfe, *One Nation, After All* (New York: Penguin, 1998), pp. 226–227.

16. E. J. Dionne Jr., *Why Americans Hate Politics* (New York: Touchstone, 1991).

17. Kathleen Jamieson, Campaign Mapping Project, a presentation at the International Communication Association (ICA) meeting, Montreal, May, 1997.

18. James B. Twitchell, *Carnival Culture: The Trashing of Taste in America* (New York: Columbia University Press, 1992), p. 272.

19. Ibid., p. 272.

20. Fallows, op. cit., pp. 32–33.

21. Ibid., p. 120.

22. Ibid., p. 120.

23. Ibid., p. 44.

24. M. L. Stein, "The Culture of Timidity," *Editor & Publisher* (May, 1997), pp. 14–15.

25. Ibid., p. 15.

26. Observations gleaned from more than 15 years of monthly *St. Louis Journalism Review* (*SJR*) meetings with dozens of veteran newspaper reporters and editors, including Ed Bishop, Irving Dilliard, Larry Fiquette, David Garino, Charles Klotzer, Ted Gest, Roy Malone, Selwyn Pepper, Joe Pollack, E. F. Porter, Lou Rose, Michael Sorkin, Rick Stoff, Ellen Harris, Gregory Freeman, Bonita Cornute, and more.

27. James Fallows, "The Puff Adders Nest of Modern Journalism," *Civic Catalyst* (July, 1996), p. 7.

28. Davis Merritt, "The Misconceptions about Public Journalism," *Editor & Publisher* (July 1, 1995), p. 80.

29. Ibid., p. 80

30. Calder Pickett, *Voices of the Past* (New York: John Wiley & Sons, 1972), p. 103.

31. Davis Merritt, *Public Journalism & Public Life: Why Telling the News Isn't Enough* (Hilldale, New Jersey: Lawrence Erlbaum Associates, 1995), p. 19.

32. Ibid., pp. 113–114.

33. Stein, op. cit., pp. 15–16.

34. Merritt, op. cit., 19.

35. Pat Browne, and Robert Browne, *Digging into Popular Culture: Theories and Methodology in Archeology, Anthropology and Other Fields* (Athens, Ohio: Bowling Green State University Press, 1991), p. 81.

36. David L. Protess, et al., *The Journalism of Outrage* (New York: Guilford Press, 1991), pp. 14–15.

37. Pickett, op. cit., 207.

38. Shelley Ross, *Fall from Grace: Sex, Scandal and Corruption in American Politics from 1702 to the Present* (New York: Ballantine Books, 1988), pp. 27–28.

39. Ibid., pp. 64–130.

40. Pickett, op. cit., p. 71.

41. Ibid., p. 82.

42. Ibid., pp. 83–84.

43. Staci Kramer, remarks made at the monthly *St. Louis Journalism Review* (*SJR*) editorial board meeting in St. Louis, September, 1995.

44. Don Corrigan, "Public Journalists Suffer Setback," *St. Louis Journalism Review* (September, 1997), p. 13.

45. Jay Rosen, comments made at public journalism roundtable at 1996 International Communication Association (ICA) meeting, Chicago, May, 1996.

PART II
Surveying Public Journalism

Much of Part II is derived from a survey study of public journalism conducted by the *St. Louis Journalism Review* (*SJR*) in cooperation with the Webster University School of Communications in St. Louis. The project involved an extensive survey of daily newspaper editors and university professors of journalism and mass communication. The survey project took place in the 1996–1997 academic year. Some of the results were published in monthly issues of *SJR* into late 1997.

Data were collected by a questionnaire mailed to daily newspaper editors and professors of journalism and mass communication. The sample consisted of respondents randomly selected from a mailing list provided by the Association for Education in Journalism and Mass Communication (AEJMC). Only professors who were listed in the "newspaper" or "mass communication and society" divisions of the AEJMC listing were considered eligible for inclusion in the study's universe. The sample also consisted of respondents randomly selected from a mailing list of daily newspaper editors in the United States provided by the weekly *Editor & Publisher* journalism trade magazine.

A simple random sampling strategy was used to select 720 names from this compiled listing of 2,923 individuals who constituted the study's universe. Because the percentages of professors and editors were roughly equivalent (51 percent were editors and 49 percent were professors), it was not deemed necessary to stratify the sample on this key population characteristic. The survey mailing promised confidentiality, but not anonymity; therefore, it was possible to initiate one follow-up mailing to those who did not respond to the first mailing in order to increase the study's response rate.

The overall response rate for the survey was 45 percent. The 720 survey mailing produced 327 respondents. A higher percentage of professors responded to the survey than editors (50 percent for the professors and 37 percent for the editors) The overall response rate was, however, adequate for the exploratory nature of this survey project.

The survey instrument consisted of a series of questions about the field of journalism generally and about public journalism specifically. For the most part, multiple choice questions using Likert rating scales were used throughout the survey instrument. An ecosystem rating scale was also used to format some survey questions. For a definition and more information on ecosystem rating scales, see Linda A. Suskie's, *Questionnaire Survey Research, What Works*, published by the Association of Institutional Research in Tallahassee, Florida. The ecosystem rating scale was used particularly for those questions asking respondents to describe a concept or practice as an example of public journalism, as well as to judge whether the concept or practice was good or bad for the field of journalism. These are primarily the questions that are analyzed in Chapters 4 and 5 of this book.

A number of professors and editors included written comments about public journalism and the state of journalism in general on the survey. These professors and editors also volunteered to participate in more thorough phone interviews as a part of the study, and to exempt themselves from the survey project's promise of confidentiality. Because the intent of this book is to serve as a critical review of the public journalism phenomenon, most interviews were conducted with those professors and editors who indicated that they had reservations about the theory or practice of public journalism.

It might be interesting to note that the individuals who initiated this survey project originally expected the survey findings to reveal that public journalism was favored by university journalism and mass communication professors, while it was not so popular with daily newspaper editors. On the contrary, the results of the survey show that of those editors and professors indicating familiarity with public journalism, roughly 50 percent of editors and 50 percent of the professors are favorably disposed toward public journalism. More detailed survey questions, however, reveal that these professors and editors have differing views on what actually constitutes public journalism. This points to the nagging "definition problem" of public journalism. Both constituencies express concern about potential trouble areas that could make public journalism a bad idea for the practice of journalism in general.

4
Public Journalism
and Its Concepts

THE DEFINITION PROBLEM

Both supporters and opponents of public journalism have expressed dismay over the challenge of defining what public journalism and its concepts are all about. Some supporters argue that public journalism is more a range of practices, rather than a series of concepts that can be melded into a definition. Other supporters contend that too much attention has been paid to practices, many of them ill-conceived, when public journalism is really about an intellectual frame of mind developed after a study of the best contemporary thought on democracy, politics, and the news media.

Davis "Buzz" Merritt, one of public journalism's key practitioners, has accepted invitations to media seminars and press panels across the country. He is not enthusiastic when he's asked to talk about specific public journalism projects. He argues that too much attention has been focused on "media combines, public forums or the simplistic airing of the views of uninformed citizens."[1] According to Merritt, journalists must understand the conceptual framework and underpinnings of public journalism before committing to its practice. In other words, serious journalists must understand the philosophic talk, before taking the public journalism walk. He complains that too many practitioners have tried to take an intellectual shortcut with the consequence that a lot of attempts at public journalism have been botched. A true public journalist must take the intellectual journey.

How, in fact, does one take the "intellectual journey" necessary to understand what constitutes public journalism? What are the basic concepts that must be grasped by any would-be practitioner? For starters, Merritt recommends studies about citizens, politics, and public life, many of them produced by the Harwood Group and the Kettering Foundation. Also recommended are books by authors such as Daniel Yankelovitch, E. J. Dionne, and David Mathews. Dionne's, *Why Americans Hate Politics*, is high on the list of required reading.

The scholarship of theoretician Jay Rosen of New York University is indispensible. Rosen has written much about the contrasting views of Walter Lippmann and John Dewey regarding the role of the news media in a modern democracy. Educator Dewey's views are readily championed over the more elitist approach to press function allegedly advocated by commentator Lippmann. According to Rosen, Dewey made the case that journalism and democracy will suffer if the ordinary citizen is treated as a spectator, rather than as an actor, in the political process. The news media have a responsibility to engage and involve citizens in public life, rather than to just talk to them about what's happening in the public arena.[2]

Any discussion of the concepts and intellectual origins of public journalism must be deemed incomplete without some mention of the development of social responsibility theory and the impact of the 1947 Hutchins Commission. Scholars in the emerging field of mass communication after World War II, intellectuals such as Fred Siebert, Theodore Patterson, and Wilber Schramm, helped lay the foundation for a perceptible shift away from libertarianism in the latter half of the Twentieth Century. As Renita Coleman observes in her study of the intellectual antecedents of public journalism, libertarianism gave way to an emerging "social responsibility theory of the press, which was akin to Dewey's proposal of the role of the press in helping build a more pluralist and tolerant society."[3]

A socially responsible press moves away from the "marketplace of ideas" concept of news media function to an obligation, now especially familiar to public journalists, "of making public life go well." For free press libertarians, the alarming aspect of the social responsibility philosophy or view of the press is in its call for self-restraint or even self-censorship when that is in the interest of the "common good" or the betterment of society. The general welfare of society, under social responsibility, sometimes has to take precedence over the dissemination of information that could result in a clear and present danger to the domestic tranquility.

Robert M. Hutchins and his 1947 study task force, the Hutchins Commission, are sometimes described as the the the formal articulators of social responsibility theory for the American news media and the progenitors of public journalism. Hutchins was the chancellor of the University of Chicago from 1945 to 1951 and founded the Center for the Study of Democratic Institutions. Hutchins' friend, Henry Luce, publisher of *Life* and *Time* magazines, had the idea of establishing a council to study press function in America in the early 1940s. Luce's idea became a reality when it found funding from various sources, and Hutchins was selected to form a study commission composed of 12 intellectuals in the areas of history, philosophy, and law.

Commission members found much wrong with newspapers, then the dominant news medium of the time. Some commissioners, such as Archibald Mac-Leish, argued that the press turns coverage of events into a drama, while ignoring more placid developments that are crucial to public understanding. Instead, newspapers concentrate on "stories of race riots, of violent strikes, of over-wealthy and foolish women, of nightclub murders, of quarrels and disagreements between public officials."[4]

The commission's complaints against the press—news selected for its entertainment value, a distorting hunger for scoops, cover-ups of the press's own missteps, and poor coverage of minorities—sound remarkably similar to the charges leveled by public journalism advocates such as James Fallows or Davis "Buzz" Merritt in their books. Although the Hutchins report generally rejects regulation of the news media, several commissioners favored it during the study group's deliberations. According to Stephen Bates, who authored a recent study of the Hutchins Commission and its deliberations, commission members spoke enthusiastically behind closed doors about creating a Federal Communications Commission (FCC) for newspapers, requiring monopoly newspapers to carry government-provided news, and enacting criminal libel statutes. Bates notes that in the final report, "to their credit, the men abandoned these blatantly unconstitutional proposals."[5]

According to the Hutchins Commission's final report, the poor performance of the press presented a public danger because "the preservation of democracy and perhaps of civilization may now depend upon a free and responsible press."[6] According to the report, for the press to serve democracy well it must first provide a truthful and comprehensive account of the day's events in a proper context; second, it must provide a forum for the exchange of comment and criticism; third, it must provide a mechanism for projecting attitudes and opinions of different groups in society to one another; fourth, it must provide a method of presenting and clarifying the goals and values of society; and, fifth, it must find a way of reaching every member of society with its information, feeling, and thought.[7]

Although public journalism advocate Merritt does not mention the work of the Hutchins Commission as an important stop on the intellectual journey to understanding public journalism, an examination of its work can be instructive in understanding journalism's latest reform movement. The commissioners of 50 years ago, like the public journalists, felt democracy was threatened by an unruly, libertarian press that concentrates on conflict-oriented reporting. Like the public journalists, the commissioners came up with ideas to rectify press performance, including a new dedication to reaching the average citizen and an obligation to articulate and clarify goals for society.

There are, of course, important differences in the analysis and recommendations of the commissioners of a half century ago and the news media critique and prescriptions of today's public journalism advocates. For one thing, the commissioners were extremely concerned about press concentration and growing monopoly. They struggled with how to deal with this issue—the public journalists deal with problems of press concentration only on the periphery of their critique. Second, the commissioners held a fairly dim view of the citizenry. They urged the press to be better than the public and to elevate news content rather than debase it to the level of public taste. In contrast, the public journalists seem to have an excessive faith in the good taste of the citizenry. Their view seems to be that the public longs for substantive news content and is frustrated that the media insists on feeding them tabloid gossip, sensational murder stories, and political subterfuge.

There are some interesting similarities in how the mainstream news media responded to the Hutchins Commission findings of 50 years ago, and how traditional journalists are responding to today's public journalism. Today's public journalism advocates are accused of having an academic mentality and of being largely ink-free, just as the Hutchins group was accused of a deficiency in knowledge of practical journalism and the commission was faulted for not having a single member from the journalism community. Wilbur Forrest, president of the American Society of Newspaper Editors, said of the commission that he doubted if "one in ten of these authorities could run a newspaper and stay out of bankruptcy over 12 months."[8]

Today's public journalists are sometimes charged with engaging in vagaries and abstractions, just as the Hutchins Commission members were similarly accused some 50 years ago. The mainstream press of the time found the Hutchins Commission analysis and recommendations to be perplexing, unexciting, inaccessible, and difficult. "The commissioners are philosophers and obviously not journalists," declared *Fortune* magazine. The journalists' weekly trade magazine, *Editor & Publisher*, said that the report's "hodge-podge, hardly understandable language is mostly unsupported hearsay."[9]

Stephen Bates, author of a 1995 study of the Hutchins Commission deliberations and its report, notes how the mainstream press's unfavorable reaction nearly drowned out the commission's recommendations. Nevertheless, the report has appreciably influenced academic thinking about journalism in the last 50 years. Bates observes that "the experience of the Hutchins Commission makes for a revealing, sometimes poignant case study of a reformist flop."

It is too early to determine whether the public journalism movement will succeed in changing the face of American journalism, or end as another "reformist flop." There is no question that public journalism's pronouncements and philosophy are hampered by some of the same flaws that afflicted the reformist message of the Hutchins Commission. Much of the public journalism treatise is decidedly academic and provides few clues as to how it would appropriately be put into action. The concepts of public journalism are vague and abstract, and they have served to sanction a wide array of journalistic experiments.

"One measure of the discomfort that journalists feel over the concept of public journalism is the great variety of names given it, e.g., civic journalism, citizen journalism, community journalism or communitarian journalism," declares Philip Meyer. "It's as though all who try some version of it want to distance themselves from the questionable practices of the others."[10]

Meyer, a longtime professor at the University of North Carolina and a public journalism supporter, concedes that there is much confusion about what qualifies as a public journalism concept or practice. He notes that one consequence of the definition problem "is that debating public journalism is like arguing over a Rorschach test. Each [debate participant] sees in it manifestations of his or her fondest hopes or worst fears."[11]

WHAT IS A PUBLIC JOURNALISM CONCEPT?

The *St. Louis Journalism Review* (*SJR*) survey presented editors and professors with a wide array of questions about the emerging public journalism phenomenon in order to reach some understanding of what actually constitutes public journalism. For the purposes of this chapter, the focus is on that part of the survey project which involves the responses of editors and professors regarding public journalism concepts. Table 4.1 shows the extent to which editors and professors are familiar with the term public journalism.

Of the 143 editors responding to the survey question measuring familiarity with the term "public journalism," 71 percent indicated they were "very familiar" or "somewhat familiar." About 18 percent said they were "slightly familiar" with the term, while 11 percent said they were "not at all familiar" with the term.

Of the 184 professors responding to the survey question measuring familiarity with the term "public journalism," about 86 percent indicated they were "very familiar" or "somewhat familiar." Almost 12 percent said they were "slightly familiar" with the term, while only about 2 percent said they were "not at all familiar" with the term.

The *SJR* survey examined how those editors and professors, who are "very familiar" or "somewhat familiar" with public journalism, react to a variety of statements promoting concepts or ideas that are derived from the literature of public journalism. Six concept statements thought to be representative of key attitudes and practices of public journalism were analyzed using two different response item scales. Survey participants were asked whether the concept: (a) Describes what is public journalism; (b) Is the concept good or bad for journalism? Table 4.2 and Graphs 4.1 and 4.2 summarize how the respondents' answers break down on these six concept statements related to public journalism.

Table 4.1
Editors and Professors Who Are Familiar with the Term Public Journalism

Degree of Familiarity	Editors	Professors
Not at All Familiar	16 11.2%	4 2.2%
Slightly Familiar	26 18.2%	22 11.9%
Somewhat Familiar	55 38.4%	60 32.6%
Very Familiar	46 32.2%	98 53.3%
Total	143 100.0%	184 100.0%

Table 4.2
Attitudes and Practices that Comprise Concepts of Public Journalism[a]

Concepts	Describes Public Journalism[b]				Is Good or Bad for Journalism[c]			
	Disagree	Don't Know	Agree	Total	Bad	Not Sure	Good	Total
Participants versus Watchdogs	79 30.7%	43 16.7%	135 52.6%	257 100.0%	138 53.7%	60 23.3%	59 23.0%	257 100.0%
Reporting Good Things	77 30.1%	79 30.9%	100 39.1%	256 100.0%	90 35.4%	79 31.1%	85 33.5%	254 100.0%
Polling and Focus Groups	62 24.2%	36 14.1%	158 61.7%	256 100.0%	110 43.5%	51 20.1%	92 36.4%	253 100.0%
Actors versus Consumers	28 10.9%	50 19.5%	178 69.6%	256 100.0%	42 16.5%	74 29.1%	138 54.3%	254 100.0%
Ordinary Citizen Coverage	40 15.9%	41 16.3%	171 67.9%	252 100.0%	38 15.2%	59 23.6%	153 61.2%	250 100.0%
Issues versus Horse Races	14 5.4%	27 10.5%	217 84.1%	258 100.0%	11 4.3%	22 8.6%	224 87.1%	257 100.0%

[a] Only those editors and professors who were very familiar or somewhat familiar with the term pulic journalism were included in this table and in graphs 1–2.

[b] A five response Likert scale was also originally used for this item in the survey instrument. The possible response items ranged from: "strongly disagree," "disagree," "don't know," "agree," to "strongly agree." In order to simplify data analysis, the "strongly disagree" and "disagree" categories were collapsed into a single "disagree" category. The "strongly agree" and "agree" categories were also collapsed into a single "agree" category. The "don't know" response was left unchanged.

[c] A five response Likert scale was also originally used for this item in the survey and included the following categories: "very bad," "bad," "not sure," "good," and "very good." These categories were subsequently collapsed from "very bad," to "bad," and "very good," "good" to "good." The "not sure" category was left unchanged.

Graph 4.1
Do You Agree or Disagree that This Concept
Describes What Is Meant by Public Journalism?

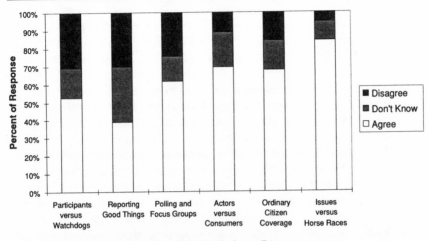

Questions Describing Public Journalism

Graph 4.2
Is This Public Journalism Concept Good or Bad for Journalism?

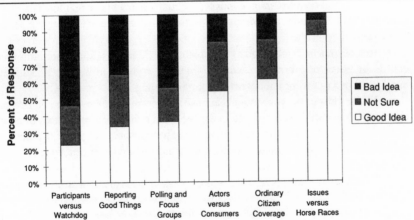

Questions Evaluating Public Journalism

1. Journalists should see themselves more as participants in the democratic process, rather than watchdogs of democratic government. (*Participants versus Watchdogs*)

Theoretician Jay Rosen is perhaps the most outspoken in pronouncing on the concept that would have journalists rethink their roles in the democratic process. In his tract, *Getting the Connections Right: Public Journalism and the Troubles in the Press,* Rosen criticizes what he sees as a fixation by many members on their role as "watchdogs," protecting against misdeeds in government. "They need to rejoin the democratic experiment," declares Rosen. "But first they will have to drop the devastating illusion of themselves as bystanders, 'watching the idiots screw up.' Public journalism begins there."[12]

Practitioner Davis Merritt also has spoken out against what he calls a "post-Watergate syndrome" among traditional news reporters—an obsession with watching government for every misdeed with a readiness to pounce at the slightest provocation. According to Merritt, "the heady rush of bringing down a president gave way to a two-decade post-Watergate syndrome that molded generations of journalists, their readers and their news sources. Suddenly, journalism schools were overflowing and newsrooms were superheated by the feverish belief that if one cannot bring down a president, a dog catcher isn't bad for starters."[13]

Despite Merritt's concern over post-Watergate reportorial overkill, those journalism editors and professors familiar with public journalism, are not supportive of the public journalism concept that puts less emphasis on the journalists' role as a watchdog and more emphasis on a participatory role in helping the democratic process go well.

In the *SJR* survey on public journalism, only 23 percent considered this concept to be good for journalism, while 54 percent considered it to be a bad idea; another 23 percent were not sure if it's good or bad.

While most of the respondents are not in support of this concept, 52 percent agree that the statement, weighing in for the democratic participant role over the watchdog role, provides a description of public journalism. Thirty-one percent disagreed that this was descriptive of public journalism, while 17 percent were not sure.

2. Public journalism is an improvement over traditional journalism, because it tries to report good things about disadvantaged communities rather than concentrating on the negative things that happen. (*Reporting Good Things*)

A frequent complaint against the press is that it primarily reports crime, dysfunction, and failure when covering disadvantaged communities. This negative publicity only dooms these communities to more failure and does nothing to solve problems or make things better. Under the premises of public journalism, the news media have an obligation to seek out and to report on community assets, especially in disadvantaged areas, to help in the rebuilding of troubled communities.

Philip Meyer of the University of North Carolina notes that the public journalism he is interested in revolves around such ideas as communicating in a fashion that helps rebuild a community's sense of itself. "This amounts to a long-delayed realization by news organizations that they and the cause of their problems are parts of a single system," Meyer explains.[14]

In their study, "Good News from a Bad Neighborhood: Civic Journalism as a Vocabulary of Community Assets," James Ettema and Limor Peer of the Department of Communications at Northwestern University write that journalists can employ public journalism to find a "revised and renewed sense of public purpose for the news."

Ettema and Peer argue that the conventions of journalism have placed a priority on news that is violent and spectacularly problematic. This serves to further hinder troubled communities. A contrasting emphasis on community assets in these locales "can enable reporters to think more expansively about urban neighborhoods and urban journalism. Neighborhoods would be understood, not simply as a set of problems that demand action, but as a set of assets that must be protected and that might be enlisted in the service of community-building," Ettema and Peer write.[15]

Journalism editors and professors, familiar with public journalism, are not especially supportive of the idea that public journalism is an improvement over traditional journalism, because it tries to report good things about disadvantaged communities rather than concentrating on the negative things that happen.

In the *SJR* survey on public journalism, only 34 percent considered this concept to be good for journalism, while 35 percent considered it to be a bad idea; another 31 percent were not sure if it's good or bad. Surprisingly, only 39 percent agree that the statement on journalistic coverage of disadvantaged communities provides a description of public journalism. Thirty percent disagreed that this was descriptive of public journalism, while 31 percent were not sure.

3. Journalists should poll citizens and use focus groups to select the type of stories that the press should cover. (*Polling and Focus Groups*)

This statement better describes a technique that has been attributed to the public journalism approach, rather than describing a concept of the movement. However, the concept or idea behind the technique is that of "reconnecting." Journalists are out of touch with their public, and they should explore the methods of social science research to reconnect. Journalists need some new tools to find out what issues and concerns really touch the public imagination.

Public journalism advocates have used polls and surveys after the completion of projects to measure how well their initiatives have been received by the public, and to find out how effective they have been in achieving certain goals of public journalism projects. These polls have been used to discern what the public likes and dislikes in a project. The Pew Charitable Trusts have funded surveys evaluating the community reception to public journalism projects in San Francisco, California, Charlotte, North Carolina, Madison, Wisconsin, and Binghamton, New York.[16]

This aspect attributed to public journalism—the use of focus groups and polling to find out what the public wants to read—has come in for heavy criticism.

Some daily newspapers engaged in public journalism have decreased international coverage and opened more space for "softer" news as a result of polling, focus groups and use of consultants. This result certainly alarms traditional journalists.

Public journalism critic Rosemary Armao says that any "disconnect" between newspapers and their readers can be better solved by hiring more reporters, rather than by paying consultants to conduct polls and focus groups. She argues that newsroom cutbacks by "MBA management-types" are responsible for the alleged loss of connection between newspapers and the public. She adds that if a newsroom has adequate staffing the reporters should be able to find out what the public is thinking and what it wants from its news services, without surveys, polls, and focus groups.[17]

David Remnick, an editor of the *New Yorker* and former *Washington Post* correspondent, has said much the same thing as Armao. Remnick believes that polls and surveys designed to find out what the public desires in news will only hurt the news business in the long run. "Like it or not, part of the job of a great editor is to listen to public desires—and then, if necessary, act against them," declares Remnick in a *New Yorker* piece that takes apart public journalism.[18]

Many public journalists bitterly complain that their movement has been falsely characterized as an effort to connect with the public through pollsters and consultants conducting focus groups. Although the protests seem to fly in the face of the reality of any number of public journalism initiatives, these protests may be having an impact.

A majority of respondents in the *SJR* survey were not favorably disposed toward the statement, "Journalists should poll citizens and use focus groups to select the type of stories that the press covers." However, even though a large percentage of respondents thought this idea was a bad practice for journalism, a majority (62 percent) thought this idea was characteristic of public journalism.

In the *SJR* survey on public journalism, 36 percent considered this concept to be good for journalism, while 44 percent considered it to be a bad concept for journalism; another 20 percent were not sure if it's good or bad.

Sixty-two percent agree that the statement on using polls and focus groups to tailor news coverage provides a description of public journalism. Twenty-four percent disagreed that this was descriptive of public journalism, while 14 percent were not sure.

4. Journalists should not see people as potential consumers of news, but as potential actors in the democratic process who can solve community problems. (*Actors versus Consumers*)

If there is one message that seems to consistently echo throughout the literature of public journalism, it is that news is not simply a product—and readers do not simply constitute a passive market. Journalists must take care to avoid viewing citizens as machines for good quotes or sound bite responses. Journalists must take a step back from the story assembly line and think hard about the consequences of their work.

As Merritt wrote in a "Shop Talk" piece for *Editor & Publisher* in July 1995, "If journalists view their objective as merely providing and interpreting information—simply telling the news in a detached way—we will not be particularly helpful to public life or to our profession. . . . We need to see people not as readers, nonreaders or endangered readers; not as customers to be wooed or an audience to be entertained; not as spectators at an event; but as a public, as citizens capable of action."[19]

This theme is once again played out in the overview of Arthur Charity's text, *Doing Public Journalism*, where he states: "Conventional journalists see the people who buy their newspapers as readers; public journalists see them as citizens. . . . To the public journalist, people have their different roles, but the goal is for them to reason and work together as fellow citizens and equals."[20]

A majority of journalism editors and professors, familiar with public journalism, support the idea that journalists should see people as potential actors in the democratic process—who can solve community problems—rather than as potential consumers of news.

In the *SJR* survey on public journalism, 54 percent considered this concept to be good for journalism, while 17 percent considered it to be a bad idea; another 29 percent were unsure.

Seventy percent agree that the concept—favoring a view of people as actors or participants in democracy, rather than as consumers of news—is descriptive of public journalism. Nineteen percent disagreed that this was descriptive of public journalism, while eleven percent were not sure.

> 5. Journalists should write more on what affects ordinary citizens rather than on the major news events of the day. (*Ordinary Citizen Coverage*)

One of the most scathing critiques of current journalism practice is that penned by James Fallows, former editor of *U.S. News & World Report*. Fallows' book, *Breaking the News*, criticizes today's news media for being "arrogant, cynical, scandal-minded and destructive." Fallows says that today's journalism has become irrelevant for the ordinary citizen; much of what is reported and emphasized is of limited consequence for the ordinary citizen. "Reporters operate as experts, or at least as insiders, in their field, and often act as if their real audience is made up of other reporters or government officials they consider their peers," Fallows writes.[21]

Fallows' disenchantment with news media performance has led him to embrace public journalism, which he praises in the last chapter of his book. He argues that news should be about what affects real people and not about official events and pronouncements by political bureaucrats, which he says make up entirely too much of the typical news fare.

A dissident voice in this trend of public journalism toward stories that are geared more for the common man is that of William Woo, former editor of the *St. Louis Post-Dispatch*. Woo contends there is a current misconception that readers want common man, people stories, rather than accounts about institutions and official happenings. Woo believes papers may be sacrificing important coverage in the name of reader interest and public journalism. Many government stories, for example, may be dull, but if the goal of the news media is to present subjects that relate to people's lives, the government story may actually be most relevant. "What six or eight people do around a table at a legislative session or regulatory board will have greater effect on the lives of ordinary people in public services, taxes, and recreational opportunities" than any number of everyday, common man stories, according to Woo.[22]

Regardless of Woo's point, the concept of reporting and writing more on what affects ordinary citizens, rather than on "the major news events of the day," does strike a chord with editors and journalism professors. A clear majority of respondents in the *SJR* survey agree that this proposition is good for the practice of journalism and represents a public journalism concept.

In the *SJR* survey on public journalism, 61 percent considered this concept to be good for journalism, while 15 percent considered it to be a bad idea; another 24 percent were unsure.

Sixty-eight percent agree that this concept provides a description of public journalism. Sixteen percent disagreed that it was descriptive of public journalism, while another 16 percent were not sure.

6. Public journalism means more meaningful issue-oriented stories about elections and is less concerned about the "horse-race" aspect of elections. (*Issues versus Horse Races*)

Disenchantment with contemporary journalism's approach to the coverage of elections has inspired a number of editors and reporters to pick up the public journalism gauntlet. Some journalists speak of an epiphany, a specific event that turned them to the public journalism idea.

For practitioner Merritt, that moment came during coverage of the 1988 Bush-Dukakis race for president when candidate Dukakis took to riding in a tank for an election photo opportunity. For Merritt, that incident symbolized the lack of substance in coverage of U.S. elections. Merritt subsequently tried some new ways of doing election coverage at his own paper, *The Wichita Eagle*. These issue-oriented approaches have been incorporated into the catalog of public journalism experiments deemed successful by public journalism advocates. Merritt explains his unhappiness with the horse-race approach to elections, politics, and related coverage in his book, *Public Journalism & Public Life*.

"A popular reportorial device—thought to engage readers and make the news personal to them—is to sort out 'winners' from 'losers'. . . . The journalistic notion is that it is a service to citizens and readers because each can quickly decide whether he or she 'won' or 'lost.' Actually, that approach is a disservice," writes Merritt. "It is a disservice to citizens because it vastly oversimplifies a complex situation. It assumes citizens are one dimensional in their interests, and encourages them to be so."[23]

Theoretician Rosen puts the matter a bit more succinctly in *Public Journalism: Theory and Practice*, a 1994 publication of the Kettering Foundation, co-authored by Rosen and Merritt. According to New York University's Rosen, "Public journalism tries to put 'what matters to citizens,' 'the choices the community faces,' in place of 'what professionals are telling and selling' and 'who's up and who's down.'"[24]

One the largest segments of public journalism experiments at daily newspapers has focused on election coverage. These experiments are aimed at implementing the concept of moving away from horse-race coverage of politics and campaigns, and moving toward more issue-oriented coverage.

In the *SJR* survey on public journalism, 87 percent considered this concept to be good for journalism, while a mere 4 percent considered it to be a bad idea; another 9 percent were unsure.

Eighty-four percent agree that the statement on the journalistic coverage of elections, emphasizing issues rather than the horse-race aspect, provides a description of public journalism. Five percent disagreed that this was descriptive of public journalism, while 11 percent were not sure.

WHAT IS PUBLIC JOURNALISM?

The *SJR* survey project reveals some clear divisions over what is considered a legitimate public journalism concept, even among professors and editors who profess to have some knowledge about what public journalism is all about.

There is obvious concern, and division, over any journalistic concept that lessens the importance of the "watchdog" role of the news media. There is obvious concern, and division, over any journalistic concept that would use polls and focus groups to connect with the public and to determine how news content should be shaped to satisfy the public appetite. There is concern over what is meant by public journalists when they talk about new approaches to news aimed at solving community problems.

The uncertainty over what is a legitimate public journalism concept, and what concepts should inform a public journalism project, confounds many who have tried to understand public journalism. This uncertainty has been called "the definition problem" by both friends and foes of the movement; even those sympathetic with the aims of public journalism warn that the definition problem is critical and must be addressed, even while its most vocal proponents express irritation at demands for clarity and insist that the movement is a work in progress.

The University of North Carolina's Meyer argues that because public journalism lacks clear concepts and even a definition, it is vulnerable to exploitation by a range of special interests that would like a piece of media power. Meyer provides examples: "The chamber of commerce wants to tear up a park to build a convention center? Support it in the name of public journalism. You don't know what issues to cover in the coming election? Let the readers, while under the spell of the most vocal interest group, vote on it in a poll commissioned in the name of public journalism. Is reporting on the local crime problem bad for retail business? Suppress it in the name of public journalism."[25]

Public journalists argue that theirs is a reform movement that will change the culture of newsrooms. Reporters will adopt a new set of journalistic reflexes that will allow them to connect with citizens and to help them with their problems. Editors who subscribe to public journalism, and who refer to themselves as "change agents," will revitalize communities and pump up a flagging democracy. Are observers of this new phenomenon asking for too much when they seek a definition of public journalism from its advocates? Should those on the sidelines simply get out of the way and trust that this new movement is for real, even if its formula for a new kind of journalism is ill-defined and elusive?

The most "real" and valid public journalism concept, according to respondents to the *SJR* survey, is that public journalism entails more meaningful issue-oriented reporting about elections. It is less concerned about the horse-race aspect of elections—who's ahead at the moment and who's behind. This is the only concept in the *SJR* survey that draws overwhelming support. More than 80 percent of respondents feel that this concept is descriptive of public journalism and constitutes a good idea for journalism practice.

Few can argue with the wisdom of this approach to journalism practice. It should be pointed out, however, that advocates for more issue-oriented coverage of elections have been around for a long time. The critics of horse-race coverage of elections were crying out against it long before public journalists began having epiphanies over the shortcomings of presidential election coverage.

This begs the question as to whether public journalism ideas are as novel, innovative, or revolutionary as proponents claim. Aren't we just talking about old-fashioned, traditional practices of good journalism? Is a new movement in journalism really required to implement these good ideas?

EDITORS VERSUS PROFESSORS

One of the more interesting and significant revelations of the *SJR* survey section on concepts of public journalism involves a split between the daily newspaper editors and those who teach journalism in academia. In the 1996–1997 survey study, professors of journalism and mass communication are much more sympathetic to public journalism concepts that might be described as having a sociological orientation. Daily newspaper editors, on the other hand, are more sympathetic to public journalism concepts that are more market-oriented. These attitudinal differences can be seen in Table 4.3.

For example, almost 45 percent of the editors in section (a) of Table 4.3 think it's a good idea to poll citizens and use focus groups to select the type of stories that the press should cover. By contrast, less than a third of journalism professors think this is a good idea. Approximately 60 percent of each group agree that this concept is descriptive of public journalism.

In addition, more than 76 percent of the editors in section (b) of Table 4.3 think it's a good idea for journalists to write more about what affects ordinary citizens rather than on the major news events of the day. By contrast, only about 51 percent of the journalism professors think this is a good idea. Once again, about

Table 4.3

Editors' and Professors' Value Judgments Concerning Public Journalism Concepts[a]

(a) Journalists should poll citizens and use focus groups to select the type of stories that the press should cover (*Polling and Focus Group*)

| | Good or Bad for Journalism? | | | |
	Bad	Not Sure	Good	Total
Editors	39	14	44	97
	40.2%	14.4%	45.4%	100.0%
Professors	71	37	48	156
	45.5%	23.7%	30.8%	100.0%
Total	110	51	92	253
	43.5%	20.1%	36.4%	100.0%

(b) Journalists should write more on what affects ordinary citizens than on the major news events of the day (*Ordinary Citizen Coverage*)

| | Good or Bad for Journalism? | | | |
	Bad	Not Sure	Good	Total
Editors	9	14	75	98
	9.2%	14.3%	76.5%	100.0%
Professors	29	45	78	152
	19.1%	29.6%	51.3%	100.0%
Total	38	59	153	250
	15.2%	23.6%	61.2%	100.0%

(c) Public Journalism is an improvement over traditional journalism because it tries to report on the good things about disadvantaged communities rather than concentrating on the negative things that happen in them (*Reporting Good Things*)

| | Good or Bad for Journalism? | | | |
	Bad	Not Sure	Good	Total
Editors	47	33	19	99
	47.5%	33.3%	19.2%	100.0%
Professors	43	46	66	155
	27.7%	29.7%	42.6%	100.0%
Total	90	79	85	254
	35.4%	31.1%	33.5%	100.0%

(d) Journalists should not see people as potential consumers of news, but as potential actors in the democratic process who can solve community problems (*Actors versus Consumers*)

| | Good or Bad for Journalism? | | | |
	Bad	Not Sure	Good	Total
Editors	26	39	35	100
	26.0%	39.0%	35.0%	100.0%
Professors	16	35	103	154
	10.4%	22.7%	66.9%	100.0%
Total	42	74	138	254
	16.6%	29.1%	54.3%	100.0%

[a] Only those editors and professors who were familiar or somewhat familiar with the term public journalism were included in this table.

two-thirds of each group agree that this concept is descriptive of public journalism.

The *SJR* survey, therefore, lends credence to Professor Meyer's contention that different interest groups can find different things to like in public journalism, since it remains an ill-formed theory that lacks a clear definition. Even interest groups as similar in outlook as newspaper editors and college journalism professors see different things in public journalism. The editors gravitate to public journalism concepts that are market-oriented, while the journalism professors favor ideas that would seem to address sociological issues.

Another set of survey data supporting this finding can be found in section (c) of Table 4.3. This section shows that only 19 percent of editors are favorably disposed to the statement: "Public journalism is an improvement over traditional journalism, because it tries to report good things about disadvantaged communities, rather than concentrating on the negative things that happen." By contrast, 43 percent of professors think this concept is good for journalism. Twice as many professors favor a journalism concept that allows journalism to tailor reporting around perceived needs of given coverage areas.

This split is even more dramatic on the concept statement "Journalists should not see people as potential consumers of news, but as potential actors in the democratic process who can solve community problems." Only about 35 percent of the editors feel this idea is good for journalism, as shown in section (d) of Table 4.3. By contrast, 67 percent of the professors find this idea to be good for journalism.

This obvious split between the practitioners and the academics serves to underscore the criticality of public journalism's definition problem. If the movement has no clear definition, then would-be practitioners can interpret it as they wish. They can justify any number of practices in its name.

Results of the *SJR* public journalism survey provide confirmatory empirical evidence for a finding that many have observed anecdotally while attending editors' conferences and professors' seminars. The finding or conclusion is that many journalism and mass communication professors see public journalism as a mobilizing force to address inequities in society and to effect social change. Many daily newspaper editors, on the other hand, see public journalism as a new box of tools and marketing devices to get readers back into the newspaper habit.

NOTES

1. Davis Merritt, "Missing The Point," *American Journalism Review* (July/August, 1996), p. 30.

2. Jay Rosen, *Imagining Public Journalism* (Bloomington, Indiana: Indiana University Press, 1995), pp. 17–20.

3. Renita Coleman, "The Intellectual Antecedents of Public Journalism." Paper presented at a civic journalism interest group session at the AEJMC convention in Anaheim, California, August, 1996.

4. Stephen Bates, *Realigning Journalism with Democracy: The Hutchins Commission, Its Times, and Ours* (Washington, D.C.: The Annenberg Washington Program in Communications Policy Studies of Northwestern University, 1995).

5. Ibid.

6. Ibid.

7. Ibid.

8. Ibid.

9. Ibid.

10. Philip Meyer, "Discourse Leading to Solutions," *The IRE Journal* (November-December, 1996), pp. 3–5.

11. Ibid.

12. Jay Rosen, *Getting the Connections Right* (New York: Twentieth Century Fund Press, 1996), p. 6.

13. Davis Merritt, *Public Journalism & Public Life: Why Telling the News Isn't Enough* (Hillsdale, New Jersey: Lawrence Erlbaum Associates, 1995), p. 58.

14. Meyer, op. cit., p. 3.

15. James Ettema, and Limor Peer, "Good News from a Bad Neighborhood: Civic Journalism as a Vocabulary of Community Assets." Paper presented at the annual conference of the International Communications Association (ICA), Chicago, May, 1996, p. 29.

16. "New Civic Journalism Research," *Civic Catalyst* (January, 1997), p. 1.

17. Comments made by Rosemary Armao at a panel on public journalism at the 1995 Investigative Reporters and Editors (IRE) Convention in Miami, June 1995.

18. David Remnick, "Scoop," *New Yorker* (January 29, 1996), p. 42.

19. Davis Merritt, "The Misconceptions about Public Journalism," *Editor & Publisher* (July 1, 1995), p. 80.

20. Arthur Charity, *Doing Public Journalism* (New York: Guilford Press, 1995), p. 12.

21. James Fallows, *Breaking the News* (New York: Vintage Books, 1997), p. 240.

22. M. L. Stein, "The Culture of Timidity," *Editor & Publisher* (May 24, 1997), pp. 14–15.

23. Davis Merritt, *Public Journalism & Public Life: Why Telling the News Isn't Enough* (Hillsdale, New Jersey: Lawrence Erlbaum Associates, 1995), p. 100.

24. Davis Merrit, and Jay Rosen, *Public Journalism Theory and Practice* (Dayton, Ohio: Kettering Foundation, 1994), p. 16.

25. Meyer, op. cit., p. 3.

5
Public Journalism
and Its Practices

GENESIS OF A REVOLUTION

From its inception, public journalism has been accompanied by plenty of controversy. The first experiment is often traced to a daily newspaper in Columbus, Georgia, that abandoned the role of detached observer and pursued an activist mode. The Columbus experiment is now hailed as the genesis of a journalistic revolution.

The late editor of *The Columbus Ledger-Enquirer*, Jack Swift, was behind a series entitled, "Columbus Beyond 2000: Agenda For Progress," which included a survey of 400 households on issues ranging from race relations to employment to the health of the local economy. Reporters put in many hours assembling the massive project as the 1980s came to a close.

After more than a year of work, the series ran in the paper with little community response. A list of recommendations for the greater Columbus community went nowhere. Editor Swift was unwilling to sit back and let the series of stories fade into oblivion in the news morgue. He initiated and directed a 1990 community task force that sponsored town hall meetings and backyard barbecues. Its purpose was to engage citizens to become participants in directing their community's future, thus, the 1990s phenomenon of public journalism emerged.

The *Ledger-Enquirer* experiment drew criticism from some in the Georgia community as well as from reporters on the paper itself. Reporters expressed an uneasiness with the paper's coverage of its own events. They grew tired of the project's length, as did many readers. They felt coverage of traditional beats was being lost in an effort to promote the kinds of goals that are more familiar to a chamber of commerce.

According to the University of South Florida's Lynn Waddell, who researched *The Ledger-Enquirer* experiment, tension in the newsroom reached unbearable levels when the newspaper's parent company, Knight-Ridder, conducted an attitude survey among newspaper staff in the summer of 1990 and Swift came in for harsh criticism. In November 1990, Swift killed himself with a bullet to the head and many speculated that a factor in his suicide was despair caused by the response to the newspaper project. Before the suicide of Swift, *The Ledger-Enquirer* gave up on the project, causing some supporters in the community to feel abandoned.[1]

Waddell interviewed *The Ledger-Enquirer* reporter Billy Winn in the course of her research on the project. Winn told Waddell that public journalism can become a crutch for journalists who really don't know a community and that the term itself has become a corporate buzz word. Winn had praise for some of the results of the first public journalism project, but he was less than happy with the hype and intense scholarly interest in the newspaper's initiative. Winn told Waddell: "We've had every guru through here, and they have analyzed it to death. I happen to believe in public journalism. I just don't like all this talk about it being something new. We did a lot more when I first came into journalism in the '60's. Public journalism is a bad substitute for true journalism."[2]

One of the gurus who took a keen interest in *The Ledger-Enquirer* project was the Kettering Foundation's David Mathews, who saw the approach by Swift as a dramatic departure from traditional journalism—a departure that could help communities resolve their own problems through public deliberation. Jay Rosen and James Fallows are two other gurus of the new movement in journalism who find *The Ledger-Enquirer* experiment to be a model for change in journalism.

In his book, *Breaking the News*, Fallows describes the "transforming experience" that led Swift to plunge the newspaper into an activist mode for the betterment of the community. Fallows draws on Rosen's observation that what the Columbus newspaper had done was to "reconstrue the position of the journalists within politics. Instead of standing outside the political community and reporting its pathologies, they took up residence within its borders. This was a courageous move that made a difference to the citizens of Columbus."[3]

Rosen's confident observations notwithstanding, there is still much debate over just how courageous *The Ledger-Enquirer* experiment was and whether it should be held up as an example for contemporary journalism. The journalists who put in 12- and 14-hour days to get the project assembled have some reservations. The readers also had some reservations as they watched regular news being bumped from the front pages in favor of what editor Swift saw as a pressing need for community conversation about the future of Columbus, Georgia.

There is so much uncertainty within the public journalism movement itself as to what constitutes a legitimate project worthy of emulation that even the highly-praised, initial project in Columbus is a source of contention. Uncertainty has been so prevalent in public journalism from the beginning that it has been elevated to a virtue. If journalists are uncertain and ambivalent about what they are doing and what it will accomplish, then they have passed a major fork in the road of public journalism's intellectual journey, according to advocates.

In less than a decade of public journalism's existence, its proponents have declared that their initiatives comprise a dramatic paradigm shift in the way journalism is conceived and practiced. Then, they've backed off from such pronouncements and suggested that public journalism is simply "good journalism" and that in time its very name—public journalism—will melt away as its better practices are adopted. This sort of retreat has subsequently infuriated another portion of its supporters, who have retorted that "we have been too quick to seek accord with some of our critics by agreeing that civic [public] journalism is 'just good ol' fashioned journalism' freshened for the '90s. That's a wonderful way to dismiss the most provocative elements of the experiment."[4]

In less than a decade of public journalism's existence, its advocates have declared that it is nothing less than a fully launched reform movement that will revive democracy and fix a journalism practice that is broken. Then they've backed off from such sweeping declarations and suggested that "public journalism can't do it all." After some significant project failures, they've conceded that "our results suggest that there are significant limits—at least in the short term—to the ability of journalists to reconnect citizens with democratic institutions solely by altering the way they write about them."[5]

Public journalism advocates have praised projects that have connected the news media with foundations, commercial entities, and public relations firms, and then backed off insisting that being "connected" doesn't mean abandoning independence and detachment. Public journalism advocates have praised projects that have involved focus groups and polling for setting a citizens' agenda for subsequent public forums, and then backed off insisting that public journalism is not about "focus groups," "polling," and "setting a citizens' agenda."[6] Public journalism advocates have praised projects with headlines that purport to take back neighborhoods and restore citizen involvement in the political process, and then backed off insisting that public journalism is not aimed at solving problems.[7]

Public journalism's friends in consulting firms and in supportive foundations have put out elaborate brochures touting specific newspaper, radio, and television projects around the country. The projects have included such initiatives as "Taking Back Our Neighborhoods/Carolina Crime Solutions," "Your Voices Count," and "Voice of the Voter." Public journalism advocates have then backed off from the multitudinous projects, suggesting that public journalism isn't about projects at all; instead, it's about learning to incorporate public journalism concepts, modes of thinking, and habits of mind into the daily and weekly practice of mainstream journalism.

"So much of public journalism has been defined in project terms or focused on fixed-time election efforts," laments Steve Smith, a public journalism advocate at the *Colorado Springs Gazette Telegraph.* "That makes it easier for the critics to separate civic journalism from the journalistic mainstream. . . . I've come to see that our efforts are totally compatible with mainstream journalism."[8] Many advocates echo the same refrain, suggesting that the project-oriented beginning of public journalism has delayed the movement's maturation, and now its supporters should simply focus on making public journalism a part of news-room routine.

Prominent public journalism practitioner Davis "Buzz" Merritt praises the motivation and the energy behind many public journalism projects, but he resists endorsing them. "Some recent experiments under the name of public journalism, unfortunately and avoidably, have left themselves open to criticism," Merritt stated candidly in a 1996 *American Journalism Review (AJR)* piece.[9]

In his *AJR* article, Merritt argues that some public journalism projects have been true to the intellectual concept, while conceding that others have strayed far beyond where he would go as a newspaper editor. Who is the final judge in the public journalism movement, the final arbiter who bestows the blessing: "Yes, this, my friends, is public journalism?" Is Merritt the authoritative voice that pro-nounces what constitutes public journalism? What makes a bona fide public jour-nalism project?

WHAT IS A PUBLIC JOURNALISM PROJECT?

In order to provide another perspective on public journalism, the *SJR* survey presented editors and professors with a wide array of questions about the emerging public journalism phenomenon and about public attitudes regarding the news media. In addition to asking them their opinions about what actually constitutes the concepts of public journalism, the *SJR* survey also posed a series of questions about public journalism projects. Once again, only the responses of those editors and professors who were either "very familiar" or "somewhat familiar" with the term public journalism were examined.

The *SJR* survey examined how editors and professors react to a variety of project ideas derived from the literature of public journalism or from actual news-paper projects that have been conducted as public journalism initiatives. Six proj-ect ideas were selected as examples of public journalism projects. Survey partici-pants were asked whether the project ideas are representative of what is meant by public journalism and to evaluate whether the project ideas are good or bad for the practice of journalism.

Table 5.1 and Graphs 5.1 and 5.2 summarize how their answers break down on these six public journalism project statements.

> 1. A project in which a newspaper promotes racial progress by asking readers to sign a pledge to work for racial harmony and racial understanding wherever pos-sible. (*Racial Pledge*)

The racial progress project question is derived from the 1993 story series entitled, "A Question of Color," which was published by the *Akron Beacon-Journal*. Hailed as a classic example of public journalism at its best, the Pulitzer Prize-winning story series used focus groups in studying community attitudes on race. The 10-month project suggested that part of the problem with race relations in Akron related to the lack of personal relationships between people of different

Table 5.1
Project Ideas of Public Journalism[a]

Project Ideas	Describes Public Journalism[b]				Is Good or Bad for Journalism[c]			
	Disagree	Don't Know	Agree	Total	Bad	Not Sure	Good	Total
Racial Pledge	70 27.3%	67 26.2%	119 46.5%	256 100.0%	116 45.4%	70 27.3%	70 27.3%	256 100.0%
Pizza Papers	68 26.7%	46 18.0%	141 55.3%	255 100.0%	124 48.4%	58 22.7%	74 28.9%	256 100.0%
Abortion Summit	51 19.9%	58 22.7%	147 57.4%	256 100.0%	102 39.9%	61 23.8%	93 36.3%	256 100.0%
Gang Summit	40 15.6%	47 18.4%	169 66.0%	256 100.0%	88 34.4%	58 22.6%	110 43.0%	256 100.0%
Business Meeting	23 9.1%	45 17.7%	186 73.2%	254 100.0%	68 26.7%	49 19.2%	138 54.1%	255 100.0%
Political Forum	8 3.1%	17 6.7%	230 90.2%	255 100.0%	21 8.2%	11 4.3%	224 87.5%	256 100.0%

[a] Only those editors and professors who were very familiar or somewhat familiar with the term public journalism were included in this table and in Graphs 5.3–5.4.
[b] A five response Likert scale was originally used for this item in the survey instrument. The possible response items ranged from "strongly disagree," "disagree," "don't know," "agree," to "strongly agree." In order to simplify data analysis, the "strongly disagree" and "disagree" categories were collapsed into a single "disagree" category. The "strongly agree" and "agree" categories were also collapsed into a single "agree" category. The "don't know" response was left unchanged.
[c] A five response Likert scale was also originally used for this item in the survey and included the following categories: "very bad," "bad," "not sure," "good," and "very good." These categories were subsequently collapsed from "very bad," to "bad," and "very good," "good," to "good." The "not sure" category was left unchanged.

Graph 5.1
Do You Agree or Disagree that This Project Idea
Describes What Is Meant by Public Journalism?

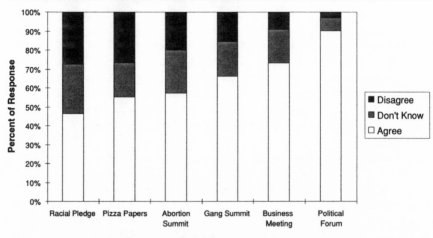

Questions Describing Public Journalism

Graph 5.2
Is This Public Journalism Project Idea Good or Bad for Journalism?

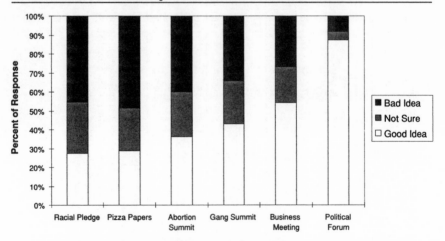

Questions Evaluating Public Journalism

races. The paper sponsored a number of meetings to encourage, among other things, more diversity in the workplace.

The *Beacon-Journal* also published a model New Year's resolution, urging readers to make this pledge: "My New Year's Resolution is to do everything I can in 1994 to help improve race relations." More than 22,000 residents signed coupons containing the resolution and returned them to the *Akron Beacon-Journal*.

The coupon project was deemed a success, and the paper also had 10,000 T-shirts, lapel pins, and caps produced with the logo, "Coming Together."[10]

Journalism editors and professors familiar with public journalism are not especially supportive of the racial progress pledge idea. In the *SJR* survey on public journalism, only 27 percent considered it to be a good idea for journalism, while 46 percent considered it to be a bad idea; another 27 percent were not sure.

Most of the respondents are not in support of the racial progress pledge idea; however, 47 percent did agree that this project idea describes what is meant by public journalism; 27 percent disagreed, while another 26 percent were not sure.

The *Akron Beacon-Journal* projects editor Bob Paynter told *SJR* in 1994 that many seasoned journalists would probably look at the paper's resolution project with cynicism and dismiss it as media gimmickry. Nevertheless, he said he felt that it had a positive effect for the community.[11]

2. A project in which a newspaper offers residents pizza, paid for by corporate sponsors, as an incentive to gather in backyards to discuss "likes" and "dislikes" about their community as well as its future. (*Pizza Papers*)

The backyard community issues project question is derived from the so-called "Pizza Papers" reporting of 1993 in the *Spokesman Review* in Spokane, Washington. In a column introducing the project entitled, "A Pepperoni for your Thoughts," the newspaper offered free pizzas in exchange for readers assembling together to discuss visions of the future of their city and region.

More than 1,500 residents gathered in backyards to discuss what they liked and didn't like about where they live. An urban consultant gathered their ideas in a lengthy report on the region's future. The pizza papers project was heavily subsidized by the corporate community in a number of ways. The newspaper paid less than half of the $75,000 it cost to produce the report that was summarized in the paper; the rest of the money came from banks and other downtown Spokane interests.[12]

Mark Jurkowitz, ombudsman for *The Boston Globe*, took aim at the pizza papers example of public journalism in a winter 1996 edition of the Forbes' magazine, *MediaCritic*. Describing the project as "disturbing," Jurkowitz noted, "In seeking contributions from institutions they typically cover, newspapers compromise their independence and the notion that they will report the news impartially."[13]

Journalism editors and professors familiar with public journalism show a little more support for a pizza papers idea than for the racial progress pledge idea. In the *SJR* survey on public journalism, 29 percent considered it to be a good idea for journalism, while 48 percent considered it to be a bad idea; another 23 percent were not sure.

The pizza papers idea scores fairly high as a description of what is meant by public journalism among the respondents. Fifty-five percent agreed that this project idea describes what is meant by public journalism; 27 percent disagreed, while another 18 percent were not sure. In some ways, the pizza papers project harkens back to the original Columbus, Georgia project of *The Ledger-Enquirer* which asked readers to discuss the future of their city in informal gatherings involving backyard barbecues.

The high percentage of respondents who believe that the pizza papers idea is descriptive of public journalism is startling, because of the phrase "paid for by corporate sponsors" in the project statement presented to survey participants. It could be argued that this phrase added a negative bias to the questions on the pizza project, it was thought to be an important element of a number of public journalism projects of this kind. Negative bias or not, a clear majority of respondents (57 percent) still thought the project statement was descriptive of a public journalism project.

> 3. A project in which a newspaper sponsors a meeting of abortion clinic protesters and pro-choice activists to find areas of agreement between the two groups. (*Abortion Summit*)

The abortion issue summit question in the *SJR* survey is derived from the literature of public journalism. In an article entitled, "Reluctant Sea Change," which was published in the January/February 1996 issue of *The Quill*.[14] Arthur Charity refers to such a summit idea in *The Quill* article as an inspiration for aspiring public journalists.

Charity, an avid public journalism proponent and author of the text, *Doing Public Journalism*, urges the study of a public television program video entitled, "What's the Common Ground on Abortion?" The public television program put the leaders of the National Abortion Rights Action League and the National Right To Life Committee on the same stage and, according to Charity, it "succeeded against all odds in getting them to identify areas in which they might work together."[15]

The videotape of the program is available from Search for Common Ground in Washington, D.C. Charity insists that the tape can show journalists how to ask "a wiser set of questions" in framing a story on such a divisive issue. Charity and other public journalists argue that traditional journalism only reports on the extremes of divisive issues, only making matters worse for society. They argue that journalists should move away from conflict-driven reporting on issues such as abortion, and move toward story projects that can bring people together.

Journalism editors and professors familiar with public journalism show a little more support for the abortion issue summit idea than the two previous project ideas discussed in this article. In the *SJR* survey on public journalism, 36 percent considered it to be a good idea for journalism, but 40 percent considered it to be a bad idea; 24 percent were not sure.

The abortion issue summit idea scores high as a description of what is meant by public journalism among the respondents. A 57 percent majority agreed that this project idea describes what is meant by public journalism; only 20 percent disagreed, while 23 percent were not sure.

4. A project in which a newspaper sponsors a gang peace summit to try to end violence and drive-by shootings by gang members. (*Gang Summit*)

The gang peace summit project question is derived from several such projects that have been sponsored by California dailies. Editors of these papers say
their reporters grew weary of reporting gang-related crimes and murders and won-
dered if there wasn't some sort of action they could take to end the spiral of violence in their communities.

An editor told a Miami IRE seminar in 1995 that her paper's gang summit
project was successful in achieving an uneasy truce between rival gangs and in
reducing the violence. She said reporters also were relieved to be engaged in positive reporting about the gang summit, rather than writing more distressing stories
of continuing gang violence. She said such repetitive, negative reporting is one of
the factors that leads to "burnout" among journalists.[16]

One pitfall of such summit projects was pointed out in a 1995 edition of the
Columbia Journalism Review (*CJR*) in the article, "Are You Now or Will You Ever
Be, A Civic Journalist." *CJR*'s senior editor, Mike Hoyt, wrote about a public journalism experiment that aimed to make peace between Koreans in a suburban
community and local political leaders.

The Koreans were angry over a police action. The newspaper offered
meeting space to "facilitate" a get-together for better understanding. Unfortunately, the newspaper's peace summit degenerated into wrangling, verbal spar-
ring, and shrill demands. The newspaper reporter wrote an account of the meeting
as essentially a food fight, but the editor reworked the article into a brighter
account of the meeting as a "celebration of diversity."

As *CJR*'s Hoyt declared, "the incident points to a fine line that civic journalists sometimes walk. It is in the interest of the newspaper to portray its public
journalism efforts as helpful, perhaps even when they are not. With a few twists
of the semantic dials, public journalism can become public posturing."[17]

Journalism editors and professors familiar with public journalism show an
increased support for the gang peace summit idea compared to the three previous
project ideas discussed in this chapter. In the *SJR* survey on public journalism, 43
percent considered it to be a good idea for journalism; 34 percent considered it to
be a bad idea; while 23 percent were not sure.

The gang peace summit idea scores high as a description of what is meant
by public journalism among the respondents. A 66 percent majority agreed that
this project idea describes what is meant by public journalism; only 16 percent disagreed, while 18 percent were not sure.

5. A project in which a newspaper brings business interests and environmental
   activists together to reach a consensus on the use of community resources. (*Business Meeting*)

The business and environment consensus project question is derived from
the literature of public journalism as well as from some newspaper projects such

as the 1993 "Our Jobs, Our Children, Our Future," by the daily *Huntington Herald-Dispatch* in West Virginia. The Huntington paper teamed up with the local NBC affiliate to sponsor a town hall meeting on economic development after a decade of massive job losses in the community.[18]

Local environmentalists expressed concern about what kind of industry should be encouraged to settle in the Huntington area in the new push for development. At the town hall meeting, an attempt was made to find a middle ground between concerns over industrial problems and interest in new jobs and local economic development. The news media project raised eyebrows among journalism professors at the local W. Page Pitt School of Journalism and Mass Communications at Marshall University in Huntington.

One professor questioned whether the project wasn't a way "to soften up the community" for a proposed pulp mill development for the area. The mill development was opposed by a local environmental alliance because of increased logging, trucking, and pollution from the mill's chlorine-based processes. However, the mill promised to bring in 600 jobs.

"The *Herald-Dispatch* said that Huntington is dying and there has to be a pro-active approach," said Dwight Jensen, a journalism professor at Marshall. One of the things the paper did was advocate the bond issue to set up a commission to attract new business. That bothers me. The paper not only advocated it, it orchestrated it. "I have less of a problem if someone else originated the idea, and the paper endorsed it," said Jensen. "I really question whether a paper gives all sides an equal opportunity to be heard in a situation like this. For example, the paper pushed for a regional airport as part of the development, but then downplayed an FAA report that was less than enthusiastic about the idea."[19]

In a decade of downsizing and lost jobs, it's not surprising that local newspapers would feel a need to be pro-active in helping their home communities rebound. As Jensen points out, however, the credibility of a newspaper can suffer when it takes the initiative to bring opposing interests together to create some common vision for future economic development. An activist role by the newspaper erodes confidence in its ability to provide impartial or balanced reporting.

Journalism editors and professors familiar with public journalism show a level of support beyond 50 percent for the business and environment consensus project idea. In the *SJR* survey on public journalism, 54 percent considered it to be a good idea for journalism; 27 percent considered it to be a bad idea; while 18 percent were not sure.

The business and environment consensus project idea scores very high as a description of what is meant by public journalism among the respondents. A 73 percent majority agreed that this project idea describes what is meant by public journalism; only 9 percent disagreed, while 18 percent were not sure.

> 6. A project in which a newspaper joins with radio and television in sponsoring citizen forums with political candidates—and all three media cooperate in coverage. (*Political Forum*)

The political candidate forum project question is derived from any number of projects prominently showcased in such publications as *Civic Journalism: Six Case Studies*, a joint report of the Pew Center for Civic Journalism and the Poynter Institute for Media Studies in St. Petersburg, Florida.[20]

These projects sport such titles as "The Public Agenda," a Tallahassee Democrat and WCTV6 experiment; "Voice of the Voter," a San Francisco Chronicle, KRON-TV, and KQED-FM experiment; and, "Front Porch Forum," a joint experiment of *The Seattle Times* and public radio stations KPLU and KUOW.

San Francisco's 1994 "Voice of the Voter" experiment in public journalism, as summarized by the case studies report, offers a typical description of such a project: "It enabled several thousand readers, listeners and viewers to participate in the election. It used the power of the press to force political candidates to listen—and respond—to what the people had to say. And it gave birth to a newspaper-led voter registration drive."[21]

The collaborative media projects involving political candidate forums are among the most popular and least controversial of the public journalism experiments. They are praised for renewing democracy because they bring "regular folks" to the microphone to question candidates, and also because they purportedly cover issues that the people care about, rather than the horse-race aspect of elections that political insiders care about.

This isn't to say that these projects are immune from criticism. Among the complaints is that many of these projects are obsessed with citizen polls to find out what's on the average voter's mind, but these polls don't always identify the most important issues in an election.

Michael Gartner, former president of NBC News and editor of the Ames, Iowa, *Daily Tribune*, pinpoints other faults: media coalitions homogenize the news and actually reduce the number of voices; the stories generated by the projects tend to read like civics textbooks; and, there's little evidence that these projects have any real impact on elections. Gartner said he believes that media coalitions fail to serve the public because they diminish the diversity of information from news outlets.[22]

Journalism editors and professors familiar with public journalism show an overwhelming support for the political candidate forum project idea that involves several media working together on elections. In the *SJR* survey on public journalism, 88 percent considered it to be a good idea for journalism; 8 percent considered it to be a bad idea; 4 percent were not sure.

The political candidate forum idea also scores extremely high as a description of what is meant by public journalism among the respondents. A 90 percent majority agreed that this project idea describes what is meant by public journalism; only 3 percent disagreed, while 7 percent were not sure.

WHAT IS PUBLIC JOURNALISM?

Professor and veteran journalism researcher Philip Meyer suggests that if we're confused or befuddled by the philosophical musings about public journalism, then we ought to go study the projects done in its name to find out what it's all about. The projects give us concrete examples of what is being proposed, according to Meyer.

The problem with this avenue of inquiry is that even the public journalism experts distance themselves from many projects that have been held up as examples of this new approach and movement in reporting. Public journalism practitioner Merritt, author of *Public Journalism & Public Life: Why Telling the News Isn't Enough*, concedes that many public journalism projects go far beyond what he finds acceptable as an editor. He, nevertheless, praises the motivation of the project editors in seeking new paths away from the tired forms of traditional journalism.

"But because their understanding of the theory was so shallow, and their hunger for immediate change so great, many of them overshot, which meant that what they labeled 'public journalism' became a huge, fat, almost unmissable target for would-be critics," Merritt told a seminar at the AEJMC's 1995 convention in Washington, D.C.[23] Merritt did not elaborate on what kinds of projects deserve the imprimatur of public journalism and what kinds of projects fall short.

What, therefore, constitutes a legitimate public journalism project? A project that receives the nod from practitioner Merritt? A project that is blessed by leading theoretician Rosen? A project that receives the funding and endorsement of the Pew Center, the Kettering Foundation, or the Poynter Institute?

The dilemma of discovering just what constitutes a bona fide public journalism project is reflected in the *SJR* survey results. Editors and professors familiar with the public journalism concept are divided in their evaluations of public journalism project ideas and whether the ideas are representative of what public journalism means.

The idea of a newspaper promoting a racial progress pledge project enjoyed the support of only about one-quarter of the respondents, although almost half the respondents viewed it as a good description of what is meant by public journalism. However, half of the respondents were either not sure or disagreed that the pledge project idea was an example of public journalism.

These divisions and indications of uncertainty were expressed in varying degrees on all but one of the public journalism project ideas presented in the *SJR* survey. The confusion about what embodies public journalism, and what conforms to the tenets of a true project for public journalism, has been called the definition problem by both friend and foes of the movement.

"Public journalism is struggling to overcome many things. It is new and not well understood, in part because there is no consensual definition of it," the University of Missouri's Renita Coleman told the Civic Journalism Interest Group at the 1996 AEJMC convention in 1996. "Those who are engaging in public journalism projects are essentially working without a blueprint, inventing it as they go. There are many criticisms—both from those within the movement and those outside," added Coleman, emphasizing that public journalism proponents must address the definition problem if the movement is to have a future.[24]

Public journalism advocates are fond of insisting that telling the news is not enough; that simply imparting clear and accurate information is somehow inadequate for these times. There is, however, both anecdotal and empirical evidence that public journalists need to address their own difficulties in simply communicating what public journalism is—the definition problem.

In the *SJR* survey one project idea did enjoy a clear consensus of what was descriptive of public journalism—and good for the practice of journalism— the collaborative media project involving political candidate forums. These kinds of projects are among the most highly-touted in the panoply of public journalism initiatives. These projects are often described as "front porch forums" in which newspapers seek out the average person to give voice to their viewpoints and to the issues they would like to see political candidates address.

In the story collections that revolve around these forum projects, public journalists resolve to find out what the voters think—often through polls, formal and informal surveys, and focus groups. They also pledge to avoid the temptation of reporting election races as political dogfights, and they insist on a kind of reporting that relies less on the political experts and more on the collective wisdom of average citizens.

Few can argue with the wisdom of this approach to journalism practice as embodied in the political forum projects. This may explain why the collaborative media political candidate forum project idea enjoyed overwhelming support among respondents in the the *SJR* survey of editors and journalism professors.

However, if there is a consensus that these kinds of projects embody the essence of public journalism, then it begs the question as to whether a new movement called public journalism is really required. It also begs the question as to whether public journalism is as innovative and revolutionary as its proponents claim. Aren't we just talking about old-fashioned, traditional practices of good journalism? Some proponents of public journalism answer "yes" to this question. Others answer a resounding "no" and bristle at the implication of this question.

"That's a wonderful way to dismiss the most provocative elements of the experiment," to repeat the irate rejoinder of public journalism advocate Steve Smith of the *Colorado Springs Gazette Telegraph*. Editor Smith adds defiantly that public journalism "isn't heresy. And it doesn't deserve the hack criticism we've seen."[25]

NOTES

1. Jay Black, ed. *Mixed News: The Public/Civic/Communitarian Journalism Debate* (Mahwah, New Jersey: Lawrence Erlbaum Associates, 1997), pp. 70–71.

2. Ibid.

3. James Fallows, *Breaking the News* (New York: Vintage Books, 1997), p. 251.

4. Steve Smith, "Getting Down and Dirty with the Critics," *Civic Catalyst* (January, 1997), p. 3.

5. David Bloomquist, and Cliff Zukin, *Does Public Journalism Work? The "Campaign Central" Experience* (Washington, D.C.: Pew Center for Civic Journalism, 1997), p. 28.

6. Davis Merritt, "Missing the Point," *American Journalism Review* (July/August 1996), p. 30.

7. Ibid.

8. Smith, op. cit., p. 3.

9. Merritt, op. cit., p. 30.

10. Arthur Charity, *Doing Public Journalism* (New York: Guilford Press, 1995), p. 140.

11. Don Corrigan, "St. Louis Native Wins Pulitzer for Racial Study," *St. Louis Journalism Review* (May, 1994), p. 9.

12. Mark Jurkowitz, "From the Citizen Up," *MediaCritic* (Winter, 1996), pp. 79–80.

13. Ibid.

14. Arthur Charity, "Reluctant Sea Change," *The Quill* (January/February, 1996), p. 25.

15. Ibid.

16. Comments made at a panel on public journalism projects at the 1995 Investigative Reporters and Editors (IRE) convention in Miami, 1995.

17. Mike Hoyt, "Are You Now or Will You Ever Be, a Civic Journalist," *Columbia Journalism Review* (September/October, 1995), p. 27.

18. Arthur Charity, *Doing Public Journalism* (New York: Guilford Press, 1995), pp. 142–143.

19. Interview with Dwight Jensen originally conducted by author for article: Don Corrigan, "Racial Pledges, Gang Summits, Election Forums—What Actually Makes a Public Journalism Project?" *St. Louis Journalism Review* (March, 1997), pp. 8–9.

20. Jan Schaffer, and Edward Miller, *Civic Journalism: Six Case Studies* (Washington, D.C.: Pew Center for Civic Journalism, 1995), pp. 12–56.

21. Ibid., pp. 38–47.

22. Michael Gartner, "Public Journalism: Seeing through the Gimmicks," *American Editor*, publication of ASNE (Summer, 1997), pp. 72–73.

23. Comments made by Davis "Buzz" Merritt at a public journalism panel at the AEJMC convention in Washington, D.C., August 1995.

24. Renita Coleman, "The Intellectual Antecedents of Public Journalism." Paper presented at a civic journalism interest group session at the AEJMC convention in Anaheim, California, August, 1996.

25. Smith, op. cit., p. 3.

6
Practitioners and Public Journalism

AN EVANGELIST MEETS A PRACTITIONER

Investigative Reporters and Editors (IRE) may well qualify as the most practical-oriented journalistic organization in a profession that boasts dozens of trade groups and associations. Many of these groups spend their annual meetings debating front-page design, codes of conduct, or the latest ethical quandary, but IRE focuses on the practical side of journalism—from using computers to report on irregularities in law enforcement to digging out county records to report on cozy deals between developers and municipal officials.

IRE, which dates from the 1970s and has more than 4,500 members worldwide, was founded in the aftermath of the murder of reporter Don Bolles in Phoenix, Arizona. Bolles was investigating mob connections to real estate deals taking place in the state. Reporters from dailies throughout the country converged in Phoenix to investigate Bolle's death, and IRE became an outgrowth of that cooperative project. The group has drawn the practitioners of journalism, ambitious reporters, and enterprising editors to itself like a magnet.

At IRE's June 1995 convention in Miami, supporters of public journalism and their opponents squared off both formally and informally at a number of sessions. However, the best fireworks by far over public journalism came at a special issues forum entitled "Public Journalism: Death or Savior of American Newspapers." Rosemary Armao, then-executive director of IRE, challenged public journalism guru Jay Rosen of New York University to show examples of newspapers that have increased readership by employing public journalism techniques. Rosen told the IRE audience that public journalism's success, where it has been put into practice, could probably not be effectively measured for another decade.

"I don't have to wait ten years. I'm ready to say to Jay right here and now that much of what passes for public journalism is crude, naive, and dumb," said

Armao, her voice rising and her eyes shooting sparks.[1] "It's boring. It's transcripts. It's very much lazy journalism." Armao was referring to a public journalism technique that involves newspapers conducting focus groups with readers. The idea is to find out—and write about—what readers are thinking and to have them help set the agenda for what should be covered as well as how it should be covered. Armao described this kind of journalism as "at its best, lazy; at its worst, public relations." She said she hesitated to even dignify it by calling it journalism or reporting.

"It's wimpy," declared Armao. "It's not courageous to go out and list the views of a whole lot of people without really writing what's at stake. You're not going to get sued that way. [But] it's at best lazy journalism. It's a way to fill up a whole lot of space and look like you're doing something new. Wow, we're pioneers! We're trying this whole new concept. We're invited to API (American Press Institute) to tell other reporters all about it."

New York University's Rosen, who was introduced by *The Miami Herald*'s executive editor, Doug Clifton, as the chief "academic theoretician for public journalism today," cautioned the reporters to not reject out of hand public journalism and its possibilities. Rosen told the IRE audience in Miami that all responsible journalists must seek answers on how to address the decline of public life in America and the increasing irrelevance of journalism in the lives of most Americans.

"What is to be done when American society is increasingly unable to solve its most basic problems?" Rosen asked the IRE conference. "What is to be done when 71 percent of the people believe the press gets in the way of solving problems, according to a Times-Mirror poll? What is to be done when in March of this year only 45 percent of Americans reported reading a newspaper yesterday—down 13 percent from just a year ago? What is to be done when Howard Kurtz of *The Washington Post*, taking note of the 'disconnect' between journalists and the public, describes the news business as an incestuous profession, that is increasingly self-absorbed, remote and arrogant?"[2]

Rosen's prescription at the IRE convention for "what is to be done" was, naturally, public journalism. In a report published by Indiana University's School of Journalism in April 1995, Rosen provided examples of public journalism. A number of those examples, quoted here, illustrate Rosen's concept in action:

- Public journalism practices have involved creating televised forums that show citizens engaged in deliberative dialogue, sponsored by a media partnership in Madison, Wisconsin. The goal here is to show democratic habits of mind in action.
- There have been several interventions in a lethargic public climate in places like Boulder, Colorado, and Olympia, Washington. These bring together civic leaders, experts, and groups of citizens to chart a long-term vision for a community, which is then published in the newspaper.
- There have been various efforts to focus political reporting on the search for solutions to public problems; and a variety of measures to heighten the visibility of citizens in the news by, for example, telling the story of individuals who got involved and made a difference.

- There have been campaigns to get people to vote, including some that allowed people to register in the lobby of the newspaper.
- There have been other efforts to engage citizens as participants—for example, a Neighborhood Repair Kit published by the *Star Tribune* in Minneapolis, which sought to give residents the information and incentive they needed to improve their neighborhoods.[3]

IRE's Armao said she believed some of public journalism's experiments, described by Rosen at the conference and elsewhere, cross the line of detachment. She emphasized that crossing this line is part of what has damaged press credibility with the public in the first place. She also took a slap at the bureaucratic language of public journalism, which she said only distances the practice from the regular people who both read and write journalism.

"Public journalism is a cult-like movement, you're either a believer or a heretic. It even has its own jargon like a cult," said Armao. "You've heard some of the code words. Do you want to hear the word 'connectedness' again? How about 'engaged' or 'set the public agenda'? It's a cult-like movement and if you happen to disagree with it, you have some doubt about it—you aren't exactly burned at the stake but you are sent back into the job market to find another job."

Armao described herself as a "refugee from public journalism" and described her experience as a reporter for public journalism advocate Cole Campbell's *Virginian-Pilot* in Norfolk, Virginia. After witnessing an education reporting team project at *The Virginian-Pilot*, which she said was almost spiked because it was inconsistent with the goals of public journalism, Armao said she became wary of public journalism. She said that reporters at the paper studied the effectiveness of the local school board, and found it made no effective difference in its functioning whether board members were appointed or elected.

"It was read by a member of the Public Life Team, a team that has the mission of revitalizing the flagging democracy, and he argued that we should not print the story because it would not encourage people to exercise their right to vote, and it would encourage apathy," said Armao. "It really frightened me at the time. I could be a refugee from public journalism."

Rosen argued that journalists have to recognize that there is a flight from journalism because of public cynicism and the belief that America's problems are intractable. He said journalism must break out of its traditional routines and begin providing hope about public life and some solutions to public problems. He said the concept that he advocates puts the public first—public conversation, public problem solving, and using journalism to engage people in public life.

"The debate over what's called public journalism has gotten sidetracked," explained Rosen. "We've argued too much about advocacy journalism, when we should be talking about journalism and democracy. We seize upon the most fruitless cliché imaginable, 'objectivity,' when we should be talking about things like public judgment and civic capacity. We debate whether readers should drive the agenda, when we should be talking about what makes the reader into a citizen."

"Traditional journalism believes that people need to be informed so that they can participate effectively," continued Rosen. "In public journalism, we believe that people have to participate effectively so they'll want to become informed. Traditional journalism assures that democracy is what we have, and information is what we need; in public journalism, we think that the reverse is true. Information is what we have—we live in a sea of information. Democracy is what we need. Public journalism is about forming the public, as much as informing the public. The assumption that the public exists, and always will, is a complacent one."

Rosen said that IRE should form a task force to examine a new kind of journalism that looks at local and national problems and investigates "possible solutions, obtainable futures, and unimaginable coalitions among real political actors." He said such a task force would investigate how journalism is serving some communities in finding answers to problems, while it is failing other communities that are drifting into failure.

In assessing the progress of communities, Rosen said journalism might adopt a new "index of leading civic indicators: citizen participation, coalition building, problem solving, inclusiveness, setting a common agenda, planning the future, etc." Rosen conceded that public journalism is in its infancy, that there is room for debate about it, and he emphasized that not all of its practitioners "know exactly what they are doing." But he added that journalists must dare to try something different to reinvigorate public spaces and public dialogue, because "when the life of the community no longer matters, neither does journalism."

Armao said she agreed with Rosen that "a lot of people who are leading these movements don't know what they are doing." She also agreed there was a need for change because, she said, journalists are much more insular and out of touch with the readership they are supposed to serve. "[But] I disagree with a lot of what we've heard about how we got into this situation," Armao told the IRE audience. "We were a part of the community and we were read. And then the MBAs started coming into our newsrooms and they cut the number of reporters, and they cut the amount of space they had in the newspaper. And, whoa, now we're unconnected from our public.

"I think that public journalism and some of the other calls for change are a business response and at least, in part, inspired by a business response to get back our audience," continued Armao. "Why don't we go back into the public? Why don't we do deep reporting? One newspaper has recently spent enough to pay for two new reporters in order to hire a consultant to go out and find for the paper where people meet to exchange ideas—whether whites do this kind of exchange at dinner parties and whether low-income blacks meet in donut shops. That's something reporters used to know and they still ought to know."

Armao said newspaper managements are looking at the bottom line and the quick fix in trying to figure out how to shore up declining circulations. She said much of what public journalism has to offer is attractive because it sounds nice and can be done cheaply. Armao insisted that good reporters are leaving the profession because newspaper managements no longer value good journalists, instead they would rather invest in consultants and gimmickry. She said reporters at the *Minneapolis-Star* banded together in self-defense against this trend. She said they issued a manifesto declaring that some of these efforts to gain readership "can easily become a slavish effort to sell ourselves to our customers."

"If we're truly interested in expanding a public dialogue and engaging the public in a dialogue with us, then why don't we expand the editorial pages—have more letters to the editor. Maybe because that involves using more newsprint," stressed Armao. Armao's comments came at a time when newsprint prices were skyrocketing and causing many newspaper corporations to cut back on news pages.

Rosen, for his part, told the reporters and editors that they should ask themselves if they are confident that in 10 years they will still be asked to do a journalism that is worth doing. He said that if they are not so confident, they should consider the message of public journalism. Rosen criticized what he called an attitude of "fortress journalism" that leads journalists to believe they don't need anything but the First Amendment. He criticized journalistic elitists such as Max Frankel of *The New York Times*, "who said in a recent column about public journalism that the press should leave reform to the reformers." He urged the reporters and editors to reject a fortress journalism mentality, reject the cynicism of the scions of the media elite, and take the bold risks of their colleagues who are experimenting with public journalism.

ELITISTS IN THE FORTRESS

Rosen found an audience at the 1995 IRE convention which was not especially receptive to his message that public journalism can be the salvation for the difficulties of the news industry. As a bona fide reporter and "refugee from public journalism." IRE's Armao was a formidable opponent in the presentation of two perspectives on public journalism. "The reason I describe myself as a refugee is because I am a hard news reporter, and I had to leave *The Virginian-Pilot* when Cole Campbell instituted these mushy ideas of connecting with the public and finding out the public agenda," says Armao. "In the spring of 1996, Cole brought a casket into the newsroom and he had all the staff scribble down their journalistic regrets and put them in the casket. This is incredible. It's another example of how public journalism gets so involved in process, when the time and energy could be better spent on simply writing a good story."

In countering Armao and other critics, public journalism supporters contend that most of their opposition comes from other disgruntled journalists. They are fond of quoting Rosen's assertion that "all of the resistance to public journalism has come from other journalists, not from the public or politicians."[4] In *Breaking the News*, public journalism advocate James Fallows contends that in several years of projects, *The Virginian-Pilot* has received only one letter to the editor claiming that its new reporting techniques on community problems have compromised the paper's objectivity or integrity. This protest did not come from an authentic citizen, but from a retired newspaper editor who had a professional axe to grind.[5]

In other words, criticism of public journalism comes from those who are indoctrinated in the canons of traditional journalism, and not from the citizens who positively relish a new approach to journalism. In fact, public journalists maintain that the resistance, even within the journalism profession, can be isolated to the handful of practitioners who work in the elite press—the major dailies, magazines, and broadcast outlets of the East Coast. Public journalists like Fallows find particular satisfaction in going after *The New York Times* or *The Washington Post*, where executive editor Len Downie is a favorite target.

Downie has denounced public journalism, while insisting that the job of a newspaper is to report the news and to strive toward the ideal of objectivity in presenting the news. "I know there are times when individual feelings among reporters and editors may cause them to want to take a side," Downie concedes. "We work very hard to drive that out of our work."[6] Public journalists lampoon Downie's concern with suppressing personal feelings in reporting, and in story composition, as a sort of quaint notion completely out of touch with reality. Downie is a favored adversary because of his rather extreme personal method for insuring objectivity in election coverage. Downie refuses to vote in elections, convinced that this involvement in the political process could taint his effort at fairness in political coverage.[7]

Downie is among the small "elite" of traditionalists whom public journalists like to target, a group that includes some of their most articulate critics, such as David Remnick of the *New Yorker*; Mike Hoyt of the *Columbia Journalism Review*; Max Frankel of *The New York Times*; Michael Gartner, formerly of NBC News; and Howard Schneider of *Newsday*.

"When big-paper editors hear that the public journalists want to 'listen' to the public and be guided by its concerns, the editors imagine something that they dread," declares Fallows in his book.[8] According to Fallows, the elite journalists on today's big-city papers are too attached to outdated axioms of objectivity, professional detachment, and unlimited toughness to care about the impact of their work on the health of democracy.

The evangelists of public journalism regularly denounce the traditional news media for "framing stories" in a "bi-polar," "us against them" style of reporting that harms democracy and distorts reality. They contend that mainstream journalists cannot help themselves because they have been "reflexively conditioned" to see "conflict as the highest coin in the journalistic realm," according to Davis "Buzz" Merritt, author of *Public Journalism & Public Life: Why Telling the News Isn't Enough.*[9]

Despite their denunciations, public journalism's partisans go into the same reactionary mode when defending their movement against critics. They frame the controversy as a battle between the elitist newspapers of Washington or New York and the more pragmatic, civic-minded newspapers of America's heartland—Colorado Springs, Dayton, Wichita, Sioux City, and now St. Louis with the arrival of practitioner Cole Campbell as *Post-Dispatch* editor.

One of the most heated "us against them" commentaries was penned by Jan Schaeffer for *The Quill*, the magazine of the Society of Professional Journalists.

Schaeffer, now director of the Pew Center for Civic Journalism, once again framed the battle over public journalism as a sort of populist struggle between an elitist, big-city press and the rest of the civic-minded journalists toiling out in the provinces. Schaffer quotes Gil Thelen, then-editor of *The State* in Columbia, South Carolina, who laments the attitudes of writers and editors at *The Washington Post, The New York Times,* the *New Yorker,* and *The Wall Street Journal.* She describes Thelen as "steamed and irritated" at the elite press's resistance to public journalism.

"What's really hurting this [public journalism] is the way the elite press is smashing around anything that smacks of experimentation," notes Thelen in *The Quill* article. He argues that elite publications have been able to set the standards, framework, and values of journalism for too long.

"And a lot of the people in my newsroom want to work for them," adds a disappointed Thelen. "Everybody defers to them. Maybe that's the source of resistance [to public journalism]." Thelen adds that newspapers like *The New York Times* can afford to be smug and resistant to change. The *Times* can afford its elite audience with only 25 percent penetration in its base city, but most newspapers don't have that luxury, Thelen emphasizes.

"In the elite conversation, there can be all of the sanctimoniousness about the extreme separation of church and state [newspaper and community] and an exaggerated kind of independence of action and folderol about voting that prejudices my objectivity. That isn't the kind of bullshit that plays with regular people," Schaeffer quotes Thelen. "Regular people view and experience the world differently from regular readers of *The New York Times.*"[10]

There's no shortage of examples of public journalism proponents framing the battle over public journalism as an "us against them," "the civic-minded vs. the big-paper elitists." Consider these observations:

- "Look where the criticism [of public journalism] is coming from. It's coming from the stewards of current convention, the Eastern establishment press—*The New York Times, The Washington Post,*" Cole Campbell told the *St. Louis Journalism Review.* "These people say, in essence, we are the definers of what are the proper conventions. Who are these people in Wichita, Kansas; Charlotte, North Carolina; Norfolk, Virginia? Who are these people? It has almost as much to do with class and status as it does with ideas."[11]
- "From where I sit, it seems as if public journalism is being victimized by the media elite," declared Steve Smith in the January, 1997 issue of *Civic Catalyst.* "the big guns from Washington, New York and Boston—and the big gun wannabees—are the folks who have targeted journalists like me, and like you. . . . I don't know how to define civic [public] journalism for a national newspaper like *The New York Times, The Wall Street Journal,* or *The Washington Post.* As far as I'm concerned, how or even whether these concepts are embraced by *Times, Journal,* or *Post* editors is their affair."[12]
- "I think it hurts our business when we only look to those rather unusual publications (*The New York Times, The Washington Post*) with their specialized audiences and let them influence what flies for the rest of us," *Boston Globe* Editor

Matthew V. Storin told a public journalism awards dinner in 1996. "In the eyes of some critics in those two cities, public journalism is the most dangerous thing to hit our business since establishment papers began quoting the *National Enquirer*.

"Now, of course, I don't challenge their right to offer criticism," added Storin. "I just don't think everyone should jump off a bridge just because two mammoth, 18-wheelers are rolling over it at the same time."[13]

Not since Spiro Agnew, henchman and vice president for Richard M. Nixon's Administration, have there been so many denunciations of the media elite, the journalistic values of New York and Washington, D.C., and the ways of the Eastern establishment press. It seems rather bizarre to hear other journalists picking up where Agnew left off, chastising the elite media outlets for being out of touch with real people—Nixon and Agnew's disenchanted "silent majority." But apparently the oddity of this turn of events escapes the public journalism advocates, as they rail against the bogeyman of the "media elite" whenever their reporting experiments in the provinces come in for criticism.

No matter how much Nixon and Agnew blamed their problems on the media elite, it was not sufficient to divert attention from their own venality and corruption. The transgressions of public journalism have nothing in common with the antics of Nixon and Agnew; however, the howls of the public journalists against the "media elite" inevitably invite a comparison with the protests against an out-of-touch "media elite" by the doomed Nixon Administration and its cronies in the early 1970s.

No matter how many times public journalism advocates dismiss their critics as the "stewards of current convention" and the "big-paper elitists," their protests cannot conceal a widespread uneasiness among reporters and editors nationwide regarding their new press philosophy and their journalistic experiments.

The uneasiness is not confined to an East Coast "media elite." The controversy over public journalism is not simply a battle between the nattering nabobs of negativism at *The New York Times* and *The Washington Post* and the more civic-minded newspaper editors and reporters in the heartland. With all their polls, focus groups, and deliberative dialogue, it would seem that the public journalists should know this.

In addition to the set of questions on public journalism concepts and projects, the 1996–1997 *SJR* survey asked participants a series of general questions evaluating public journalism. The data from the responses reveal that the public journalists appear to have created a false dichotomy. Public journalism advocates like to frame their battle as one between elitist, big-city dailies and civic-minded, smaller dailies that are supportive of the movement, however the *SJR* survey results present data supporting a contrary finding.

The *SJR* survey data in Table 6.1 show that there is no consensus among all daily newspaper editors that public journalism is good for the practice of journalism. More than half of the newspaper editors indicated that they thought public journalism is a good idea; the other half were either "not sure" or thought that public journalism is a "bad idea" for the practice of journalism.

Table 6.1

The Relationship between Editors Classified by Their Paper's Circulation Size and Their Attitudes about Public Journalism

In general, do you believe that public journalism is a good idea or a bad idea for the practice of journalism?

Editors by Paper size[a]	Bad Idea[b]	Not Sure	Good Idea	Total
Editors from Large Papers	2	1	12	15
	13.3%	6.7%	80.0%	100.0%
Editors from Medium Papers	6	9	18	33
	18.2%	27.3%	54.5%	100.0%
Editors from Small Papers	15	29	52	96
	15.6%	30.2%	54.2%	100.0%
Total	23	39	82	144
	16.0%	27.1%	56.9%	100.0%

[a] Editors were classified into the following categories based on their paper's circulation size: Large papers >80,000; Medium papers ≦80,000 and ≧25,000; Small papers <25,000.

[b] The "Bad Idea" category consists of two categories that were collapsed ("Very Bad Idea" and "Bad Idea"). The "Good Idea" category consists of two additional categories that were collapsed ("Very Good Idea" and "Good Idea"). The "Not Sure" category was not changed.

Second, and perhaps more important, the data in Table 6.1 reveal that editors from medium to small city newspapers are not any more likely to rate public journalism a good idea than editors from larger city newspapers. Newspaper editors from small to medium papers gave public journalism the same "good idea" rating (54 percent), whereas editors of larger newspapers were actually more positive (80 percent). This finding was not statistically significant because too few big city editors were sampled in the survey, however the magnitude of the difference in opinion between these editors groups is nevertheless large and suggests that big city editors are more supportive of public journalism than editors from smaller and medium size cities.

Table 6.2 from the *SJR* survey shows that newspaper editors were evenly divided on a series of questions asking them why they thought public journalism might be a good idea for the profession. More than 80 percent of these editors come from newspapers of under 100,000 circulation.

- 49 percent of editors think that public journalism is a good idea because it will improve the practice of journalism with new approaches.
- 46 percent of editors think that public journalism is a good idea because it will convince people that journalists care about their communities.
- 50 percent of editors think that public journalism is a good idea because it will improve people's lives by offering solutions to problems.

In the *SJR* survey of newspaper editors, results were more lopsided when respondents were asked a series of questions on why they thought public journalism might be a bad idea for the profession.

Table 6.2

Editors' Opinions Regarding Why Public Journalism Is a Good Idea or a Bad Idea

In general, do you believe that public journalism is a good idea or a bad idea for the practice of journalism?

Is public journalism a good idea because:	Yes	No	Total
(a) It will improve the practice of journalism with new approaches.	70 48.6%	74 51.4%	144 100%
(b) It will convince people that journalists care about their communities.	66 45.8%	78 54.2%	144 100%
(c) It will improve peoples lives by offering solutions to problems.	72 50.0%	72 50.0%	144 100%
Is public journalism a bad idea because:			
(d) Government may have more justification to try to control the press.	33 22.9%	111 77.1%	144 100%
(e) The press will be seen as biased.	86 59.7%	58 40.3%	144 100%
(f) The press may become corrupted by special interests if it gets involved as an actor in the political issues of the day.	102 70.8%	42 29.2%	144 100%

- 23 percent of editors think that public journalism is a bad idea because government may have more justification to try to control the press.
- 60 percent of editors think that public journalism is a bad idea because people will see the press as biased.
- 71 percent of editors think that public journalism is a bad idea because the press may be corrupted by special interests if it gets involved as an actor in the political issues of the day.[14]

DEMONIZING GREAT JOURNALISM

The *SJR*/WU survey reveals substantial division among newspaper editors as to whether public journalism is a good or bad idea as a press practice. A breakdown of survey respondents clearly shows that the controversy over public journalism is not simply a fight between the elitist press of Washington and New York and the more civic-minded newspapers of the American heartland. Some of the toughest criticism of public journalism practices in the *SJR* survey project comes from newspapers in the heartland.

"Public journalism advocates are trying to change the nature of the debate by criticizing *The New York Times* and *The Washington Post*," said Craig Klugman, editor of *The Journal Gazette* in Fort Wayne, Indiana. "It's demagoguery to beat up on the *Times* and the *Post* and to portray them as the great enemy of their public journalism.

"It makes no sense to demonize two great journalistic enterprises. I'm tired of it," said Klugman. "You could take some very good *New York Times* and *Washington Post* projects that could easily fall into certain categories of public journalism. I'd prefer to just call it 'good journalism.' I am not against solution-oriented journalism. For Christ's sake, I think that's rudimentary to journalism. I am concerned about what happens when newspapers decide to become a player in events."

Klugman cited a public journalism project by another Indiana newspaper that decided to sponsor events to encourage better race relations. He said the paper was prompted to take the action after a Ku Klux Klan march in the area. According to Klugman, the paper sponsored community forums in which a sizeable number of blacks advocated black separatism. They were not interested in fostering interracial cooperation for the good of the community.

"When I asked the editor why all the talk of separatism was not mentioned in the paper's coverage, she said she didn't know," related Klugman. "Well, I know why it wasn't covered. It wasn't consistent with the good intentions of the newspaper's public journalism project. It's tough to cover something impartially when your newspaper is part of the story."

Klugman said public journalism projects that involve newspapers sponsoring public forums can easily backfire, such as the forum on bettering race relations. If the forum does not succeed in producing the kind of results the newspaper intended, then the newspaper has a dilemma in reporting accurately on what happened. Klugman added that most public journalism initiatives involve projects in which the solutions to the local public problems are readily apparent.

"I haven't seen public journalism take on too many projects where the solutions to the public problems weren't obvious. These things are full of goodness and platitudes," said Klugman. "I've never seen them take on a public issue such as gay rights in a community. That's because there is no easy solution that's going to make everybody happy. You'll never see the public journalists trying to find common ground on the issue of gay rights, because the divisions run too deep. Nothing the news media does is going to end a lot of the divisions in our society."

An outspoken critic of public journalism, Klugman said he always runs the risk that advocates will tell him that it's unfair to criticize an idea or a project, because "it's not really public journalism"—even though the project or idea was originally labeled as public journalism. "A major criticism I have with public journalists is that they change how they define themselves and what they're about," said Klugman. "And I'm sick and tired of hearing them cry that they're not reported correctly. I think most of the critiques that I have read have been fair and correct.

"I don't disagree with everything they say and do," added Klugman. "Anything that gets reporters out into the community talking to citizens is not all bad. We can't just interview the bureaucrats. I had a metro editor with a long article about school disciplinary policy with no feedback from students or parents. I sent the article back for more interviews with regular folks about school discipline. But if public journalism wants a newspaper to convene a public forum of state bureaucrats, school officials, parents, and students to discuss what school disciplinary policy should be, I am totally against it. That is not a newspaper's prerogative."[15]

Denny Bonavita, editor with *The Courier Express*, which publishes daily in Dubois, Pennsylvania, said public journalism has yet to answer fundamental questions: "Who elected us?" Who elected the newspaper to sort out and to find solutions to public policy questions? Who elected the news media to bring industry and environmentalists together or to solve the problem of poor discipline in a community's public schools?

"Some of us have spent 30 years covering boards and civic groups, and we know they don't always function effectively. I think this has inspired some editors to think the newspapers should get involved, because they know how to do it better," said Bonavita. "That's wrong. That's not our job. Our job is to try to tell the news and that's hard enough.

"We're dealing with an issue of the merger of the city and the township, and we have supported it very strongly on the editorial page," said Bonavita. "But we wouldn't get behind this public journalism style on the front page, because I think we would be disposed to not cover anything negative about the merger brought up at the public hearings and meetings."[16]

Steve Gray, editor of *The Monroe Evening News* in Monroe, Michigan, said he's not only troubled by the definition of public journalism, he said the whole premise for how public journalism is going to bring back more readers to newspapers is wrong.

"Public journalism doesn't address the real reasons for the declining interest in newspapers," said Gray. "It only perpetuates the press's myopic obsession with 'public affairs' as the primary interest of our readers. The press needs to address the whole appetite for information. We need to expand the definition of news."[17]

While the definition of what makes news may need to be expanded, Lon Slepicka of the Prince Georges *Daily Journal* in the suburbs of Washington, D.C., is one of many editors who distrusts the methods used by public journalism to find out what the news should be. Slepicka is one of many editors who say most people are too busy making a living and carpooling kids to worry about what makes news—and they expect trained news professionals to make those kinds of decisions for them.

"Two things that really bother me are the use of focus groups, surveys and outside editorial boards to determine our news judgement," said Slepicka. "I think we're trained news professionals and have some expertise about what issues deserve public attention.

"The other problem I have is with this whole 'good news vs. bad news' complaint by public journalists—that we cover the negative," said Slepicka. "Prince Georges has a lot of crime and we cover it. Some of our readers complain about it, but I think if you take crime off the front page, you do a disservice to readers who may not take the precautions that they need to. And I don't know that our readers really want crime off the front page if they really sit back and think about it."[18]

Public journalism advocates insist that traditional journalists worry too much about "the proper separations" and not enough about "the proper connections." This constant concern about conflict-of-interest, according to public journalists, makes citizens think newspapers are aloof and uncaring about community concerns. But even small town editors think the "proper separations" are important to readers when they look at a newspaper's coverage.

"I think we have to be concerned about conflict-of-interest, both real and perceived," said editor Alan Blanchard of *The Daily News* in Greenville, Michigan. "I just recently was asked to serve on the Coalition for a Greater Greenville. I told them that the newspaper would be happy to cover it, but our role is to report the news and to not be a part of making it. It will hurt us with our readers if they think we've already got an agenda when we're covering these things. They'll say: "Why bother, we know what they're going to have to say."

"These civic groups are telling me now: 'Why aren't you getting behind us? We know that other newspapers in other towns are getting on the bandwagon and helping their communities.' That's what bothers me about public journalism," said Blanchard. "It is having an effect on changing people's perceptions about what a newspaper is supposed to do."[19]

Ava Betz, editor of *The Lamar Daily News* in Lamar, Colorado, said small town newspapers don't need public journalism, because they have always been close to their citizens. At the same time, Betz insisted that even a small town paper, serving a cohesive community with common interests, has to be careful not to blur the line between news columns and editorial columns.

"I see public journalism as a 'back to grassroots' movement by big city papers to try to win back lost readers," said Betz. "But at small newspapers, we never moved away from the public. Our readers grab us in the grocery store and on the sidewalk. We've always been in touch, we don't need a movement."

"I have misgivings about what public journalism says can go on the front page," added Betz. "I think editorializing in favor of civic projects doesn't belong on the front page. That stuff belongs on the editorial page."

Betz said she is also concerned about the trend toward foundations funding public journalism projects for newspapers and their reporters. This is a common concern among many editors and it raises many questions for them. What are the implications of newspapers taking foundation money to develop special projects? What kind of precedent does this establish in the news business? Are newspapers charitable causes?

"I worry about what strings would be attached to getting the foundation money," said Betz. "I do know that if somebody wanted to give me money to cover some projects that I think need covering, I would be tempted. But aren't there always strings attached?"[20]

Phil Willis, editor of the *Athens News Courier* in Athens, Alabama, echoed Betz's concern regarding the influence of foundation money in the newsroom. It may be okay for foundations to fund programs for reporters to update themselves on news technology or to take a sabbatical to learn new background knowledge for reporting. But when foundations fund specific kinds of reporting projects, problems can arise.

"I would never encourage my reporters to get a grant from a foundation to help them do their reporting," said Willis of the Athens daily. "I think foundations like the Freedom Forum, with its First Amendment Center in Nashville, offer reporters some good programs and information. But I wouldn't want a foundation funding our reporting projects.

"I have concerns about papers sponsoring civic studies and projects to better the community," added Willis. "I worked at a paper that sponsored an adult spelling bee to encourage adult literacy. I don't have a problem with that. But anything that gets into serious political issues we should cover, not sponsor."[21]

Norman Baggs, who edits the *Gwinnett Daily Post* in Lawrenceville, Georgia, is another editor who has difficulty with the definition of public journalism. Baggs is a country editor who said he is troubled by all the nonsense perpetrated by university schools of journalism to make reporting more difficult than it has to be in practice.

"What the hell is public journalism? For that matter, what the hell is private journalism? I can't conceive of what these people are talking about," said Baggs. "To me, all journalism is public. I think this is all for a bunch of academic-minded people with high ideals who haven't run a newspaper for years.

"I work for a living," added Baggs. "Newspapers are not brain surgery. We don't have to make social science out of this. It doesn't take that much to go out of the newspaper office and find out what people are thinking."[22]

Baggs said he is disturbed that, under public journalism, foundations are getting into the newsroom and paying for reporting projects. He said newspapers should pay their own way for their reporting.

Baggs' protest over foundations helping to pay for news coverage is also a major concern of Klugman at Fort Wayne's *Journal Gazette*. "I've heard Ed Fouhy of the Pew Center make a defense of this practice by saying we're not really talking about that much money," said Klugman. "That's outrageous. Fouhy said we're talking about small potatoes—maybe $25,000 here or there. Talk about elitist! I work at one of the bigger newspapers in Indiana, and $25,000 would not be small potatoes in our newsroom.

"The amount of money is not the main issue, though," said Klugman. "The main issue really is: Why do newspapers need foundations to cover the news? And why do newspapers want to become part of the news instead of covering it?"[23]

NOTES

1. Comments made by Rosemary Armao at a journalism forum, "Public Journalism: Death or Savior of American Newspapers," at the 1995 Investigative Reporters and Editors Convention, Miami, in June 1995.

2. Comments made by Jay Rosen at a journalism forum, "Public Journalism: Death or Savior of American Newspapers," at the 1995 Investigative Reporters and Editors Convention, Miami, June 1995.

3. Jay Rosen, "Public Journalism as a Democratic Art." Pamphlet adapted from a Rosen presentation at the American Press Institute, Reston, Virginia, November 11, 1994, p. 15.

4. James Fallows, *Breaking the News* (New York: Vintage Books, 1996), p. 264.

5. Ibid.

6. Ibid., p. 263.

7. Ibid.

8. Ibid., p. 266.

9. Davis Merritt, *Public Journalism & Public Life: Why Telling the News Isn't Enough* (Hilldale, New Jersey: Lawrence Erlbaum Associates, 1995), p. 20.

10. Jan Schaffer, "The Best or Worst?" *The Quill* (May, 1997), pp. 25–28.

11. Ed Bishop, "Doing Journalism to 'Public Journalism,'" *St. Louis Journalism Review* (March, 1997), p. 11.

12. Steve Smith, "Getting Down and Dirty with the Critics," *Civic Catalyst* (January, 1997), p. 3.

13. Matthew Storin, "Civic Journalism: Part of the Solution," *Civic Catalyst* (July, 1996), p. 11.

14. Don Corrigan, "Public Journalism Opponents and Advocates Not Easily Stereotyped," *St. Louis Journalism Review* (October, 1997), pp. 12–13.

15. Comments by Craig Klugman of *The Journal Gazette*, Fort Wayne, Indiana, in a phone interview originally for an article in the *St. Louis Journalism Review*. Don Corrigan, "Public Journalism Opponents and Advocates Not Easily Stereotyped," *St. Louis Journalism Review* (October, 1997), pp. 12–13.

16. Comments by Denny Bonavita of *The Courier Express*, Dubois, Pennsylvania, in a phone interview originally for an article in the *St. Louis Journalism Review*. Don Corrigan, "Public Journalism Opponents and Advocates Not Easily Stereotyped," *St. Louis Journalism Review* (October, 1997), pp. 12–13.

17. Comments by Steve Gray of *The Monroe Evening News*, Monroe, Michigan, in a phone interview originally for an article in the *St. Louis Journalism Review*. Don Corrigan, "Public Journalism Opponents and Advocates Not Easily Stereotyped," *St. Louis Journalism Review* (October, 1997), pp. 12–13.

18. Comments by Lon Slepicka of the *Daily Journal*, Prince Georges, Maryland, in a phone interview originally for an article in the *St. Louis Journalism Review*. Don Corrigan, "Public Journalism Opponents and Advocates Not Easily Stereotyped," *St. Louis Journalism Review* (October, 1997), pp. 12–13.

19. Comments by Alan Blanchard of *The Daily News*, Greenville, Michigan, in a phone interview originally for an article in the *St. Louis Journalism Review*. Don Corrigan, "Public Journalism Opponents and Advocates Not Easily Stereotyped," *St. Louis Journalism Review* (October, 1997), pp. 12–13.

20. Comments by Ava Betz of *The Lamar Daily News*, Lamar, Colorado, in a phone interview originally for an article in the *St. Louis Journalism Review*. Don Corrigan, "Public Journalism Opponents and Advocates Not Easily Stereotyped," *St. Louis Journalism Review* (October, 1997), pp. 12–13.

21. Comments by Phil Willis of the *Athens News Courier*, Athens, Alabama, in a phone interview originally for an article in the *St. Louis Journalism Review*. Don Corrigan, "Public Journalism Opponents and Advocates Not Easily Stereotyped," *St. Louis Journalism Review* (October, 1997), pp. 12–13.

22. Comments by Norman Baggs of the *Gwinnett Daily Post* in Lawrenceville, Georgia, in a phone interview originally for an article in the *St. Louis Journalism Review*. Don Corrigan, "Public Journalism Opponents and Advocates Not Easily Stereotyped," *St. Louis Journalism Review* (October, 1997), pp. 12–13.

23. Comments by Craig Klugman of *The Journal Gazette*, Fort Wayne, Indiana, in a phone interview originally for an article in the *St. Louis Journalism Review*. Don Corrigan, "Public Journalism Opponents and Advocates Not Easily Stereotyped," *St. Louis Journalism Review* (October, 1997), pp. 12–13.

7
Professors and Public Journalism

HANDLING BAD NEWS

Public journalism supporters in the academic community were licking their wounds at the 1997 annual media professors convention in Chicago. Recent bad news about the impact of public journalism on the disconnected citizens of New Jersey was producing some long faces. The bad news involved a study evaluating the "Campaign Central" project of *The Record* in Hackensack, New Jersey, *The Record*'s public journalism project provided at least one full page of "civic-style" coverage daily from Labor Day through the November 1996 election.

The public journalism coverage also included supporting activities such as televised town meetings, chat rooms on a web site, and an eight-page voters' guide. The study evaluating all of this activity under the newspaper's umbrella heading of "Campaign Central" was conducted by David Bloomquist, *The Record*'s public affairs editor, along with Cliff Zukin, a consultant from the Eagleton Institute of Politics at Rutgers University.

Among Zukin and Bloomquist's findings about campaign coverage in New Jersey à la public journalism:

- Readers of *The Record* actually were no better informed about the elections than readers of "traditional" coverage in other papers.
- 42 percent of *The Record* readers could not name either U.S. Senate candidate in the 1996 race—neither Democrat Robert Tornicelli, the winner, nor Republican Dick Zimmer.
- Readers of *The Record* were no more likely to vote in November, or even to discuss the campaign with friends, than were non-readers of *The Record*.
- Fewer than one in five of *The Record* subscribers could even remember reading the "Campaign Central" election coverage.[1]

If that weren't enough, public journalism supporters felt "twice burned" at Chicago's AEJMC (Association for Education in Journalism and Mass Communication) Convention. Not only were they smarting from the dismal study results of *The Record*'s public journalism project, but also by a *Columbia Journalism Review* (*CJR*) article accusing the Pew Charitable Trusts of trying to keep the lid on the study's results.

Pew is a major funder of public journalism projects nationwide. In the July/ August 1997 *CJR*, Pew was accused of "disinviting" the study's authors to a May convention of the Association for Public Opinion Research at the Marriott in Norfolk, Virginia. Zukin told the *CJR* that "Pew wanted to contextualize our findings," so more time was needed before the study could be reported."[2]

At the AEJMC meeting, Ed Fouhy, who then directed the Pew Center for Civic Journalism, bristled at the *CJR* article and dismissed it as bunk. He declared that public journalism in newspapers works, and he said the *CJR* article was "a canard."[3] At the AEJMC panel session on the public journalism experience of *The Record*, the Pew Center made available a press release entitled: "Public Journalism Can't Do It All" with the subhead, "In-depth issues coverage fails to counter multi-million dollar TV ad campaigns."

The press release lamented that 54 pages of issue-based coverage could not break through the noise of television campaigning. It emphasized that $17 million spent on political television commercials "made it [the election] seem like a showdown in a sandbox." Panelists at AEJMC made an effort to "contextualize" the discouraging results of the New Jersey public journalism experiment with a discussion of possible explanations for the failure. Among the points made:

- *The Record*'s experiment was too short to produce significant results.
- *The Record*'s coverage wasn't sufficiently "public."
- Public journalism was drowned out by competing messages from other media.
- The essential information citizens wanted was still too difficult to find, understand, and act on.
- The public simply is not sufficiently interested in politics for public journalism to be of service in an election context.
- "The public may be so 'checked out' of the political process that no amount of tap dancing will bring readers to take an interest in political elections," said Bloomquist at the AEJMC panel.[4]

Despite the discouraging news, the professors supporting public journalism were relatively undaunted. The Chicago AEJMC convention schedule was literally packed with scholarly paper presentations on the new public journalism movement. All of the papers presented at AEJMC seemed to accept as a given that public journalism is good for citizens and journalism. Only a few of the paper presenters engaged in anything vaguely resembling criticism of the movement, and their complaints in no way challenged the fundamental premises of public journalism.

A paper by Renita Coleman of the University of Missouri-Columbia examined treatment of public journalism in three media reviews, the *CJR*, the *American Journalism Review* (*AJR*) and the Nieman Reports. In reviewing 45 articles,

Coleman said the treatment has, in most cases, matured from "name calling and black-and-white reporting" to more reflective pieces on public journalism.

James Engelhardt of the University of Oregon applied Steven Lukes' multi-dimensional conception of power to the public journalism movement. Engelhardt argued that there is a difference between civic journalism and public journalism. Civic journalism is more scientific and based on polls and collecting data, while public journalism is based more on citizen input and citizen forums. He rallied to the advocates' cause by insisting that public journalism consists of more than just good journalism.

Janice Hume of the University of Missouri presented a paper authored by several academics who used q-methodology to explain how news practitioners view public journalism.The paper came up with four typologies in the examination: civic journalism supporters, concerned traditionalists, neutral observers, and the responsible liberals.

Christine Newby-Fiebich examined the "agenda-setting function of local and national media" on the Wichita, Kansas area, where *The Wichita Eagle* practices public journalism. Newby-Fiebich found that local television has the biggest impact on setting the agenda for citizens, while the daily newspaper appeared to have an impact on the way citizens rank concerns.

Cheryl Gibbs of Earlham College said one of her biggest challenges in the classroom is to teach young journalists to be listeners rather than interviewers. She said students have a hard time becoming "public listeners" and instead want to "control" the interview process. The insistence on "control" leads to disconnect and disaffection with the public. "We've taught them to control the interview to get the quotes they want," said Gibbs. "It takes a lot more patience and energy to be a 'public listener.' It's hard for a reporter to shut up and be a public listener."[5]

Despite the canards and attacks on public journalism in the *Columbia Journalism Review* and the discouraging results of the New Jersey election coverage study, the public journalism supporters at the AEJMC meeting were, for the most part, unflinching and undaunted. They found much to rejoice about as they filed into the AEJMC Civic Journalism Interest Group and the Council of Affiliates meeting. At this session, Gil Thelen, a newspaper editor and public journalism convert, and Judy VanSlyke, dean of the College of Journalism and Mass Communication at the University of South Carolina, were among those heralding a new venture, Project Reconnect.

They noted that the Pew Center for Civic Journalism had allocated up to $8 million for public journalism projects as of August 1997; and they explained that Project Reconnect had received an allocation of $80,000 from the Pew Center to support the expenses incurred in six newspaper change projects aimed at reconnecting with various segments of the citizenry.

The six Pew Center projects involved newspaper-university teams, and their target projects included addressing the disconnect of African Americans and news coverage of Civil War topics; addressing the disconnect involved in town-and-gown relationships; addressing the disconnect of environmental protection groups and environmental businesses and industry; addressing the disconnect of news reporters in their coverage of blue-collar neighborhoods; and addressing the disconnect of the press with conservative Christians and people of religious faith.

Steve Smith of the *Colorado Springs Gazette Telegraph* and Patricia Raybon of the University of Colorado's School of Journalism and Mass Communication eyed collaboration on an effort to address a disconnect between the Colorado paper and the merchant community over business coverage.

"We could have chosen our disconnect with the religious community or other ethnic communities, but we chose the business community because we were ranked as one of the top impediments in the community to progress on the economic front," explained Smith of the *Colorado Springs Gazette Telegraph*. Smith said business groups in Colorado Springs once looked at the paper as "dedicated to negativity" in its coverage of commerce. He said that it was true that the paper was "once libertarian and dedicated to total disconnect."[6]

However, Smith said the paper was now more interested in being a partner in a boom-town community. He said that hiring interns to work in covering the business community, and engaging in some public listening to the gripes about the paper's news coverage of business, has helped to reconnect the newspaper with a vital constituency in Colorado Springs.

Project Reconnect was hailed by journalism professors as a prototype vehicle for initiatives to reach out to traditionally disaffected audiences. Academics at the civic journalism interest group meeting of the AEJMC echoed the language of public journalism proponent Davis "Buzz" Merritt, who insists that reporters need to stop worrying about the proper separations in their work and instead need to get the connections right. The approaches discussed by the journalism professors for getting the connections right in the six Pew-sponsored Project Reconnect programs include moderated discussions with opinion leaders, focus groups and community forums, surveys, and public listening techniques.

DO PROFESSORS LOVE PUBLIC JOURNALISM?

The public journalism movement's never-ending road show made a stop several months after the 1997 AEJMC convention in Denver at the Society of Professional Journalists (SPJ) annual convention. Advocates of public journalism at the Denver SPJ convention took up a panel proposition entitled: "Why Journalists Hate Public Journalism and Why Academics Love It."

The premise of the SPJ panel was faulty, but participants were nevertheless able to tout the new reporting techniques of public journalism before an audience of working reporters. Several national surveys reveal that both the academic community and working journalists are divided in their opinions on whether public journalism is good for the reporting profession. There are a number of explanations for the misconception that professors are universally gaga over the public journalism movement.

Jay Rosen, who is often credited as the intellect behind the movement, is a professor. Rosen chose the academic life after a short stint working in traditional journalism, an encounter which he found distasteful. Rosen has written the most tracts on public journalism, and most papers and monographs supporting public journalism have been written by professors.

Journalism professors have flocked to write grant applications to foundations sponsoring public journalism projects. Joint projects between newspapers and schools of communication fulfill university mission requirements for community outreach. Successful grant applications also make academic deans smile and pave the road to tenure for many faculty.

One of the fastest-growing interest groups of the AEJMC (Association for Education in Journalism and Mass Communication) has been in the public journalism area. Panels on public journalism have proliferated at AEJMC conventions, and papers accepted for presentation have almost always been supportive of the movement.

Professors who oppose public journalism have been less visible and vocal than those who are supportive. Part of their reticence is a concern over appearing reactionary, especially to colleagues who view public journalism as a progressive movement. Professors who are disposed to favor public journalism also tend to have more academic credentials than opponents within academe, and credentials can mean more clout within the academic setting.

"I go to AEJMC's annual professors conventions and I've seen the civic journalism people's slate of programs, but why should I go and be a naysayer?" asks Stephen Bloom, a professor at the school of journalism at the University of Iowa in Iowa City. "I don't have the time or the patience and I will just be dismissed by the true believers. They are the gods of the new gimmickry and I'm not going to spoil their program. The fact is, there's always going to be some academics who jump on a new bandwagon if there's a way to get some foundation money for a panel or a project, but I don't think any real practitioner would do this, no matter what kind of foundation money is out there."

Bloom said that "respected practitioners who now work in academia absolutely loathe public journalism." He said he knew of no public journalism advocates on the faculty at Iowa. "There are some academics who get excited about it because it's a new idea for a panel, but it's real boring for anybody who has spent some time in the trenches. But it's more than just boring; it's pernicious. I find it unethical to convene news events and then to cover them. It's worse than boosterism."[7]

Bloom is joined in his suspicion that public journalism borders on boosterism by Gerald Stone, a professor who is director of journalism graduate studies at Southern Illinois University–Carbondale. Stone says he was originally "quite impressed" with public journalism, but has become more of a skeptic as he's watched different projects unfold. He says he dislikes projects that involve a newspaper covering forums and town hall meetings that the newspaper has helped sponsor. "That coverage just isn't news, it's promotion," explains Stone. "When there isn't foundation money to support these projects, then there's a promotion department that's ready to support them because it seems like good public relations. A newspaper should not turn itself into a moderator for special interest groups to have a dialogue—that should be left to the League of Women Voters or a non-profit group, and the paper should cover it."

Stone says public journalism has established a foothold in journalism academia, and its philosophy and techniques are not simply a trend that will soon disappear. "There's a hardcore of journalism professors who are fully committed to public journalism. They give papers, hold workshops and give classes on public journalism. I think they'll be doing this for some time to come," observes Stone. "I don't think this movement has gotten the scrutiny and criticism that it should. Quite frankly, I think this is because some academic heavyweights have gotten behind it, and some foundations are out there with them, and so a lot of professors are reticent to say too much against it. It deserves more scrutiny."[8]

The 1996–1997 *SJR* public journalism survey indicates that a sizable number of professors of journalism are skeptical of the new movement, although clearly a majority take a favorable view of public journalism. Table 7.1 shows that 56 percent of professors indicated that they found public journalism to be a good idea; 24 percent were undecided over whether it's a good or bad idea; 20 percent indicated that it's a bad idea for journalism.

When journalism professors responded to a series of questions asking them why they thought public journalism might be a good idea for the profession (Table 7.8), they were almost equally divided in a series of propositions on what makes public journalism a positive development for journalism.

Sixty percent of professors think that public journalism could be a good idea because it will improve the practice of journalism with new approaches. Forty-seven percent of professors think that public journalism could be a good idea because it will convince people that journalists care about their communities. Fifty percent of professors think that public journalism could be a good idea because it will improve people's lives by offering solutions to problems.

However, results as shown in Table 7.2 were more lopsided when journalism professors were asked a series of questions on why they thought public journalism might be a bad idea for the profession.

Twenty-two percent of professors think that public journalism could be a bad idea because government may have more justification to try to control the

Table 7.1
**Professors' Opinions Regarding Public
Journalism's Influence on the Practice of Journalism**

In general, do you believe that public journalism is a good idea or a bad idea for the practice of journalism?

Responses	Professors	Percent
Bad Idea[a]	36	19.6%
Not Sure	44	23.9%
Good Idea	104	56.5%
Total	184	100.0%

[a] The "Bad Idea" category of two categories that were collapsed ("Very Bad Idea" and "Bad Idea"). The "Good Idea" category consists of two additional categories that were collapsed ("Very Good Idea" and "Good Idea"). The "Not Sure" category was not changed.

press. Fifty-two percent of professors think that public journalism could be a bad idea because people will see the press as biased. Sixty-five percent of professors think that public journalism could be a bad idea because the press may be corrupted by special interests if it gets involved as an actor in the political issues of the day.[9]

While the *SJR* survey reveals that slightly more than half of journalism professors have a favorable view of public journalism, it also reveals that professors have some concerns. They are concerned about special interest influence on reporting when the press gets involved as an actor in the community. They are concerned about the issue of bias—real or perceived. They are concerned about public journalism's dismissal of objectivity and detachment as principles primary to the practice of journalism.

"Objectivity and detachment may not be completely possible for journalists, but they shouldn't give up striving for it and seeing it as an ideal," says Marshel Rossow, chair of the department of mass communication at Mankato State University in Minnesota. "Public journalism just seems to be giving up on these ideals.

"I'm very troubled when I see a newspaper setting up meetings where causes are going to be pushed," adds Rossow, who worked on dailies for 15 years before entering academia. "I'm against this even when the causes are good for a community. It's just not a newspaper's function to do this."[10]

Bloom, professor of the school of journalism at the University of Iowa in Iowa City, says public journalism projects with the best of intentions can end up making matters worse. Bloom detailed a public journalism project at the Iowa City's daily, the *Press-Citizen*, which backfired on the newspaper. After a black

Table 7.2
Professors' Opinions Regarding Why Public Journalism Is a Good Idea or a Bad Idea

Is public journalism a good idea because:	Yes	No	Total
(a) It will improve the practice of journalism with new approaches.	110 60.1%	73 39.9%	183 100%
(b) It will convince people that journalists care about their communities.	87 47.5%	96 52.5%	183 100%
(c) It will improve peoples lives by offering solutions to problems.	91 50.0%	91 50.0%	182 100%
Is public journalism a bad idea because:			
(d) The government may have more justification to try to control the press.	41 22.4%	142 77.6%	183 100%
(e) The press will be seen as biased.	95 51.9%	88 48.1%	183 100%
(f) The press may become corrupted by special interests if it gets involved as an actor in the political issues of the day.	119 65.0%	64 35.0%	183 100%

minister's car was spray-painted with racial epithets, the newspaper decried racism in the community and convened a forum to discuss bettering race relations.

"After an investigation, it turned out that the minister had done the damage to the car himself to collect insurance. The *Iowa City Press-Citizen* had egg on its face big time," says Bloom. "There's a natural skepticism among reporters in the trenches, because they see these scams going on all the time. Those who've worked in the trenches know that their job is to report the news and not to get on some high horse that the community can unite on," Bloom adds.[11]

Professor Robert Daly of Kansas State University says the journalism professors who advocate and teach public journalism are "the touchy, feely types who think the goal is to make everybody feel good." Daly echoes other professors who complain that too many teachers would rather talk about "great ideas" in their classrooms, than teach the skills necessary to writing a good story. "I believe in teaching 'just the facts' kind of reporting, and I'm a 'we're here to learn a skill' kind of teacher," Daly adds.

Daly says his objections to public journalism as a news practice are three-fold. "I see it as market-driven, rather than as something that's going to serve people. Secondly, I think it's an abrogation of the newspaper's role to determine what a news story should be. I object to surveys asking people what stories should be covered, and then covering whatever a survey determines is news. Third, I think public journalism is just going to backfire on journalism generally," says Daly. "It gives people false hope. Newspapers build these projects up like something really big is going to happen to better some people's lives. It's not going to happen. Public journalism doesn't deliver and we're already seeing it."[12]

Sherrie Wilson, a journalism professor at the Omaha campus of the University of Nebraska, says she is attracted to some of the ideas of public journalism, particularly its critique of traditional journalism's penchant to frame stories in a confrontational mode using sources at the extremes. Nevertheless, Wilson complains that she is turned off by the movement's dismissal of traditional ideals such as detachment as well as the messianic rhetoric of public journalism advocates.

"I am getting tired of hearing that it's journalism's responsibility to save democracy," says Wilson. "I think we explain to people what's going on in the democratic process and we let the chips fall where they may."

Wilson says that if public journalism catches on, then she fears a lot of journalism textbooks are going to have to be rewritten. She also suspects that a lot of journalism professors would not teach from those rewritten textbooks. "My sense is that professors are pretty well divided on public journalism, although many are not speaking out on it too much," adds Wilson. "I think the civic journalism interest group of AEJMC has made it a topic that has to be discussed. But a lot of those people come from an academic perspective rather than from a practicing journalistic perspective.

"When I was still a graduate student at the University of Minnesota I worked at the *Pioneer Press* and I watched a lot of these grant projects being carried out. When the grants are gone, that's when the projects are over," notes Wilson. "I think that if reporting projects are worth doing, they should continue after the grant money dries up," said Wilson. "Beyond that, I'm concerned about grant money subsidizing the newsroom. I hate to see newspapers getting into a dependency on that kind of money."[13]

PUBLIC JOURNALISM'S IDENTITY CRISIS

Criticism of public journalism comes from all sides, and this is another indication of public journalism's continuing identity crisis. A movement that cannot be easily defined is going to yield to any number of interpretations. As a work in progress, its major philosophers have tended to describe it in abstract terms. Public journalism has supporters both on the left and the right of the ideological spectrum in academia and elsewhere.

Supporters on the left are attracted to public journalism because of its rhetoric for solution-oriented journalism that solves people's problems. All of this sounds like a challenge to the existing power structure—the source of people's problems—from the perspective of the left. Supporters on the right are attracted to public journalism because of its marketing emphasis, and its suggestion that old separations of church and state—such as news and advertising—are obsolete. They also are focused on its journalistic message of "solving problems ourselves," which sounds like a move away from the welfare state. Not surprisingly, public journalism has detractors, as well as supporters, on both the left and the right of the ideological spectrum.

Some academic critics have interpreted public journalism to be a marketing gimmick. These professors are inclined to criticize public journalism's emphasis on polls, focus groups, and related techniques to find out what the public wants in news. For them, public journalism is pandering to the public's fickle, calorie-laden media appetite at the expense of more substantive reporting on domestic and international policy issues—all in the name of profit. Critical professors, who tend to be liberal or to the left ideologically, see a marketing emphasis in public journalism that makes it just another ploy by corporate news operations. That ploy is to please commercial interests, while at the same time persuading the public of a heartfelt concern for community interest.

"When I think of public journalism, I think of a bunch of editors and reporters holding hands together and singing, 'We Are The World,'" says Jay Brodell of Metropolitan State University in Denver. "The idea that a newspaper should be some kind of corroborator in community building is not journalism. The role of the press should be to stand back and observe as fairly as humanly possible what's going on in a community," explains Brodell. The Denver professor says public journalism diminishes that function and instead turns the press into "a bunch of community cheerleaders."[14]

The idea that public journalism may just be an exercise in "community cheerleading" alarms many of those on the left who had hoped that it would be a catalyst for real societal change. Critics on the left in the academy have complained that public journalism's initiatives for change are warm and fuzzy palliatives which will do nothing to challenge basic wrongs perpetuated by an entrenched power structure. In other words, the projects of public journalism are not much different than the work done by the United Way or the 100 neediest cases campaigns by daily newspapers during the holiday season. Such projects may do some isolated good, but they do not addresses the fundamental causes of societal problems such as job displacement, underemployment, urban crime, racism, and chronic drug abuse.

These critics on the left are wont to refer to Jay Rosen's admission of journalism's great weakness as "a public practice housed within a media industry devoted to private gain."[15] This inherent weakness prevents public journalists from demonstrating any self-consciousness about the ideological implications of their approach and their refutation of traditional journalism. The new movement's "focus on community resources leaves established structures of political power and economic interest as unexamined as do mainstream narratives of strategy and conflict," declares Peter Parisi, a professor in the department of film and media studies at Hunter College in New York.[16] Parisi is concerned that public journalism will address some current contradictions in established news practice, while failing to bring about any genuine change.

Parisi's reservations are echoed by Professor Richard Shafer, who teaches journalism at the University of North Dakota. Shafer refers to public journalism as a "contrived revolution from the top," that is helpless to mobilize citizens to confront the real external causes of their problems. "Certainly a Marxist critique would reveal the fallacy of attempting to solve community level problems that have their roots in structural social, political and economic factors at the national and international level," declares Shafer.[17]

Critics on the left complain that public journalism does not go far enough in effecting societal change; however, more conservative critics argue that it goes too far. They bristle at the idea of "journalists as social workers" or as catalysts for change. The more conservative critics abhor the idea of journalists as activists, particularly if that activism is focused on bringing more government resources to bear on issues such as public health, public welfare, or public works.

Some academic critics have interpreted public journalism to be an excuse for discarding any allegiance to objectivity in favor of a journalism that crusades for causes such as income redistribution and various notions of social justice. These professors are inclined to criticize public journalism's emphasis on solution-oriented reporting and a journalism beholden to making public life go well. For them, public journalism is simply an admission that the news media has an elitist, left-wing agenda and is finally prepared to drop any pretense of objectivity. Professors, who tend to be conservative, libertarian, or to the right ideologically, see a dangerous collectivist bent in public journalism that will complete the takeover of the news media by left-leaning social engineers.

"My principal concern is this: What you have is journalists increasingly becoming this unitary, enclosed elite," says Ted Smith, a journalism and communication professor at Virginia Commonwealth University. "This elite is increasingly telling itself that it needs to take control of the political system and a situation that's in decline. The thing that's crucial with public journalism is that it gives journalists a very activist role, and, even though they say they're going to consult with the public about what the public agenda is, the crucial thing is the new activist role. There's a real problem with a small, self-selected elite determining what's in the best interests of the public and taking on an activist role.

"I think all of this appeals to a lot of people in academia because the public journalism movement has its intellectual roots there," adds Smith. "Academics tend to be more idealistic and change-oriented, while wanting to do things differently. The thing that's different now is that a lot of editors are desperately seeking ways to hold onto readers and they're trying out the academics' ideas. I also think this whole movement is going to be around for a while because there's lots of foundation money behind it."[18]

Professor John C. Merrill of the University of Missouri, a critic of public journalism, sees the movement as having its intellectual origins in the communitarian journalism philosophy. Merrill has little use for this philosophy, which he says puts far too much emphasis on the need for a press promoting societal harmony and progress at the expense of the traditional Miltonian view of the press as an outlet and a marketplace for all sorts of ideas—many of them potentially disruptive or politically incorrect.[19] Beyond the socialist agenda and socialistic impulses of the communitarians and their new allies in public journalism, the heart of the dilemma is that these people are basically opposed to a libertarian ethic of information dissemination.

It's ironic that some professors see public journalism as a Trojan Horse for a left-wing or Marxist-oriented journalistic activism, while others see it as a thinly-veiled corporate initiative for the total subversion of news information into a saleable commodity. There already are plenty of tracts written on public journalism, which interpret the movement in so many different ways so as to provide confirmation for either of these viewpoints. Yet it's possible to subscribe to neither of these somewhat conspiratorial viewpoints and still find the philosophy and practice of public journalism to be fundamentally flawed.

NOTES

1. David Bloomquist, and Cliff Zukin, *Does Public Journalism Work? The "Campaign Central" Experience* (Washington D.C.: Pew Center for Civic Journalism Report, May, 1997), pp. i–iv.

2. Edwin Diamond, "Civic Journalism: An Experiment that Didn't Work," *Columbia Journalism Review* (July-August, 1997), pp. 11–12.

3. Comments made by Ed Fouhy at a public journalism panel at the 1997 AEJMC Convention, Chicago, August 1997.

4. Comments made by David Bloomquist at a public journalism panel at the 1997 AEJMC Convention, Chicago, August 1997.

5. Comments made by Cheryl Gibbs at a panel on teaching public journalism at the 1997 AEJMC Convention, Chicago, August 1997.

6. Comments made by Steve Smith at the Civic Journalism Interest Group and the Council of Affiliates meeting at the 1997 AEJMC Convention, Chicago, August 1997.

7. Comments by Stephen Bloom of the University of Iowa in a phone interview originally for an article in the *St. Louis Journalism Review*. Don Corrigan, "Public Journalism Opponents and Advocates Not Easily Stereotyped," *St. Louis Journalism Review* (October, 1997), pp. 12–13.

8. Comments by Gerald Stone of the University of Southern Illinois at Carbondale in a phone interview originally for an article in the *St. Louis Journalism Review*. Don Corrigan, "Public Journalism Opponents and Advocates Not Easily Stereotyped," *St. Louis Journalism Review* (October, 1997), pp. 12–13.

9. Don Corrigan, "Public Journalism Opponents and Advocates Not Easily Stereotyped," *St. Louis Journalism Review* (October, 1997), pp. 12–13.

10. Comments by Marshel Rossow of Mankato State University in Minnesota in a phone interview originally for an article in the *St. Louis Journalism Review*. Don Corrigan, "Public Journalism Opponents and Advocates Not Easily Stereotyped," *St. Louis Journalism Review* (October, 1997), pp. 12–13.

11. Comments by Stephen Bloom of the University of Iowa in a phone interview originally for an article in the *St. Louis Journalism Review*. Don Corrigan, "Public Journalism Opponents and Advocates Not Easily Stereotyped," *St. Louis Journalism Review* (October, 1997), pp. 12–13.

12. Comments by Robert Daly of Kansas State University in a phone interview originally for an article in the *St. Louis Journalism Review*. Don Corrigan, "Public Journalism Opponents and Advocates Not Easily Stereotyped," *St. Louis Journalism Review* (October, 1997), pp. 12–13.

13. Comments by Sherrie Wilson of the University of Nebraska at Omaha in a phone interview originally for an article in the *St. Louis Journalism Review*. Don Corrigan, "Public Journalism Opponents and Advocates Not Easily Stereotyped," *St. Louis Journalism Review* (October, 1997), pp. 12–13.

14. Comments by Jay Brodell of Metropolitan State University In Denver, Colorado, in a phone interview originally for an article in the *St. Louis Journalism Review*. Don Corrigan, "Public Journalism Opponents and Advocates Not Easily Stereotyped," *St. Louis Journalism Review* (October, 1997), pp. 12–13.

15. Jay Rosen "Public Journalism as a Democratic Art." Pamphlet adapted from a Rosen presentation at the American Press Institute, Reston Virginia, November 11, 1994, pp. 9–10.

16. Peter Parisi, "Toward a 'Philosophy of Framing': News Narratives for Public Journalism," *Journalism & Mass Communication Quarterly* (Winter, 1997), p. 682.

17. Richard Shafer, "Structural Problems and Civic Journalism's Failure to Address External Factors of Community Underdevelopment," *Democratic Communique* (Spring, 1998), p. 30.

18. Comments by Ted Smith of Virginia Commonwealth University in a phone interview originally for an article in the *St. Louis Journalism Review*. Don Corrigan, "Public Journalism Opponents and Advocates Not Easily Stereotyped," *St. Louis Journalism Review* (October, 1997), pp. 12–13. Note: None of Smith's quotes were used for the actual *SJR* article.

19. Jay Black, ed. *Mixed News: The Public/Civic/Communitarian Journalism Debate* (Mahwah, New Jersey: Lawrence Erlbaum Associates, 1997), pp. 60–64.

PART III
Confronting the Crucial Issues

The public journalism philosophy has found a receptive audience in academia. To be sure, there are dissident voices within the academy, mostly from professors who have brought some years of professional journalism experience with them to their academic posts, but an even larger segment appears to be embracing it and looking for ways to incorporate it into classroom teaching.

The popularity of public journalism among academics is not particularly surprising. Journalism education in the United States has come to be dominated by theorists and intellectuals in mass communication studies. Educators increasingly view the teaching of traditional journalism as a second-rate undertaking, according to studies such as Betty Medsger's, *Winds of Change: Challenges Confronting Journalism Education* Advanced degrees and scholarly publishing are favored over professional experience in the hiring and promoting of journalism educators.

In some sense, public journalism is an outgrowth of these trends in schools of journalism. The major tenets and philosophic arguments of public journalism have been promulgated in academic papers for years. In fact, for decades theorists in academia have been talking and writing about alternative framing of stories, the myth of objectivity, communitarian approaches to journalism, and the idea of reporters as community activists.

Part III of this book is, in part, an analysis of the phenomenon of the "academizing" of journalism. Chapter 8 specifically examines the impact of university journalism and communication programs on the news industry in recent years. As one professor notes in the chapter, the news industry has traditionally ignored much of the scholarship by professors. Their ideas and research have been dismissed as arcane and impractical. However, with the loss of readers at many major dailies, the industry is taking a hard look at such academic constructs as the public journalism philosophy and its application.

Additionally, some scholars are now attempting to apply public journalism concepts on a global scale. Chapter 9 examines the push to take public journalism global. The public journalism idea, as applied to international communication settings, has many similarities with development journalism. There are many parallels also with the ideas that came out of the NWICO (New World Information and Communication Order) debates of the 1970s and 1980s. The U.S. press editorialized vigorously in the 1980s against these ideas for how the press should conduct itself. However, many of these ideas now seem to have been embraced by the public journalism movement.

Chapter 10 makes the case that public journalism is a diversion that takes our attention away from the most important failings of the news media in America. Public journalism not only fails to address the crucial issues, it is likely to make these critical problems worse. Among the issues examined are the narrowing of political discussion in the news media, the increasing influence of public relations operatives on the news media, the decline of investigative reporting, and the failure of journalism schools.

The Appendix is a glossary of some of the significant terms and phrases employed by public journalism scholars and practitioners. Jay Rosen and other academics have stated that part of their charge in this new movement is to create a new vocabulary that can aid in the reform of traditional journalism. For example, in the new paradigm of public journalism, journalists need to be aware of "leading civic indicators" that can help them assess how well public life is going in a given community.

The reformers often speak about how journalists need to become "meaningful participants" who engage in "public listening," a process that later can help them as they partake in "quality framing discussions" back in the newsroom. For the uninitiated, the lexicon in the Appendix can help with interpreting the language of public journalism.

8
The "Academizing" of Journalism

"Clarity, clarity, clarity!" thunders literary authority E. B. White from the tattered pages of a book known to all writers.

The Elements of Style, originally authored by William Strunk, Jr. and updated by White, has served young scribes as the bible on writing for a century.[1] Thousands of traditional journalists, many of them working on newspaper copy desks, continue to clutch the slim volume that they first studied in journalism school. They continue to open the little book's dog-eared pages for its cautionary notes on convoluted prose and its advice on avoiding the pretentious.

Keep it clear, keep it brief, keep it bold, Strunk hammers away. Beware of opinion, of too much explanation, of too many fancy words.[2] But the evangelists of public journalism have created their own lexicon—devoid of brevity, clarity, and common sense. Professors who employ the concepts of public journalism in their classrooms are hardly in a position to insist on the old rules of lucidity and economy in the composition of their students. Editors, likewise, indoctrinated in the new journalistic language of public connectedness, are hardly in a position to admonish their writers for crimes of obfuscation and obscure expression.

Editors and their hired communication consultants are now sending memoranda asking other editors and reporters to "finalize action plans" in an effort to redefine "the newsroom agenda." They are asking journalistic team leaders to "set areas for assessment, in line with expectations, diagnostics, and development." They are asking journalistic performance teams to "select and vet (sic) assessment tools."[3]

Reporters, who may be impaired by an education in traditional journalism, must now stifle any preferences for concise interviewing, straightforward reporting, and plain-speaking in prose. These tendencies must be checked at newsroom doors where public journalism is practiced. Forget the usual story sources. Reporters must now engage in community mapping to identify civic assets that can be tapped for solution-oriented interviews. Never mind the deadlines. Reporters must now patiently engage in public listening that involves such citizen-oriented techniques as open-ended questioning that allows ordinary folks to genuinely express themselves.

We must now position people as citizens, declares Jay Rosen in his *Public Journalism as a Democratic Art*. Positioning people as citizens, according to Rosen, means to treat them "as unique contributors to public life; as potential participants in public affairs; as stakeholders with a personal interest; as citizens of the whole, with shared interests; as a deliberative body; as choosers, decision-makers; as learners, with skills to develop; as connected to place and responsible for place."[4]

Stakeholder, contributor, deliberator, decision-maker, learner—quite a list for the ossified mind of a traditional reporter to remember on the way to interview a striking Teamster, a grade school teacher, or a cop on the beat. For the reporter first adapting to the new, improved news culture, perhaps it is simply enough to remember, at least initially, the "journalist's dominion" as defined by Editor Cole Campbell's Public Life Team at *The Virginian-Pilot* in Norfolk: "We will revitalize a democracy that has grown sick with disenchantment. We will lead the community to discover itself and act on what it has learned."[5]

Campbell is a champion of the new public journalism approach to written expression. He brought the new approach with him from Norfolk to St. Louis in 1996 when he took the reins of the *Post-Dispatch* from public journalism nemesis William Woo. Soon the *Post-Dispatch* was filled with stories of citizens convening to discuss a Peirce Report analysis of metro problems and possible solutions. Hard news stories on the front page made way for citizen action groups meeting to determine a public agenda for revitalizing St. Louis by the year 2004. Editorial writers began pronouncing on what steps the citizenry should take to revive their flagging democracy.

The *Post-Dispatch*'s Campbell draws heavily from the deep well of public journalism jargon whether it be in interoffice memos to staffers, in presentations before civic groups, or in communiques to the readers of the *Post-Dispatch*. The jargon appeared most conspicuously in the forward to a lengthy newspaper report on efforts to revive downtown St. Louis and the metro region.

In his May 1, 1997, introduction to the paper's publication of former Missouri Senator Jack Danforth's, "Report to the Community: St. Louis 2004," Campbell stuffed 13 paragraphs chockfull of public journalism buzzwords. There were "agendas," "conversations," "deliberations," and "action teams." He wrote that the *Post* "called for a continuing conversation," that it wanted to "spur that conversation," and that it "intended to spark good conversation." He added that "direct conversations" were needed for "effective deliberation."

On the deliberation side of the public journalism approach, Campbell wrote that "deliberation can happen anywhere two or more people talk," that "effective deliberation requires genuine, direct conversation," and finally, that "deliberation moves us beyond looking out for our own interests."[6] Apparently, Campbell was asking readers to talk about the future of St. Louis.

All of this conversation, deliberation, and other assorted lingo of public journalism draws huge sighs from traditional reporters at the *Post-Dispatch* and other papers with public journalism evangelists at the helm. The traditionalists cry out, "Can't we just do journalism today?" On the other hand, newsroom employees with ambitions beyond producing clear and concise copy are eager to cozy up to mentors and enculturate themselves in the new rules of decorum in the newsroom.

At Cole Campbell's *Post-Dispatch*, editorial writers have been transformed into Athenian oracles pronouncing on the sad state of American democracy and prescribing cures involving heavy doses of civic journalism. Throughout 1997, the *Post-Dispatch* ran "a series of occasional editorials on the state of democracy in America." The first editorial in the series, "Democracy: Triumph and Troubles" noted that public journalism is seeking to draw the press closer to the people. In the initial editorial in the series, the editorial writers drew from the public journalism lexicon and outlined the movement's first premise: "People are disenchanted by the way democracy works. Leaders seem at once too pliant and too unresponsive. Trust in the government is at an all-time low. Everyone trusted Walter Cronkite; only one in four trusts Dan Rather."[7]

In this same April 1 editorial, the writers noted that the new public journalism wants to address the disenchantment with political leaders and the news media. They emphasized that public journalism is an effort to re-energize democracy and to restore citizen faith in the role the news media can play. "It is inspired by worthwhile premises: that the press dwells too much on conflict at the ideological extremes; that the press must play an active role in democracy; that political hired guns have perverted democracy; and that it is important to fill the civic spaces left vacant by the disappearance of civic association valued by [Alexis de] Tocqueville." In the description of the redemptive nature of public journalism, the *Post-Dispatch* editorial could not resist a major descriptive of the new movement—"civic spaces." In its re-incarnation under public journalism, the revived and reinvigorated newspaper itself would become a civic space in which "the community can have a conversation with itself."[8]

AN INVASION OF JARGON

The infiltration of public journalism jargon into standard journalistic expression, as well as the invasion of its many ideas and concepts, might well be termed the "academizing of journalism." The influence of university schools of journalism on the profession has increased steadily since the decade of the 1970s.

There was a time when a university education itself was considered a liability in the newsroom. The 1930s movie classic, *The Front Page*, depicted the college boy journalist as gullible, effeminate, and eminently unadaptable to the crusty habitat of daily journalism—the domain of real men. The 1950s comedy, *Teacher's Pet*, also revealed the disdain of hard-nosed editors and reporters for what they viewed as the nonsense perpetrated by journalism schools. Clark Gable, who played the gnarly editor in *Teacher's Pet*, summed up the viewpoint of a good many old-fashioned journalists toward what goes on at journalism schools, "Amateurs teaching amateurs how to be amateurs."[9]

In the 40 years since Gable's pronouncement, however, journalism and the reading public have benefited from the influence of academe. Still, the growing influence of public journalism, which is very much an academic construct, has prompted some thoughtful observers in the industry to wonder if the pendulum has swung too far in the direction of ivory tower thinking and diminished any benefits.

Much of the jargon of public journalism can be credited to the movement's intellectual guru, Rosen, a New York University professor with little actual experience in journalism. Rosen's experience consists of an editorship at his college paper at the State University of New York at Buffalo and a few months as a reporter at the *Buffalo Courier Express*. He left the *Courier Express* after quickly tiring of school board and city council coverage and because of his frustration with the restraints of journalistic objectivity.[10] He enrolled in graduate school at New York University's Department of Media Ecology and, after writing a dissertation on John Dewey and Walter Lippmann's clashing views on journalism, he was hired by NYU's Department of Journalism.

As an academic and theoretician of public journalism, Rosen has said that much of his role in the movement is to create a new vocabulary as part of the process of re-inventing the newspaper. Rosen has been joined in the task of masterminding the new verbiage for news by other academics, editors experimenting with public journalism, public policy think tanks, foundations, and consulting firms.

One of the best books available in any effort to understand the lexicon of public journalism is Arthur Charity's, *Doing Public Journalism*, published in 1995. Charity was hired by Rosen's own public journalism think tank at New York University to put together a compendium of ideas for innovative journalistic experiments and the book was the result of his work.

A few key terms in the developing language of public journalism, and attempts at defining those terms, include:

Lethargic Public Climate. This describes a community in which citizens feel alienated from their political system and feel helpless to effect change. Such a community lacks a public life. This is a dangerous situation for journalists, according to Rosen, "because when the life of a community no longer matters, neither does journalism."[11]

Public Listening. This reportorial approach involves such techniques as posing open-ended questions to ordinary citizens to provoke detailed responses. It also involves setting up discussion groups with citizens to obtain non-expert opinion on the life of a community.

Public Agenda. Through the use of questionnaires, focus groups, and public listening, public journalists can determine what issues are on the minds of ordinary citizens, rather than relying on local leaders and political experts to dictate the issues and concerns of a community.

Deliberative Dialogue. Public journalism seeks to encourage discussion that leads to solutions, rather than to traditional conflict-oriented reportage. Journalists should encourage situations in which people on opposing sides work together to achieve a common ground, not to prove each other wrong.

Community Conversation. Citizens need to communicate and socialize with each other through the vehicle of their newspapers. They need to share ideas about the problems they face and the solutions they seek in the deliberative forum that the newspaper can provide.

Framing. Journalists need to develop new reflexes in framing stories. Traditionally, journalists have focused on conflicts, the extremes, the unusual, and the negative. Journalists now need to report in more meaningful ways on how the community responds to problems and potentially solves community dilemmas.

University communication departments are not the only source for the academizing of journalism. Consultants are getting into the act of helping to coach reporters in connecting with the community. Feedback consultants with MBAs and PhDs are in the business of invading newsrooms to help journalists define expectations and assess performance in the effort to connect with the public. The Bethesda, Maryland-based Harwood Group is among the growing number of consulting companies that are in the business of telling journalists how to do their work.

The Harwood Group counts among its clients such prestigious dailies as *The Orange County Register, The Miami Herald, The Arizona Republic,* and the *St. Louis Post-Dispatch.* Richard Harwood, president of the firm, often conducts the sessions with journalists himself. Harwood will talk with newsroom leadership teams about the need to express aspirations for the newspaper and for the journalists themselves. He will speak about the "essence" of a story, trying to connect with readers, reshaping the "news reflex," providing "coherence" and finding ways to make a newspaper "authoritative and authentic."[12]

The Harwood Group and other consultants have joined with the university schools of communication in the development of a new specialized vocabulary for journalistic practitioners. Harwood's public journalism workbook, *Tapping Civic Life,* helps reporters and editors explore the different layers of civic life, which include the official layer, such as city council meetings; the quasi-official layer, such as advocacy groups; the "third places" layer of barbershops, child care centers and diners; the incidental layer of sidewalks, the market, and backyards; and the private layer of people's homes. Each layer of civic life works differently, and The Harwood Group provides hapless reporters with useful insights on each.[13]

Harwood's public journalism workbook also helps reporters understand the four leadership layers of a community, which consist of official leaders, civic leaders, connectors, and catalysts. Journalists need to know that each leadership layer plays a distinctive role in the community, and the Harwood workbook describes the general characteristics and idiosyncrasies of each category of leadership. Connectors and catalysts are the two leadership layers traditional journalists have not tapped into in the past as important sources.[14]

Key factors for engaging people in public life have been condensed into a set of nine terms: connections, personal context, coherence, room for ambivalence, emotion, authenticity, sense of possibility, catalysts, and mediating institutions. By understanding and using these factors, journalists can strengthen their stories. "For instance," explains *Tapping Civic Life*, "journalists will see the context in which a concern or event holds importance to people, people's struggle with being ambivalent [so that an issue is not always framed at the extremes], the connections people make among their various concerns."[15]

There was a time when such gobbledygook was confined to the scholarly papers of communication professors seeking publication in obscure quarterlies. Research and writing may not have been particularly useful in newsrooms or for the communication industry, but it was essential in the professors' quest for job security and tenure at academic institutions.

Among the more intriguing intellectual explorations offered at the annual conventions of the Association for Education in Journalism and Mass Communication (AEJMC) in recent years have been such titles as: "Toward a Systemic Method of Measuring Free Recall from Printed News Stories," "Using Concept Mapping to Go Beyond the Source Credibility Model in Assessing Celebrity-Message Congruence," "Objectivity and Epistemology: Stance Adverbs in News Discourse," "Effects of Message Discrepancy on Recall of News Information over Time," "Nonreaders, Single Newspaper Readers and Multiple Newspaper Readers: A Discriminant Analysis," "Putting News into Context: Apparent Reality Versus Source Credibility in Judgments of News Believability," and the "Community Editors' Views on Extralogical Coverage."[16]

For years, journalism and communication professors lamented that their research and scholarly papers did not draw the attention or weigh in with those in the news industry. At an AEJMC convention held in Washington, D.C., in 1989, a broadcast professor stood up in a conference session and harangued former CBS anchor Roger Mudd at length on how the broadcast industry had much to learn from the in-depth research and ideas of professors. Mudd replied that he was aware of just how valuable the research was, having just browsed through the conference paper room, reading the interesting paper abstracts, and noting that each study was priced at 25 cents per copy.[17]

Mudd's attitude was indicative of the dim view of journalism academe among many news practitioners. Their complaints have been that journalism academe has strayed from a primary mission of training students to perform well in entry-level journalism positions. Instead, professors have put much of their energy into developing communication theories and engaging in arcane research. To an alarming extent, journalism professors have either succumbed to working out personal agendas in their research, or to conducting research that has a semblance of sophistication, but which has little real world value.

CRISIS IN THE ACADEMY?

Tonda Rush, executive officer officer of the National Newspaper Association (NNA), sounded the alarm about the direction and influence of the journalism academy at the 1993 AEJMC Convention in Kansas City. Rush, like Mudd, expressed little patience with academic journalism studies that focus on media schemata, framing philosophies, portrayals of apparent reality, or extralogical news coverage. She said journalism professors needed to spend more time on teaching students the nuts and bolts of traditional story writing, with more attention to concepts such as fairness, balance, and how news content should be shaped.

According to Rush, the news industry has certain expectations of journalism schools and their graduates. The news industry wants a "22-year-old to emerge with some idea of how the world works, who can turn on a computer, find area codes in the phone book, hail a cab in the city, ask delicate questions without offending someone, and comb his hair before he stands in front of 500 people with a Nikon in his hand."[18] Rush said journalism school graduates should know something about Watergate, the importance of Omaha Beach in World War II, how congressional districts are set up, and why it's important to spell things right.

"Neither the publisher nor the editor gives a damn about how many theories about electoral politics a kid knows . . . or whether he thinks old-growth forests are essential for survival," Rush hammered away at her AEJMC faculty audience. "They're looking for pragmatists, not eggheads. And finally, they want someone who understands that journalism is a craft and a business—not a religion."[19]

Rush's concerns were echoed a few years later in *Winds of Change: Challenges Confronting Journalism Education* The critical report was written by Betty Medsger, a former chairwoman of the journalism department at San Francisco State University and a former reporter for *The Washington Post*. Medsger's report, funded and released by the Freedom Forum, concluded that journalism schools needed a major overhaul, that changes were needed in curricula, and that many faculty members lacked substantial practical reporting experience.[20]

Medsger revealed that too many professors who lacked professional experience were teaching skills courses on reporting, writing, and editing, with the result that students aren't getting the basics down very well. At the same time, courses in reporting, writing, and editing were low on the totem pole of academic prestige. Professors were much more interested in teaching mass communication theory courses and wanted more time to research issues in journalism and communication.

Medsger's study found that many journalism education programs were in need of a defined mission. Many of the journalism master's degree programs were described as unfocused, impractical, and in need of restructuring or elimination.

In a section of her study entitled "Voices," Medsger gave journalism academics and news professionals the opportunity to comment and to provide their individual assessment of the state of journalism education. Some of the comments of the news professionals were particularly telling. "If engineering, medicine, or law were to become as theoretical as journalism has, I'd be afraid to cross a bridge, be treated for the injuries I receive when it collapses, or sue the contractor responsible," said Eric Meyer, managing director of Newslink, a Wisconsin media operation. "Elimination of the lumping together of communications and journalism would help, as would stressing practical research among faculty."[21]

Meyer is among those news practitioners who feel that journalism education has been dominated by theorists with doctoral degrees awarded for research that has little do with the practice of journalism. Meyer advocates full tenure appointments for college teachers with MAs who have substantial professional experience. Meyer and other professionals interviewed by Medsger expressed the view that journalism faculties are full of people who have been "out of the business too long and haven't the faintest idea of what hiring editors are looking for from school graduates."[22]

"The fundamental question is: Is the role of journalism schools to produce students who are trained to work as competent journalists, or to produce 'scholarship' consisting of irrelevant and, in my opinion, bogus 'quantitative and qualitative' research?" declared Jane E. Kirtley of The Reporters Committee for Freedom of the Press. Kirtley commented further in Medsger's study, "When I receive an issue of *Journalism Quarterly*, almost invariably there is at least one article that strikes me as so ridiculous that I feel compelled to hurl the journal across the room. I recall one article a few years ago that, as I remember it, attempted to draw a correlation between the number of misspelled words in a newspaper and the number of Pulitzers it had won. This, to me, is suggestive of how far academics will stretch into absurdity to come up with "quantitative" studies. Journalism is not social science, and social science models don't work."[23]

Despite all these past calls for change and reform in university journalism education by those in the news business, academia has been less than responsive. The news practitioners have called for a journalism education that should be less theoretical and more practical; that should produce fewer eggheads and, instead, nurture more pragmatists for work in newsrooms; that should treat journalism as a craft and business profession, rather than as a social science or a religion. How has journalism academia responded to these calls? It has responded with a new movement called public journalism to teach journalism students the art of "public listening" so they may "engage in deliberative dialogue" with citizens in order "to revive the flagging democracy."

Many journalism professors, particularly those with less journalistic work experience and a more theoretical bent, have gone gaga over public journalism. More than 150 university teachers became members of the civic (or public journalism) interest group of the American Educators in Journalism and Mass Communication shortly after it was founded. The new division, first organized by Professor Edmund Lambeth of the University of Missouri School of Journalism, is the fastest growing interest area of the AEJMC. Division members meet around the country to discuss public journalism scholarship, showcase new public journalism syllabi and instructional methodology, and address the question of bringing public journalism to the classroom.

Many news practitioners are alarmed, though not necessarily surprised, that public journalism has so mesmerized journalism professors in the academy. They aren't necessarily surprised by its popularity, because public journalism's intellectual veneer, sociological trappings, and specialized language are naturally attractive to the academic mentality. These news practitioners are, however, alarmed because a sizeable number of their colleagues in the news business are lending a sympathetic ear. They are no longer among the professionals decrying questionable scholarship and theory-oriented teaching. Instead, they are beginning to embrace the public journalism critique of traditional journalism as well as its ideas for reforming journalism; and they are beginning to mimic the vocabulary flowing out of the journalism academy.

Professors who advocate public journalism, such as St. Louis University's John Pauly, say the critique of traditional journalism that is found in public journalism has been around for 15 years, and actually supersedes the 1990s movement of public journalism. The critique holds that traditional journalism is too conflict-oriented, that it treats readers as news consumers rather than as citizens, and that reporters are too often fixated on elusive ideals of objectivity and detachment.

"Journalists have only taken this critique seriously in recent years because of the declines in readership and economic difficulties at papers," according to Pauly. "That's why public journalism is more than just a fad, because I think there are deep structural problems with newspapers, such as readership decline, that are not going to go away. Public journalism is not only a moment in newspaper history, it's also an important moment in the history of communities," added Pauly.[24]

DOING JOURNALISM TO PUBLIC JOURNALISM

While public journalism is touted by academics and is getting a hearing from some in the news industry, particularly at newspapers suffering circulation declines in the country, it attracts derision and ridicule from traditionalists. The label of "traditional journalists" or the "journalistic elite" has been applied by public journalists to those news practitioners who are not embracing the new movement in journalism.

Public journalism advocates have complained that their concepts and ideas have been misrepresented and vilified by traditional journalists, that, in fact, the public journalism movement has "had journalism done to it."[25] The slackers, fogies, and cynical souls who still subscribe to traditional news values might well retort that, with the much-heralded public journalism, journalism itself is having "academia done to it." It's happening in newsrooms as reporters are corralled into seminar sessions to listen to public journalism consultants. It's happening in journalism classrooms where university professors are teaching deliberative approaches to interviewing and the imperative to reframe stories. It's happening at academic conferences where public journalism proponents share ideas to be advocated in both newsroom and classroom.

In forums such as the annual convention of the AEJMC, Davis "Buzz" Merritt gives journalism professors pep talks on public journalism and why it should find a receptive audience among students. "I frequently speak to college classes on journalism and I ask students why they got into journalism. None of them say: 'I got into it because I want to be objective,'"Merritt told an AEJMC session on teaching public journalism in 1997. "None of them say: 'I got into it because I want to be detached.' They say they got into it because they like to write; they got into it because they like to tell stories; they got into it because they want to change things. This points out to why there is so much dissatisfaction in the profession.

People did not get into journalism because they were enamored of an ethic of detachment and objectivity."[26]

According to Merritt, young people often lose sight of their original reasons for going into journalism once they have spent some time in classrooms where traditional journalistic tenets are taught. The worn and deadening obsession with balance, detachment, and objectivity in the classroom has its effect on students. "Jay Rosen tells the story about being invited by [Professor] Jim Carey to speak to a graduate class of journalists," explained Merritt. "The first year, he spoke in the sixteenth week of the semester—deep into the semester—and 90 percent of the students railed after his presentation that: 'You can't do that!'" Merritt said the students thought Rosen's ideas violated traditional journalism principles.

"So the next year, Carey invited Rosen to speak in the second week of the semester and 50 percent of the class, said: 'Yes. Yes. That's why I got into journalism in the first place.' The point is that enculturation takes place that quickly," concluded Merritt.[27] Merritt and the public journalism advocates want to end the enculturation of journalism students in traditional values which they disdain.

Cheryl Gibbs, a professor at Earlham College and leading proponent of teaching public journalism in schools of journalism, has documented some of the pioneering classroom efforts. In her own teaching work, Gibbs is fond of sending students out into the community to have citizen conversations that can help inform their reporting. She has also had students read the local daily newspaper throughout the term and write a final paper "comparing the conversation in the paper with the conversation in the community."[28]

Gibbs can cite the work of others, such as Professor Dave Boeyink at Indiana University, who has his students examine five ways of framing journalists' relationships with their communities—entertainers, objective conduits, watchdogs, advocates, or civic journalists. Boeyink's class is then divided into teams, with each team developing a news coverage strategy reflecting one of the five philosophies. The advantages of the civic (or public) journalism approach apparently become obvious.

Gibbs also singles out the work of Professor Jackie Farnan at St. John Fisher College in Rochester, N.Y., as exemplary in the instruction of public journalism methodology. Farnan has students engage in an extensive public listening project over a semester. Farnan told Gibbs that the biggest challenge was for the students to explore new ways of interviewing. The student journalists "felt that they should steer or shape the interview, and that meant asking focused and direct questions," Farnan related. "I said, 'Just back off a little bit. We are engaged in a different enterprise—let go of control and understand that listening is different than traditional interviewing.'"[29]

Because more and more journalism professors are embracing public journalism, editors steeped in traditional journalism will now have to be enculturated in a new and "different enterprise" in order to relate to the students coming out of journalism schools. Editors will have to understand the new vocabulary of public journalism and be able to decide when a community in the throes of "civic disintegration" requires reporters to engage in "interventions" to help citizens "chart a long-term vision." Student reporters can no longer simply be sent out on interviews; rather, they are sent out to connect with the public in deliberative dialogue in order to promote an agenda that is consistent with a defensible universalism.

In the new era of public journalism, professors are conceivably telling students to expect this hypothetical directive from a "publicly enlightened" editor: "We don't cover beats, we cover issues. But first we must determine the issues by seeking out what the public's agenda is. Since this community is a classic lethargic public climate, go out and do some public listening. If one of the major issues is, indeed, funding midnight basketball or improving bus service, let's set up a forum on it that encourages deliberative dialogue. That way we may be able to avoid framing the story in a manner that promotes confrontation."

But, while a surprising number of journalism educators are ready to teach students how to report using this kind of public journalism model, other teachers adamantly oppose bringing it into the classroom. The *SJR* survey conducted as a part of this book reveals that journalism professors are divided on whether public journalism is a good idea for the news profession and whether it belongs in the university classroom.

The opposition by those academics to teaching public journalism as a way to do news can be summarized as follows.

First, public journalists have yet to make a convincing case that traditional ways of doing news are outmoded. The best that public journalism has to offer is simply the good practice of traditional journalism. The worst that public journalism has to offer violates such traditional journalistic tenets as detachment, impartiality, and that elusive ideal of objectivity.

Second, the news concepts of public journalism are often at odds with those in the textbooks used for teaching journalism. The popular Missouri Group text emphasizes conflict, prominence, and novelty as among the important criteria for determining what makes news. Public journalism castigates these traditional attributes of news. If schools of journalism teach both the traditional and public journalism approach to news, should anyone be surprised if graduates leave academia completely confused as to what, in fact, makes news?

Third, a primary mission of journalism education is to teach students to express themselves clearly and concisely. "Clarity, clarity, clarity!" thunders literary authority E. B. White from the tattered pages of a book once known to all writers. The language of public journalism runs counter to that mission. What kind of writing can we expect from a young journalist who is focused on creating new "civic spaces" and "deliberative dialogue" techniques? Such a journalist may be able to write boilerplate editorials about "engaging" the disenchanted citizenry. Such a journalist may be able to pontificate in stories inspired by the need to "construct a defensible universalism" or to engage in "community conversations." But will such a journalist be capable of any prose that truly "connects" with readers?

Finally, what will become of journalism—its traditional values and fundamental practices—as more and more journalism school graduates seek to "academize" it with the fuzzy mindset wrought by the new public journalism mentors?

NOTES

1. William Strunk Jr., and E. B. White, *The Elements of Style* (New York: The Macmillan Co., 1972), p. 72.

2. Ibid., pp. 71–73.

3. Don Corrigan, "Campbell's Gamble: Will Fuzzy Concepts Lead to Sharper Journalism," *St. Louis Journalism Review* (June, 1998), p. 1.

4. Jay Rosen, "Public Journalism as a Democratic Art." Pamphlet adapted from a Rosen presentation at the American Press Institute, Reston, Virginia, November 11, 1994, p. 15.

5. Ibid., p 7.

6. Cole Campbell, "Our Republic and Its Press," *St. Louis Post-Dispatch* (May 1, 1997), p. 10A.

7. Editorial Board, "Democracy: Triumph and Troubles," *St. Louis Post- Dispatch* (April 1, 1997), p. 6B.

8. Ibid.

9. Quote is from editor Jim Gannon, played by Clark Gable, in the 1957 movie, *Teacher's Pet*, by Perlsea and Paramount Pictures.

10. Scott Sherman, "The Public Defender," *Linguafranca: The Review of Academic Life* (April, 1998), p. 50.

11. Jay Rosen, "What Should We Be Doing?" *The IRE Journal* (November-December), 1996, pp. 7–8.

12. Alicia C. Shepard, "The Change Agents," *American Journalism Review* (May, 1998), p. 43.

13. The Harwood Group, *Tapping Civic Life* (Bethesda, Maryland: The Tides Center and The Harwood Group, 1996), pp. 10–11.

14. Ibid., pp. 16–17.

15. Ibid., pp. 18–19.

16. Scholarly papers and abstracts taken from July issues of the AEJMC News, the regular reports of the Association for Education in Journalism and Mass Communication.

17. Roger Mudd, Plenary Session on Broadcast Journalism from remarks made at the annual AEJMC Convention, Washington, D.C., August 1989.

18. M. L. Stein, "Revamping Journalism Education," *Editor & Publisher* (August 28, 1993), pp. 12–13,

19. Ibid., p. 35.

20. Charles L. Overby, "J-schools Should Focus on Journalism's Needs" (Arlington, Virginia: The Freedom Forum, July, 1996), p. 2.

21. Betty Medsger, *Winds of Change: Challenges Confronting Journalism Education* (Arlington, Virginia: The Freedom Forum, 1996), p. 161.

22. Ibid., p. 160.

23. Ibid., p. 161.

24. Don Corrigan, "Public Journalism Must Progress Slowly," *St. Louis Journalism Review* (March, 1998), p. 11.

25. Davis Merritt, "The Misconceptions about Public Journalism," *Editor & Publisher* (July 1, 1995), p. 80.

26. Davis Merritt, remarks made at forum on teaching public journalism at the AEJMC Convention, Chicago, Illinois, August 1997.

27. Ibid.

28. Cheryl Gibbs, "Teaching Civic Journalism," *Civic Catalyst* (January, 1997), p. 10.

29. Ibid., p. 9.

9
Globalization of Public Journalism

THE COMMUNITARIANS' DREAM

Among those in the academic community who find real excitement in the growth of the public journalism movement are the communitarian philosophers, ethicists, and communication scholars who reject the "egoistic rationalism" of contemporary journalism. The communitarians speak in a language that has been an inspiration for the creators of the lexicon of public journalism. They speak of a "rich notion of accountability" that will "resonate in an organization's consciousness" and the need for a journalism "that engenders a like-minded world view."[1]

Until the public journalists came along, the advocates of a communitarian approach to journalism were, for the most part, voices crying in the wilderness— or in university classrooms. Some scholars point to the the Hutchins Commission of the late 1940s as an important purveyor of the communitarian perspective on journalism. That perspective is at odds with many of the tenets of traditional journalism. For example, communitarians stress media responsibility, rather than press freedom. They contend the traditional press in the West has been fixated on its own rights and privileges, rather than on any obligation to the society or people it serves. The communitarians also feel the press has a responsibility to create community and to involve the public in its editorial function.

The communitarians are convinced that the day-to-day, reportorial search for truth is not a function to be ceded to individualistic journalists left to their own devices. Journalists must feel a responsibility to a larger entity. In their search for truth, journalists must always be focused on whether the information they uncover can serve the greater good of society. Obviously, communitarians have no use for the libertarian approach to journalism that is often attributed to John Milton. Milton wrote that all ideas should be expressed, even the notorious lie or outrageous error, because truth will always win out in an open encounter with falsehood. The more cautious communitarians are not so sure that truth will always gain the upper hand, and, with that in mind, they advocate a press that will always be reined in by a sense of social responsibility.

There is a danger, of course, in trying to interpret exactly what the communitarians mean because, like many public journalists, they use a language that is quite foreign to the everyday pedestrian mentality. Communitarians may be interested in the welfare and greater good of the common man, but they refuse to express themselves in a manner that the common man can understand. They have found kindred spirits in the evangelists of the new public journalism—someone who speaks their language and who can share in their unique hubris.

Philosopher and journalism professor John C. Merrill of the University of Missouri is one of the most strident critics of the communitarians. Merrill has been quick to point out the similarities in the perspective of communitarian journalists and public journalists, as well as their shared language of vague and impenetrable terms. "There is a vaguely spiritual, almost theological ring, which is alluring to many people," declares Merrill about communitarians, though he could just as easily be describing public journalists. "And it is often the tone and vagueness of their language that captivate the minds (or should I say *souls*, or *hearts*?) of many university professors and students. Also, it is rather chic to challenge the best minds of the Age of Reason and to trash their philosophies."[2]

Merrill argues that those journalists who gravitate toward communitarian ideas are throwing away the intellectual underpinnings of the American press that have their source in the philosophical writings of Milton, Locke, Mill, Constant, Voltaire, and Madison. Merrill argues that communitarians are rejecting Enlightenment liberalism and a libertarian approach to information cultures, and are instead seeking a new formulation with a rhetoric that is disturbingly similar to the ideas of socialism or Karl Marx. Merrill is not engaging in some sort of 1990s McCarthyism in pointing out this parallel as part of his critique of the communitarians, and, as a libertarian, Merrill emphasizes that he has no desire to stifle or to stigmatize those who would espouse a socialist or Marxist viewpoint on the press. In fact, Merrill points out, critics of traditional journalism, such as J. Herbert Altschull, have already made his point. The communitarian ideal, as Altschull declares, is alive and well today, although "the name of the movement has been changed from 'Marxist' to communitarian."[3]

Professor Clifford Christians of the University of Illinois is one of the leading proponents of the communitarian approach to journalism and he has found a seat at many of the roundtables organized by the advocates of public journalism. Christians, who serves on the boards of numerous communications journals and who is published widely in communications ethics, finds much too applaud in the new public journalism. Christians is impressed with the shift in thinking that public journalism represents, especially in its move away from emphasis on "individual rights to the public good."[4] He is fond of quoting public journalism philosopher Jay Rosen, who declares that "good journalism requires more than good journalists—more even than enlightened ownership, First Amendment protections, and a strong economic base. For without an engaged and concerned public, even the most public-minded press cannot do its job. . . . Rather than assuming that a vibrant civic culture exists—or simply lamenting its absence—the public journalist takes responsibility for helping to support or even create it."[5]

Christians and other communitarians are quite at home with Rosen's pronouncements on the need for a press that builds community and obligates itself to social welfare. The communitarians, not content to simply ruminate in the classroom on a such a good thing, declare that public journalism should go global. In his paper, "The Common Good in a Global Setting," Christians makes the case that the public journalism philosophy can and should be adopted on a global scale. He argues for a "defensible universalism" that can permeate journalistic efforts in local cultures around the world. He then proceeds to examine three examples of values, or global notions of a common good "that can enable civic [or public] journalism to operate fruitfully by invigorating community debates in terms of universal human solidarity."[6]

The evangelists and messengers of public journalism are only too happy to oblige Christians and the communitarians in their desire to share the good news of public journalism with the rest of the world. At the 1996 AEJMC Convention in Anaheim, Ed Fouhy, then-executive director of the Pew Center for Civic Journalism, announced to professors of journalism and mass communication that the public journalism movement had gone global. Fouhy, who prefers the term civic journalism for the new movement, noted that an increasing number of journalists from other countries were visiting the Pew Center to learn more about civic or public journalism.

"There's a great deal of interest in civic journalism all over the world," Fouhy told the professors at the AEJMC meeting. "Just in the past few months, I looked in my appointment book and I see that we've received visitors from France, Finland, Japan, Bosnia, Korea, Indonesia, Mozambique and Spain . . . and we've made presentations to the Fulbright scholars who represented more than 50 countries."[7]

Public journalism concepts and ideas are also being exported to other countries via seminars and conferences sponsored by institutions such as Pew. Public journalism came to Argentina in late April 1996, when more than 60 Argentines took part in a two-day conference in Buenos Aires. According to John Dinges of National Public Radio (NPR), the meeting was the first on the topic in Argentina and may well have been the first seminar held outside the United States devoted entirely to the discussion of public journalism techniques.[8]

Public journalism also was exported to Eastern Europe in 1996. Fouhy told professors in Anaheim that presentations were made in a public journalism conference in Prague. The audience consisted primarily of journalists from the former client states of the now defunct Soviet Union. They were looking for a new way to do journalism, according to Fouhy. Fouhy said the new journalistic ideas were particularly apropos in the setting of Prague, a city at a crossroads where the old bipolar world of conflict between us and them (the Capitalist West and the Communist East) has broken down and largely ceased to exist.[9]

The headlong rush to public journalism ideas and experiments within certain sectors of the news media in the United States calls out for more critical analysis than has been proffered thus far. The export of this movement to countries in Latin America, Eastern Europe, and the various entities of the Third World must certainly raise even more concerns. Should foundations, national policy institutes, and news organizations be in the business of exporting the concepts and practices of public journalism? What exactly are these concepts and practices and do they hold any particular relevance for nations in underdeveloped areas of the world?

The concern regarding the export of public journalism abroad is two-fold. First, public journalism is still very much in its formative stages. As both a philosophy and as a practice, public journalism is in its infancy. There is considerable disagreement among its many U.S. advocates as to what precepts are consistent with the public journalism philosophy. There is even more confusion as to what constitutes a valid public journalism project. Consequently, it is clearly premature to begin exporting what might be termed a "communication formula" that is open to wide interpretation, manipulation, and potential abuse.

The second point of concern regards the many similarities between public journalism and development journalism. There are many tenets in the rhetoric of public journalism that echo the rhetoric of development journalism. During the late 1970s and into the 1980s, the American government resisted and much of the U.S. press opposed development journalism and the related ideas of the New World Information and Communication Order (NWICO). There is an inescapable irony in the prospect that now so many of these ideas appear to be embodied in the public journalism movement in America in the 1990s.

In light of the dismay and even outrage that ideas in the NWICO debate inspired in the American press two decades ago, it seems curious that these ideas are now being embraced by a portion of the domestic U.S journalism community and even being packaged for export. The effort to export public journalism concepts to other countries—particularly those emerging from military dictatorships in Latin America or those emerging from Soviet domination in Eastern Europe—should raise some legitimate concerns.

PUBLIC JOURNALISM: NOT READY FOR EXPORT

It is not difficult to argue the first point of this chapter—that public journalism is still in its formative stages and constitutes a communication formula that needs more definition and refinement before it is considered as some sort of intellectual media export. Even the most zealous advocates of public journalism concede that they're not entirely sure what it's all about; they insist that it is an evolving movement. Proponents of public journalism argue that theirs is a phenomenon "in process." It's too early to know just what public journalism is right now. It may well take 10 years to know what exactly it will become.[10]

Obviously, there is a degree of safety in all this ambiguity for public journalism advocates. The critics in the wings are advised to hold their tongues for a decade before passing judgment. A movement that can't be defined cannot be easily criticized. Some proponents have offered that the best way to define public journalism is to actually look at the projects that have been conducted in its name.

But there is considerable disagreement, even among practitioners, as to what constitutes a bona fide public journalism project. Many advocates at seminars and conferences are often in the position of distancing themselves from the many experiments and projects devised by colleagues in favor of their own particular brand of public journalism.

The most celebrated practitioner of public journalism, Davis "Buzz" Merritt of the Wichita (Kansas) *Beacon Journal*, has explained that many of the reporting projects done in the name of public journalism "have gone far beyond where I would go as an editor."[11] Merritt does not criticize the motivation of the journalists behind projects that have gone awry. "But because their understanding of this thing was so shallow and the hunger for immediate change so great, many of them overshot, which meant that what they labeled as public journalism became a huge, fat unmissable target for would-be critics."[12]

Public journalists are in the habit of using the word "experiment" to describe their practices. At this point, many of the movement's leaders argue that they are in a better position to define what they are trying to achieve, rather than to point to an established set of practices. Their goals inspire a wide range of initiatives. They want to experiment with new models for election coverage, which move the emphasis away from personalities and who's ahead in the horse race, to an emphasis on issues and finding out what constitutes the citizens' agenda. They want to experiment with new approaches to crime coverage, which transform victims into actors who are capable of addressing crime problems and who can take back their neighborhoods from the bad guys. They want to experiment with economic coverage, which doesn't simply chronicle a community's decline, but draws citizens together to chart a long-term vision to yield a brighter future.

"Those who are pushing this movement forward don't know exactly what they're doing. I'm afraid I have to insist on that point," public journalism advocate Jay Rosen told a conference of Investigative Reporters and Editors (IRE) in 1995. "We're making it up as we go along. We proceed by experiment and reflection, and it's hard to say at this stage whether any of the experiments are really working."[13] In fact, Rosen continued, public journalists are not even sure how the success of their projects should be judged. He added that, in five to ten years, much of what passes for public journalism is likely to be viewed as crude and naive.

If it's too early in the genesis of public journalism to provide a definition for it, and if the experiments in its name are still crude and rudimentary, what are we left with? According to practitioner Merritt, critics are confounded by public journalism because they don't comprehend that it's not simply some new method or some new process for doing journalism. Instead, it involves a fundamental shift in thinking about what the job of journalism really is. Merritt argues that the uninitiated journalists and the critics need to take an intellectual journey through the literature that undergirds the public journalism movement, rather than grasping for a two or three paragraph definition that will lay it all out.

Merritt's own intellectual journey to the new movement in journalism is chronicled to some extent in his book, *Public Journalism & Public Life*. Merritt describes his own disillusionment with contemporary journalism practice which led him to question such values as objectivity, detachment, balance, and the "watchdog" or adversarial role of the press. He argues that public journalism involves a number of mental shifts by traditional journalistic communicators. He categorizes a number of these mental shifts, and listing them can be useful in a discussion of what public journalism might be as a "communication formula" that can be packaged for export. According to Merritt, public journalism:

- Moves beyond the limited mission of "telling the news" to a broader mission of helping public life go well, and acts out that imperative. When public life goes well, true deliberation occurs and leads to potential solutions.
- Moves from detachment to being a fair-minded participant in public life. Its practitioners remember that they are citizens as well as journalists.
- Moves from worrying about proper separations to concern with proper connections. If we get the proper connections right, the separations will take care of themselves.
- Moves beyond only describing what "is going wrong" to also imaging what "going right" would be like. By describing realistic possibilities that lie beyond immediate solutions, it informs people of their potential choices for the future.[14]

These tenets of the public journalism philosophy, as articulated by one of its chief proponents, get us as close to a working definition of public journalism as we are likely to achieve. Since these tenets have been quoted verbatim here, there can be no argument that the public journalism concept has been misconstrued or distorted. It must be emphasized again, however, that public journalists resist attempts at defining their movement. As Merritt himself writes, after outlining these tenets, "At this early point in experimentation, for any one editor or institution to begin to define public journalism concretely would also mean limiting the possibilities."[15]

If we accept the public journalists' admonition that it's too early to define this movement and that much of what is being done in its name is unacceptable or, at the very least, naive, then are we unreasonable to suggest that it might be premature to begin exporting this new movement to other countries? If it remains vague, amorphous, and malleable at this early stage in its development, is it unreasonable to suggest that it might be less than wise to offer it as a model to those in other countries seeking the proper role for the press in their fledgling democracies?

On the other hand, if we accept the public journalists' basic contention that theirs is a revolutionary movement in journalism—a movement that puts less emphasis on objectivity and detachment, and more emphasis on advocating solutions to problems and connecting with the public—are we still being unreasonable in suggesting that this might not be such a worthy export?

The ideal of objectivity and the tradition of detachment in conventional American journalism apparently have been a useful part of our communication formula in America for many, many years—long before public journalism came along in the 1990s. Also, many developing states and the emerging countries in Eastern Europe have not had an adversarial press that acts as a watchdog on government malfeasance and political corruption. Now that the door is open to a press with more clout and independence in these countries, do we now want to tell their journalists that an adversarial press can be counterproductive to making public life go well? Can we really be confident that the largely untried communication formula of public journalism is what we now wish to hold up as an example to those seeking our counsel from abroad?

PUBLIC JOURNALISM AND DEVELOPMENT JOURNALISM

One of the paradoxical aspects of the current public journalism movement is that its critique of how news has been traditionally gathered and presented in America echoes the international "news values" controversy of the 1970s and 1980s in the forum of the United Nations. Of course, that debate continues to some degree today. But the release in 1980 of what has become known as the MacBride Report brought the controversy to a boil in the early 1980s. The irony here is that the American press soundly repudiated—and a large segment of the U.S. press actually editorialized against—many of the themes of the "development journalism" advocated by the MacBride Report.[16] Now many of those themes are central to the public journalism movement, which is being presented as a model to the news media in other countries.

The debate leading up to the MacBride Report basically was a confrontation between developing nations of the Third World and the nations of the West with their market-based press. Third World nations complained about the dominance of the Western news agencies, and the manner in which those agencies covered their concerns. News about the developing world was, they argued, poorly informed, superficial, and intermittent. It focused on violence and turmoil. The most chaotic and bloody nations were put in the media spotlight. Peaceful nations achieved independence and statehood with barely a mention.

The Western news media's emphasis on the negative and conflict-driven story coverage became a virulent international issue by the mid-1970s. Long-time international correspondent Mort Rosenblum comments on this new world information order revolt in his book, *Who Stole the News? Why We Can't Keep Up with What Happens in the World.* As Rosenblum notes, in the 1970s universities around the world began bringing together journalists, academics, and national leaders. They discussed a new development journalism—a journalism that would be driven by new values and that would have to answer to the concerns of Third World leaders. At the biennial conference of the United Nation's Educational, Scientific and Cultural Organization (UNESCO) in Nairobi, the Soviet Union capitalized on the discord to push for a resolution to give countries some form of state control over news correspondents and their dispatches.[17]

At its 1978 general conference, UNESCO declared a New World Information and Communication Order (NWICO) to promote new values in news and to address the imbalance in the international flow of information. The old Western news values were determined to be destructive to a population's self-image and self-esteem. A new development journalism under NWICO would encompass news values more consistent with the cultural requirements and the political demands of Third World countries.

The development journalism theory seemed to be that foreign correspondents had some obligation for the welfare of the countries they wrote about. The theory also inferred that if Western reporters wrote more column inches and more often about Third World countries, with greater emphasis on positive developments, the turmoil and upheaval would vanish. The old style of journalism was exacerbating problems and hindering the ability of Third World leaders to find solutions to their internal problems. The new genre of development journalism would bring harmony and progress.

In his analysis of the international news situation, Rosenblum argues that American editors were stung by the criticisms from the Third World, and made efforts to comply with the ideals of the new development journalism. Rosenblum gives the example of a U.S. editor lecturing to a foreign correspondent, "If a man writes about Somalia being backward in some respects, we want to make sure he also writes about the successful campaign against illiteracy. It is unfair to point out that the capitol has only one stoplight unless we explain that it has no cars either, and what that means to society."[18]

The spirit of this editor's argument echoes the philosophy of the new public journalism movement, especially as it pertains to the coverage of disadvantaged communities within the United States. Public journalists contend that constant negative coverage of illiteracy, crime, and drug use in America's urban ghettos only compounds the problems. Public journalism seeks to identify the positive in these situations, identifying community assets and community leaders who can foster progress and harmony. According to public journalists, the news media have a responsibility to seek out solutions for communities in trouble and to not simply exploit horror stories of crime and drug abuse for front page headlines.

There are many other parallels between the tenets of development journalism and the philosophical thrust of the new public journalism. The complaints of the developing nations about Western news values at the height of the NWICO debate are consistent with much of the critique public journalism brings to bear against the traditional practice of journalism in America. The parallels beg the question: Is public journalism really just development journalism with a new name? A few examples of the parallels are useful to illustrate this point:

"*Parachute Journalism.*" Many advocates of development journalism argue that, since reporters for Western news agencies have little real interest or stake in the countries that they cover, their reportage is understandably incomplete, distorted, and exploitative. When a crisis erupts and attention is deemed necessary, foreign correspondents leave a comfortable world capital and catch a plane to the outpost where trouble is ensuing. The reporter figuratively "parachutes in," spends a few days, files the obligatory dispatches, and then returns to the more civilized base from whence the reporter came.

Many public journalism advocates also decry a system that produces journalists who are trained in a "determined detachment" that sets them apart from the consequences of their work.[19] Journalists "parachute" into disadvantaged communities, report on the latest drive-by shooting or unruly demonstration, then return to the safety of their newsroom to file stories that hopefully will lead to a career advance to a more prestigious newspaper. This transience "chills passions about place and time.The allure of better jobs at larger places {means] that the [journalists have] no lasting stake in the community, and so the problems in the current town need not be resolved, only reported on."[20]

Coups and Earthquakes. Advocates of development journalism argue that the Western press gives inadequate and superficial attention to positive developments in Third World countries, choosing instead to focus on discord, crisis, and upheaval. As Mustapha Masmoudi, a Tunisian who served as ambassador to UNESCO at the time of the MacBride Commissions, states, "The transnational media impose their own way of seeing upon the developing countries. . . . Moreover, [they often] present these communities—when indeed they show interest in them—in the most unfavorable light, stressing crises, strikes, street demonstrations. . . . or even holding them up to ridicule."[21]

Many public journalism advocates see a coups and earthquakes syndrome in the domestic coverage of America's news media. Negative stories dominate the headlines. Disadvantaged communities provide fodder for crime news and little else; failures and intractable problems are favored as good copy, and civil unrest and airplane crashes make the front page. Merritt suggests that a truly balanced headline would be, "25,890 Airplanes Land Safely: One Crashes in NYC."[22] Fouhy, formerly of the Pew Center for Civic Journalism, proposes that the negativity of traditional American reporting "encourages what one critic calls 'learned helplessness.'" It encourages the feeling that a problem is "so big, so complicated that the viewer or reader is left with a sense that it is beyond the capacity of ordinary men and women."[23]

Capitalist Imperatives. Many advocates of development journalism are from countries where there is no private ownership of the domestic press and there is no familiarity with the market imperative. These advocates do not consider news to be a saleable commodity, but a tool for directing public attitude formation and the development of national spirit and identity. They are more concerned about what news can or will do to a population, rather than about whether people will want to buy it as information to be consumed.[24]

Many public journalism advocates express contempt for market forces and regularly denounce those forces for encouraging journalistic sensationalism and hollow tabloid news values. "I personally think newspapers should stand for something," says Jim Walser, an assistant managing editor at *The Charlotte Observer*, which practices public journalism. "In the eyes of a lot of people, they've just become another big, corporate, money-sucking institution."[25] Public journalism advocates talk about the movement as a way to recapture an audience for news; however, most of the public journalism rhetoric is about the obligation of journalism to revitalize public life and to engage the citizenry to participate constructively in civic affairs.[26]

Solution Orientation. Advocates of development journalism argue that Western press values, which emphasize conflict and negative events as news, get in the way of solving critical national problems. They argue that critical reports hamper the speed of development. From a political perspective, Western press values are thought to be destabilizing to emerging, fragile governments and counterproductive to mobilizing a population for social and economic development. Journalism must be solution-oriented.

Public journalism advocates place a premium on journalism that offers solutions to public problems. To practitioner Merritt, traditional journalists thrive on conflict and black and white contests where there is little room for ambivalence or compromise. Traditional journalists have no interest or stake in seeing issues resolved, because conflict is their stock and trade. To Merritt, public journalism requires reporting the news "in a way that facilitates people thinking about solutions, not just problems and conflict. The most crucial thing is to figure out how you frame stories in a way that accomplishes that end."[27]

DANGEROUS PRESCRIPTION FOR THE NEWS MEDIA

It is tempting to draw further parallels between development journalism and the new public journalism. There is a remarkable similarity in the catalog of criticism aimed at traditional American journalism by development journalism advocates and the new critics found in the public journalism movement. The complaints cited here—about "parachute journalism," the coups and earthquakes syndrome, the capitalist imperative, and the preference for conflict over solution-oriented reporting in the news media—are only some of the most obvious examples of the similarity. Both the development journalism and the public journalism critique of traditional Western news values get at some perceived weaknesses that have been pointed out for years by many scholars of the mass media, both in America and abroad.

The dilemma is that regardless of the validity of the diagnosis of some of these news media ills, the prescriptives that are offered by both development journalism and public journalism are often fundamentally flawed. The cures are worse than the original maladies. In the case of the development journalism of the 1970s and 1980s, Rosenblum argues that this movement, fostered under NWICO, was largely discredited by the reality of the attempts to put the new information order philosophy into action.

Rosenblum contends that the conflict between traditional Western news media and Third World countries was not simply about misunderstanding. "It was a deep philosophical difference over the role of the press in society," declares Rosenblum. "Fragile governments wanted cheerleaders to help them attract foreign aid and win over their people to various social experiments. Correspondents felt obliged to work as they did everywhere else in the world, to call things as they saw them."[28] This created a chasm that was not easily bridged.

As the development journalism critique gained currency in the late 1970s and into the early 1980s, the Western press was increasingly targeted within UNESCO. Committees drafted news media policies to help countries impose controls over all reporters working within their borders. UNESCO members from the

Third World and the Soviet bloc pushed a plan to license journalists, allowing state officials the right to determine who qualified as a reporter or correspondent and what qualified as unbiased and useful journalistic reportage.

The most extreme prescriptions proposed by NWICO advocates in UNESCO during the 1970s and 1980s alarmed U.S. government officials and leaders of the American press. Some of the more extreme proposals in the NWICO deliberations called for government controls on any information crossing national borders, the imposition of codes of conduct or the licensing of correspondents, and the establishment of fines or even imprisonment to be levied against correspondents who insult or misrepresent host countries.[29]

These proposals served to discredit the NWICO analysis of the world news media situation and naturally prompted a stern reaction in the U.S. press. *Newsweek* saw the extreme positions of NWICO advocates as an attempt by Third World nations "to replace coverage of Western affairs with a collective, government-managed conduit of information."[30] The *Newsweek* condemnation was repeated in the editorial pages of U.S. daily newspapers across the country. *The New York Times* went so far as to suggest that it might be time for the U.S. to withdraw from the United Nations' UNESCO which, of course, the United States eventually did when its membership lapsed on December 31, 1984.[31]

In light of the outrage that ideas in the NWICO debate inspired in the American press a decade ago, it seems ironic that a number of news organizations are now accepting the NWICO critique of how the U.S. media operates, albeit on a domestic basis. Among the leaders of these news organizations, there is the same concern about negativity, conflict orientation, market considerations, and detachment as with the NWICO advocates of the 1970s and 1980s. Some of these news media outlets are the same media organizations that are now declaring themselves converts to the public journalism philosophy—organizations which are declaring a commitment to doing news differently and to experimenting with public journalism solutions.

Obviously, public journalism solutions being implemented in America do not involve the licensing of reporters or the establishment of fines or prison penalties against journalists who are too insulting or too negative about civic life. However, public journalism solutions fundamentally challenge certain principles that have, in the past, ensured a viable and independent news media. Two of these principles are detachment and objectivity.

Public journalism advocates exhort communicators to jettison detachment and to become actors in public life. This means joining with citizen groups, civic leaders, and other constituencies in determining and acting on a public agenda. However, once journalism becomes wedded to any public agenda, it loses much of its ability to be critical and independent; it has become part of the process and subordinated its critical function to the need to act for the common good, whatever that is perceived to be.

Public journalism advocates also exhort communicators to jettison objectivity, calling it a fruitless cliché.[32] There is no question that objectivity is, in fact, an elusive ideal. However, if the pursuit of this ideal is abandoned, then everything becomes relative. The mission of attempting to tell the news in a fair, balanced, and objective manner becomes secondary to some broader mission of "helping public life go well." The ideal is lost to the need to act for the common good.

The danger in this is not so readily apparent in a democratic society where there are other checks and balances to compensate for a less critical and less independent Fourth Estate. However, when public journalism—with its deflation of the values of detachment and objectivity—is applied on a global scale, the dangers become much more obvious. This is because it plays into the hands of authoritarians who have always argued that too much criticism and negativity in the news media is harmful to national development. It plays into the hands of despots who argue that communicators should be instruments of the common good of the state.

This is the challenge for foundations, news organizations, and international communication scholars who seek to inject public journalism ideas into the new world information debate, or who might even wish to champion public journalism ideas on a global scale. They must confront the possibility of how these new ideas can be used to serve and justify less than noble ends. There is some substance in the public journalism critique of traditional news operations that is valid and valuable, just as there is much that came out of the NWICO debate of the 1970s and 1980s that is worth examining. The danger is in moving too quickly from the critique to solutions which discard values and ideals that have not been arrived at so easily. These are values and ideas which may, in fact, have special relevance in the new global context. They are ideals and values which are not so readily discredited.

William F. Woo, former editor of the *St. Louis Post-Dispatch*, made this same point in a speech critical of public journalism at the University of California–Riverside in February 1995. "These values have long histories, they reflect how journalists have struggled to confront the circumstances of their eras. They have become part of a moral philosophy. In short, they are a moral imperative. . . . Before we set them aside, before we declare them obsolete and rush on to something else, we need to understand carefully what we are throwing out."[33]

NOTES

1. Clifford Christians, Mark Fackler, and John Ferré, *Good News—Social Ethics & the Press* (New York: Oxford University Press, 1993), pp. 13–17.

2. Jay Black, ed., *Mixed News: The Public/Civic/Communitarian Journalism Debate* (New Jersey: Lawrence Erlbaum Associates, 1997), p. 54.

3. J. H. Altschull, *Agents of Power: The Media and Public Policy* (White Plains, New York: Longman, 1995), p. 196.

4. Clifford G. Christians, "The Common Good in a Global Setting," paper presented at the AEJMC Convention, Washington, D.C., August, 1995, p. 2.

5. Ibid., pp. 2–3.

6. Ibid., cover page abstract.

7. Ed Fouhy, remarks made at the panel session, "Teaching Civic Journalism 1: Reports from the Newsroom," presented at the AEJMC Convention, Anaheim, California, August, 1996.

8. John Dinges, "Civic Journalism Comes to Buenos Aires," *Civic Catalyst* (July, 1996), p. 14.

9. Fouhy, op. cit.

10. Jay Rosen, "Public Journalism Forum," remarks made at the Investigate Reporters & Editors (IRE) Convention, June, 1995.

11. Davis Merritt, remarks made at the panel session, "Public Journalism: Can It Cure What Ails the News Business?" presented at the AEJMC Convention, Washington, D.C., August, 1995.

12. Ibid.

13. Rosen, op. cit.

14. Davis Merritt, *Public Journalism & Public Life: Why Telling the News Isn't Enough* (Hilldale, New Jersey: Lawrence Erlbaum Associates, 1995), p. 113.

15. Ibid., p. 114.

16. "A Bow to Big Brother," *Newsweek* (September 6, 1976), pp. 69–70.

17. Mort Rosenblum, *Who Stole the News? Why We Can't Keep Up with What Happens in the World* (New York: John Wiley & Sons, 1993), p. 271.

18. Rosenblum, op. cit., p. 271.

19. Jay Rosen, Davis Merritt, "Imagining Public Journalism: An Editor and Scholar Reflect on the Birth of an Idea." Roy W. Howard Public Lecture, Indiana University, April, 1995, pp. 8–9.

20. Merritt, op. cit., pp. 42–43.

21. Masmoudi Mustapha, "The New World Information Order." Document No. 31 submitted to the MacBride Commission (Paris: UNESCO, 1978).

22. Merritt, op. cit., p. 19.

23. *Civic Journalism: A Video Study Guide* (Washington, D.C., Pew Center for Civic Journalism, 1995), pp. 2–3.

24. John C. Merrill, *Global Journalism* (New York: Longman, 1983) from chapter, "Africa," by John L. Martin, pp. 239–240.

25. Mike Hoyt, "Are You Now or Will You Ever Be, a Civic Journalist," *Columbia Journalism Review* (September/October, 1995), p. 31.

26. *Civic Journalism: A Video Study Guide* (Washington, D.C., Pew Center for Civic Journalism, 1995), pp. 2–3.

27. Hoyt, op. cit., p. 31.

28. Rosenblum, op. cit., p. 272.

29. Narinder K. Aggrawala, "A Third World Perspective on the News," *Freedom at Issue Report*, May–June, 1978.

30. "A Bow to Big Brother," *Newsweek* (September 6, 1976), pp. 69–70.

31. "UNESCO as Censor" *New York Times* (October 24, 1980), p. A32.

32. Jay Rosen, "Public Journalism Forum," remarks made at the Investigate Reporters & Editors (IRE) Convention, June, 1995.

33. William Woo, "Should the Press Be an Observer or Actor in Public Affairs," *St. Louis Journalism Review* (July/August 1995), pp. 10–12.

10
The Real Problems
Facing Journalism

This book takes issue with public journalism's critique of contemporary journalism and also with its formulations for making journalism better. This is not to suggest that today's practice of journalism is without fault. There is much that is wrong. The problems are deep and endemic.

Thinking journalists are right to be concerned about their profession and the direction in which it is heading. They are quite right to ask whether today's journalism is, indeed, serving the needs of the public. But it is this book's contention that concerned journalists would be better off studying the annual yearbooks of Project Censored, than immersing themselves in the intellectual journey of public journalism. Project Censored, of course, is the annual compilation of significant stories that never seem to find their way into the mainstream news media.[1] The concerned journalist should take the intellectual journey to find out why sparse news coverage is given to environmental crises, white-collar crimes, threats to national health, international scandals, and political corruption as specifically compiled by Project Censored.

In the spirit of Project Censored's annual listing of the top sins of omission in reporting—sins committed by the mainstream news media—this chapter presents the top 10 problems afflicting today's news media. Public journalists such as James Fallows take exception to the creation of lists and the quantifying of issues or problems. They criticize this cataloging as part of the shallowness of much of today's journalism. If the listing of the top 10 faults of today's journalism is superficial, the problems themselves are hardly ephemeral. In fact, the complaints that public journalism advocates level at today's journalism seem petty in comparison to the list assembled here. The problems defined here have been presented in more depth—and perhaps even in a more articulate fashion—elsewhere. What is presented here is a starting point for further intellectual journeys into what really ails the news media.

Lack of Competition

The problem of the lack of competition in the media industry in the United States has been repeated so many times it has become a cliché. Nevertheless, the growth of the news monopoly in America has had a profound effect on the gathering and dissemination of news. When Ben Bagdikian first published *The Media Monopoly* in the early 1980s, about 50 corporations controlled most of the major media outlets in America: 1,787 daily newspapers; 11,000 magazines; 9,000 radio stations; 1,000 television stations; 2,500 book publishers, and seven major movie studios. By the time Bagdikian released the fourth edition of his book in 1993, the number was down to 20 corporations and is still dropping.[2]

At the end of World War II, 80 percent of U.S. newspapers were family-owned. Today, most are controlled by 20 chains.[3] At the end of World War II, many cities were served by two, three, or four daily newspapers. Today, there are only a small number of cities in America with competing daily newspapers. The increase of the one-newspaper town situation is usually attributed to the loss of a reading public, but closer examination will sometimes reveal monopoly capitalism at work. For example, in cities such as Cleveland and St. Louis, competing news companies simply arranged for one daily newspaper to fold in exchange for a long-term, profit-sharing agreement.

It can be argued that the rise of the one-newspaper town is part of what has made public journalism possible. It's highly unlikely that a daily newspaper in a competitive newspaper environment would cede its front pages to public journalism projects, while rival papers consistently trumped it with real front-page news stories about events in the community. A newspaper that devoted its front pages to series stories about restoring public life, or reviving the community with a vision for the future, would quickly lose the battle for readers to competitors with hard-hitting news and human interest stories.

The public journalism movement does not address the problem of the homogenized news product that has resulted because of one-newspaper towns and the growth of newspaper chains. Instead, public journalism has exacerbated the problem by fostering collaborative projects. These collaborative ventures can involve a newspaper, radio, and television stations working on the same journalistic project in a given market. These ventures can also involve several newspapers in a state running the same election stories as part of campaign coverage. Obviously, public journalism's collaborative approach to news simply further reduces the information choices available to audiences.

There is no easy solution to the lack of media competition within the United States. The U.S. Supreme Court, the Congress, and a succession of U.S. presidents have taken measures for two decades that only make it easier for monopoly growth within the news industry. It would take an enormous public outcry to get our government to change course and restrict media ownership in the public interest, especially with the considerable political clout of giant media corporations. If there is any light in this tunnel of steamrolling media conglomerates, it is in the rise of numerous small, alternative voices within communities during the past two decades. The new technologies in desktop publishing, offset printing, and internet websites have made it possible for a democratization and decentralization in news media on a grass-roots level. Journalism schools should put less emphasis on training reporters for metro daily jobs that don't exist and put more energy into training communication entrepreneurs who can become Davids willing to challenge the media Goliaths with tools of the new technologies.

Narrowing of Political Discussion

The golden age of political discourse in this country was well before the rise of the Hearst and Pulitzer empires at the end of the nineteenth century. The era occurred in a period roughly between the first presidential administration of George Washington and the commencing of the Civil War. During that period, a politicized press in this country debated the ideas of Thomas Jefferson and Alexander Hamilton and their respective visions for America. The period of the political press was not particularly harmonious. Newspaper editors were accused of sedition and treasonous behavior by their detractors; charges and counter-charges filled the papers. The range of political discussion in the press in this country narrowed after the Civil War. It was dramatically reduced in this century with the rise of the Red Scare and the Palmer raids brought on by the Bolshevik Revolution in Russia in 1917.

Since World War II, the relatively small continuum of cultural and political currents expressed in the mainstream news media has further contracted. Compared to the depth and breadth of political discussion in the news media of Western Europe, the American diet of political and cultural discourse is paltry, indeed.

The narrowing of political discussion has resulted in cries of an information-control conspiracy from both the right-wing and the left-wing in the United States. The right cries out against what it sees as a liberal-controlled news media with a bias toward big government, secular humanism, and political correctness; and the left cries out against what it sees as a conservative-controlled news media of right-wing pundits, commentators of the status quo, and mouthpieces for big business. Both sides accuse the mainstream news media of trivializing, stifling, or ignoring their viewpoints; both sides have some foundation for their complaints. Occasionally the frustration of the two sides boils over in such displays as small-scale militia actions on the right or pointless acts of ecoterrorism on the left. There is concern that these outbursts may be on the increase.

The irony of public journalism is that the implementation of its philosophy and practice is likely to further narrow the range of political and cultural discussion in the news media. Public journalism advocates contend that today's new media already gives too much voice to the extremes, and not enough attention is given to those who are ambivalent or undecided on various political and cultural issues. "Journalists keep trying to find people who are 1 and 9 on a scale of 1 to 10, rather than at 3 to 7 where people actually are," declares public journalism advocate Cole Campbell.[4] Campbell fails to realize that many of the people in the ambivalent middle are aided in their decision-making by the opportunity to examine the logic and character of those who represent issues on the extremes. Part of the press's democratic function is to provide a forum for the extremes.

Public journalists argue that giving voice to extremes prevents any resolution of important issues. But are journalists supposed to be experts in conflict resolution? Who assigned journalists the charge of searching for common ground? Should journalists be tailoring information to promote societal harmony or is their charge to gather and accurately communicate a wide array of perspectives on issues as part of the process of democratic decision-making?

Public journalists are convinced that the public is fed up with negative, conflict-oriented, adversarial reporting, but surveys reveal that the chief public complaint against the press is actually bias. Adoption of public journalism will only add fuel to the fire for those on the right and the left who see a conspiracy of information control in this country.

American journalism should make a concerted effort to widen, not narrow, the range of political and cultural discourse. Talk radio and talk television shows, which have come under fire from public journalists, should continue to provide an avenue of expression for all manner of ideas. Daily newspapers should run excerpts of editorial opinion from around the world, and not just from domestic outlets. The nation's dailies should also drop the highly-paid, syndicated pundits of corporate journalism and expand their op-ed pages to include not only the ambivalent middle, but also the off-beat, the reactionary, and the radical.

Subservience to the Political System

The major problem of American politics is not a yapping, venal, adversarial press that drives off the good people from entering public life, as many of the public journalists maintain. The major problem of American politics is big money, no matter its source. Among the many reasons that a plurality of Americans hold politicians in contempt is the belief that politicians are for sale. No other established democracy in the world permits such a rancid, money-soaked electoral process as America.

Campaign reform is an issue that goes to the heart of democracy. Yet none of the public journalism tracts, which rave about the need to revive democracy in apocalyptic terms, focus on campaign reform. None of them decry the spectacle of the average voter as a mere spectator in a democracy dominated and overrun by big campaign donors. Instead, public journalists like Davis Merritt worry about the "grief imposed by cynical and suspicious journalists" on those in public life.[5]

The news media can play a role to revive the flagging democracy, but it will not be accomplished by reporters becoming less cynical and less suspicious of politicians. It can be accomplished by holding politicians' feet to the fire over the scandalous money-machine that turns the wheels of both political parties. If politicians are ever to recapture the confidence of the American public, they have to cease raising political contributions in sums that buy congressional votes and presidential nods on policy issues.

Public journalism advocates insist that traditional journalists fret too much about detachment—they should worry less about separations and more about proper connections.[6] There is absolutely no question that the media is properly connected when it comes to big money politics. It's no wonder that the media exhaled a collective sigh of relief years ago when the U.S. Supreme Court ruled that under our Constitution money talks and receives First Amendment consideration. The American media benefit every election cycle with millions of dollars of soft campaign money as well as the dollars dialed in directly to particular politicians. Tens of millions of dollars are spent on candidates' TV attack ads, radio spots, and full-page political endorsements.

Could it be that the news media have not made campaign reform the issue it should be, because the news media lack the the proper detachment? Could it be that the news media lack the focus and attention for the campaign reform issue because many of the biggest campaign donors are also major media advertisers and owners who prefer the status quo?

Dominance of Public Relations

As corporations take on more of our society's decision-making responsibility, their public relations departments are controlling more and more information, placing it into context, and engineering its impact. It is often impossible to report on the most important business decisions—decisions that have enormous consequences for millions of people—in any detail. Laws governing access to information focus the light on governmental entities, while corporations that are the major beneficiaries of a generous federal government operate in the dark, immune from scrutiny.

There are far more corporate spin doctors than there are reporters, and they are generally paid at least twice as much as the journalists who increasingly rely on them for information. In fact, many of the country's best and brightest journalists cross the line to public relations careers, often becoming the hired hands of the companies and agencies they once covered ostensibly in the public interest.

The continual "downsizing" at many media corporations means there are fewer journalists available to research original material and to handle news. Public relations operatives have moved into the vacuum to pick up the slack. Recent studies indicate that as much as 80 percent of national news stories originate from press releases that are "pitched" by public relations personnel.[7] Some agencies provide "info-tainment" packages and videotape interview splices that are disguised on local television news as original material. Understaffed newspaper operations are often running agency press releases unedited, or allowing agency personnel to actually write stories.

These intrusions by public relations personnel into the news process— breaches that once were considered matters of journalistic integrity or ethics— have become more acceptable in the current news environment. This is because many newspaper and television news operations have dropped the so-called watchdog function of news in favor of a role as civic booster and community cheerleader. In this atmosphere, a silver lining is found for every cloud on the horizon—corporate takeovers of hometown companies become mergers; job lay-offs become "downsizing;" in the name of efficiency, crime-ridden neighborhoods become sites for civic renewal and discovery of community assets.

In the current news environment, the line between journalist and the public relations writer become blurred—both are simply communicators and their pur-poses are not markedly different. This becomes most obvious in some public jour-nalism experiments in which news outlets and public relations firms are partnered in an effort to create news projects which will make public life go well. Other projects team up news outlets with chambers of commerce and other business organizations to promote communities as good places to locate companies and industrial sites.

In order for journalists to recapture the franchise of "news," which by any reasonable standard is strictly and properly their domain, journalism organizations must reexamine codes of ethics and make some noise when these codes are vio-lated. Schools of journalism should take up the task they've lost sight of—the task of instructing future reporters in the substantive differences between journalism and public relations. Too many schools are going in precisely the opposite direc-tion. They are teaching courses such as "media writing," which combine report-ing, public relations, and advertising writing, and which treat them as modes of expression that are interchangeable and only marginally different from each other. Some purists argue that journalism departments should not even be housed in the same university schools as public relations and advertising. They insist on "proper separations" which would house public relations and advertising in university marketing and business programs.

"There are too many journalism degrees granted by departments and schools that show little separation between church and state," declares Ben Bagdikian, former dean of the graduate school of journalism at the University of California at Berkeley. "Such institutional programs display too little regard for the difference between, on one hand, journalism as a public service and, on the other, advertising and public relations."[8]

Decline of Investigative Reporting

Investigative reporting was once the most esteemed and coveted genre in the world of journalism. Reporters who performed in exemplary fashion covering police beats and city hall hoped for promotion to investigative work, a beat area where they would be given time to research and develop stories that would serve the citizenry and that could make institutions more accountable.

The investigative bent of American journalism can be traced as far back as the colonial period. Benjamin Franklin published a rationale for investigative journalism in his Cato's letters. That rationale is still widely quoted today as a defense for the work of the muckraker. A muckraking newspaper man himself, Franklin, under the pseudonym Cato, wrote, "The exposing therefore of public Wickedness as it is a Duty which every Man owes to his country, can never be a Libel in the Nature of things, The best Way to escape the Virulence of Libels, is not to deserve them. . . . It is nothing strange that men who think themselves unaccountable, should act unaccountably."[9]

Muckraking journalism performs a useful policy purpose in American democracy by exposing its shortcomings so that they may be righted. According to *The Journalism of Outrage*, a popular investigative reporting text, the formula of the muckraking exposé includes a cast of characters inextricably bound to the failings of the American social system. They include:

1. Elected officials who may be held accountable to the legal requisites of their office and the moral principles of public service.
2. Political office seekers whose public and private integrity may be challenged.
3. Government bureaucrats expected to administer programs and enforce regulations in their domains.
4. Business executives whose commitment to corporate responsibility may be tested.
5. An array of victims, including taxpayers and consumers, who expect their public and private services to be delivered with honesty, efficiency, and fairness.[10]

The most powerful investigative journalism of our time, the Watergate exposé, brought together this complete cast of characters and more. There were many reporters on the Watergate story, and they were able to expose a myriad of failings in the American political and social system. Many of those failings remain uncorrected, but we are still better off today because we are better informed about the nature of those failings we continue to face.

In the post-Watergate era, the image of Nixon, our first president to resign from office in disgrace, has been softened by revisionist historians and pundits who emphasize his supposed foreign policy triumphs. Even as more revelations come out about Nixon—from his paranoia and anti-semitism, to his ruthless tactics to destroy his enemies at home and abroad—there are those inclined to pardon Nixon while denigrating the hard work of journalists who exposed his wrongdoing and the irresponsible actions of his administration.

Public journalism champion Davis "Buzz" Merritt in his book *Public Journalism & Public Life*, chides *The Washington Post*'s Ben Bradlee and Sally Quinn for walking out on a luncheon speech given by Nixon in 1984 before the American Society of Newspaper Editors (ASNE). He describes their symbolic act of departure as self-indulgent and a "display of congenital journalistic toughness," and contrasts it with Nixon's "astonishing, nearly inhuman display of grit."[11]

Merritt devotes much of his primer on public journalism denouncing what he describes as the "post-Watergate syndrome" among journalists. He accuses traditional journalists of a "relentless search for the next Watergate," of a relentless exhibition of toughness for its own sake," of "treating all political figures at any level as suspects in the next Whatever-Gate."[12] It is a disservice to reporting that public journalists seem intent on making the Watergate reporting triumph into a symbol and symptom of journalistic malfeasance and excess, rather than a representation of one of journalism's finest hours.

The need for real investigative journalism has never been greater. The dismal performance of the press in the last decade—missing such stories as the effects of merger mania, the decline of the American middle class, and the multi-billion dollar savings and loan scandal—underscores the need for serious investigative reporting. If journalism is to do better, publishers need to send news employees to Investigative Reporters and Editors (IRE) seminars, instead of to consultants with expertise in deliberative dialogue. If journalism is to survive and have an impact, it will have to become more adversarial, not less so, as the public journalists prescribe. It will have to make some people mad.

Media critic Howard Kurtz makes this point in his own prescription for reviving journalism, "A good newspaper should be like the feisty columnist that readers love to hate but would never dream of missing. When the president tells an obvious fib, let's call him out on strikes. When the mayor blows a big decision, why not holler: Throw the bum out! If a big corporation is giving some poor soul the shaft, let's blow the whistle."[13]

Disappearing International News

"When journalists begin acting like waiters and taking orders from the public and pollsters, the results are not pretty," declares journalist David Remnick in an analysis of public journalism for the *New Yorker*. Remnick cited the example of *The Miami Herald*, which polled its audience to decide where it should concentrate its news resources. Sports got high marks. Foreign affairs lost out.[14]

There is something seriously wrong with reacting to polls, surveys, and focus groups that say international news is simply irrelevant. All too often, news organizations are taking the view that international news is not a priority. Fewer and fewer of the major U.S. dailies and television operations are funding permanent foreign bureaus and international correspondents. News from foreign outposts is collected haphazardly from freelance correspondents whose credentials and reliability are often questionable. The news itself gets snipped, dismembered, and stuffed into little parcels in news sections headlined, "The World in Brief."

The irony in all this is that the world has become a much smaller place where events around the globe can have an immediate impact at home. Another irony is that the communication technology available for correspondents to cover faraway places has never been more sophisticated and effective. Nevertheless, news executives have been led to believe that Americans really don't care about international news. They also share an erroneous belief with many American political leaders, that, with the end of the Cold War, international news has lost much of its critical value and importance to the public.

Mort Rosenblum, special correspondent for the Associated Press, contends that news executives and American political leaders are wrong about the importance of foreign affairs in the post-Cold War era. He writes that he was troubled throughout the 1992 campaign when George Bush continually boasted that American children could now sleep safely with a new world order. "We [correspondents] might have chimed in: The Soviet arsenal is fragmented, with lots of fingers on triggers. China is buying much of it. Black marketeers are after nuclear components. Japan has plutonium. The Balkans are boiling. The Kremlin was a threat, but [at least] it policed its satellites and clients. How out of touch are we?"[15]

"Dime a Dozen" Journalists

Public journalism advocates call for reporters to make fundamental shifts in the way they perceive the subjects of their work; make changes in their newsroom culture that allow for more reflection and deliberation; and transform their journalism into a mechanism for finding solutions to public problems.

But reporters are hardly in a position to make any kind of revolution within their newsrooms. The values shaping newsroom culture come from the top, from the corporate headquarters, the publisher, or the chief news executive. In fact, at most news organizations where public journalism ideas and practices have been initiated, the drive for such change has come from the top. Reporters who've had philosophic or ethical dilemmas over such practices have either had to quietly acquiesce or they've re-entered the job market as refugees from public journalism.

The intrinsic value of journalists to news executives has greatly diminished since the days of William Rockhill Nelson, founder and owner of *The Kansas City Evening Star*. In 1880, Nelson expressed his belief that reporters should be "wholly free to labor for the interests of the people and to wage warfare upon the corrupt." In serving these noble aims, Nelson declared, "the reporter is the essential man on the newspaper. . . . [We] should go to smash if we had no reporters."[16]

In his afterword to Weaver and Wilhoit's study, *The American Journalist in the 1990s*, Trevor Brown contrasts Nelson's philosophy with that of Michael D. Eisner, chairman of the Walt Disney Company, when he acquired *The Kansas City Evening Star* as part of the second-largest media acquisition ever in 1995. To finance the takeover of Capital Cities/ABC, Eisner had to cut costs and increase the revenues of newly-acquired properties. Reporting staffs were reduced—debt service became far more important than the public service of journalists.[17] This story has been repeated in media mergers and takeovers around the country.

As Weaver and Wilhoit point out, there is a stark contrast between the income and lifestyle of the mythical Murphy Brown and that of the typical journalist, who often works in a downsized news organization. In 1992, only one percent of American journalists earned more than $100,000. The median salary was about $30,000, far less than the earnings of lawyers, engineers, or accountants. A survey of U.S. journalism professors regarding the beginning salaries for their graduates, appearing in the *St. Louis Journalism Review* in 1990, revealed that newly-hired reporters' wages were so low that some were eligible for food stamps.[18]

In their study, Weaver and Wilhoit found a significant decline in perceived job autonomy as well as diminished job satisfaction among the reporters whom they surveyed. Other comparable professional occupations have not experienced the same declines. Weaver and Wilhoit reported that the sense of public service "that has long been an attraction for journalists does seem threatened" by the

trends affecting employment in journalism.[19] The loss of autonomy and job satisfaction had many reporters in Weaver and Wilhoit's study indicating that they
were contemplating career changes.

Those concerned with changing the direction of journalism and transforming the newsroom culture would be better off devoting their energies to improving
the salaries, working conditions, job security, and autonomy of reporters. Academics might spend less time speculating about how journalists "frame" stories or
how they use "explanatory journalism in the enlightenment function," and instead
spend more time studying beginning salaries for their student graduates as well as
their access to collective bargaining.

Demise of the Written Word

The true history of American journalism is a history of words. It's not about
the highest salaries ever paid to those anchoring the evening news. It's not about
the number of channels available on a satellite transponder to convey news to
audiences a half a world away. It's not even about the latest multibillion-dollar
media merger that will give media moguls with names like Murdoch and Eisner
unparalleled power in communication. The pure, unadulterated history of journalism remains a history of words.

It's a history of Thomas Paine writing about the "summer soldier and the
sunshine patriot." It's black journalist Frederick Douglass putting words on paper
describing a slave escaping from bondage and finding a free life before the Civil
War. It's a woman named Elizabeth Cochrane, calling herself "Nellie Bly," and
writing about a fantastic trip around the world in a balloon. It's muckraker Lincoln
Steffans writing fearlessly about corruption in Philadelphia, "a disgrace not to
itself alone, nor to Pennsylvania, but to the United States and to American character." It's Ernie Pyle writing about death and farewell to Captain Waskow in
World War II. It's Mike Royko writing about Jackie Robinson under a headline,
"The Man Who Almost Ruined Baseball."

It's also the history of a loud-mouthed Walter Winchell creating words like
"Reno-vated," "Chicagorilla," "middle-aisled," "nupted," "debutramp," and "in-
fanticipating," in smarmy columns to describe life in the fast lane in the Depression era.[20] Contrast Winchell's hot-as-a-sparkler vocabulary with the invented
phraseology of public journalism, with its "civic mapping," "connectedness,"
"issue-myopia," "paradigm shift," and "trained incapacity." The public journalists
would no doubt criticize Walter Winchell today for being overpaid and conflict-
oriented, for concentrating his reporting on celebrities and mobsters. But the outrageous Winchell knew how to connect with citizens, and his vocabulary struck a
chord with the public.

Regardless of how well-intentioned public journalists may be in their effort
to re-invigorate democracy, they cannot be easily forgiven if their version of
Orwellian "Newspeak" is allowed to seep into the language of journalism. Unfortunately, this is precisely what has happened at a host of U.S. daily newspapers.
This unseemly intrusion is one indication of how the written word has been

devalued. Thoughtful and original journalistic prose is discarded in favor of the language of the social engineer and the consultant. Editors attempting to connect with the citizenry exhort them to engage in "effective deliberation" to shape and act upon "a common agenda."[21]

The barons of daily newspapering are at wits' end to figure how circulations can continue their downward spiral, even with the disappearance of that competitor across town. Instead of calling in the consultants, the leadership gurus, and the connecting experts, perhaps the new CEOs of news might consider putting some energy into discovering journalistic talent. Forget the pundits and the syndicated columnists, throw open the gates to new voices—voices that are shrill and angry as well as voices that are uproarious, bawdy, and incurably cynical.

Turn the writers loose, demands *Washington Post* press critic Howard Kurtz in his prescription for saving the nation's floundering daily newspapers. "Let individual voices emerge from the bland chorus of daily journalism," he declares in *Media Circus* in his concluding chapter on reclaiming the franchise. "We are a writer's medium; let's exploit that to the fullest."[22]

Failure of Journalism Schools

Journalism is not brain surgery, nor is it rocket science. It lacks the mathematical precision and the proven laws that govern much of the sciences. These humbling matters of fact are a source of discomfort to many journalism professors, who find that their area of study is not held in the same regard as traditional academic disciplines such as chemistry, biology, political science, or economics. This position of supposed inferiority in the academy, while unwarranted in many respects, nevertheless goads scholars of journalism to build elaborate theories and constructs about what journalism as communication is all about. The irony of this phenomenon is that it often gets in the way of teaching students the most rudimentary information about writing and reporting.

The most dramatic evidence of this comes at the annual conventions of the Association for Education in Journalism and Mass Communication (AEJMC) where all manner of esoteric research papers are presented. Papers cover topics from the effect of birth order on journalists' disposition toward careers in feature writing or investigative reporting to the latest treatises on civic journalism's impact on agenda-setting in disadvantaged communities. Only a minute portion, if any, of the research papers focus on the quest for ways to improve the skills of students who want to write for a living. If the best minds in journalism education are absorbed in such arcane research, is it any wonder that journalism school graduates often are not meeting the basic expectations of the job market?

The problems identified here are not unknown among those in journalism education. Anyone who is skeptical about the presence of these concerns can read the Freedom Forum study released in 1996. Conducted by journalism department chair Betty Medsger of San Francisco State University, the report was based on a poll of 1,041 print and broadcast journalists, 446 journalism educators, and 500 newsroom recruiters and supervisors.[23]

Medsger identified several trends that are troubling to those concerned with the validity and effectiveness of journalism education. Those disturbing trends include emphasis on communication theory at the expense of basic reporting and writing skills; emphasis on faculty members with doctorates and academic backgrounds rather than journalistic experience; and elimination of journalism as a stand-alone major and its absorption into a murky palette of communication studies.

Perhaps more telling than the statistical breakdowns of opinions by professors and editors on various issues in Medsger's study was the inclusion of a "Voices" section in which academics and practitioners commented on their unhappiness with the state of journalism education. Ben Bagdikian, former dean of the University of California at Berkeley, was particularly outspoken in his criticism of the "idiocy of requiring journalism teachers to have doctoral degrees." Bagdikian also is wary of schools of communication with advertising, public relations, and communication under the same umbrella with journalism. "Either make the Association for Education in Journalism and Mass Communication create a separate group for journalism—minus advertising, minus public relations, and minus communication theory—or have journalism faculties who hold to high values secede from AEJMC to form their own national body with accrediting powers."[24]

Over and over in the Medsger study were calls for professors to spend less time on contriving elaborate theory papers and more time on teaching journalism basics. "All young journalists should be required to cover fires and write obits," said Bob Meyers, director of the Washington Journalism Center in the nation's capitol. "If you get it wrong there, you will never learn to get it right, and no amount of technology is going to save you. I let this be known to all younger journalists I encounter. Many of them are surprised. They thought deep thinking and mastery of the Web were all they would need."[25]

Lee Stinnett, executive director of the American Society of Newspaper Editors, told Medsger that university emphasis on Ph.D.s and academic research was counterproductive for journalism. "Journalism schools are being tempted by a faulty anti-teaching, research-dominated mindset that has permeated university thinking and corrupted its values," said Stinnett. "The research that's come out of journalism schools, with few notable exceptions, has little value to the profession."[26]

Crisis of Self-Confidence

A decline in esteem and a lack of self-confidence have sent journalists into a tailspin. Instead of focusing on the fundamentals of their calling, editors and news managers have wrung their collective hands, hired consultants, formed committees, and held endless newsroom meetings to discuss abstractions which they hope will provide some remedy. The result of all this commotion is that even journalists are left questioning the role of information gathering in our society.

Yet, the role of information gathering is still very much what it was 200 years ago when Thomas Jefferson concluded that one could not have a democratic government without a free and unfettered press. If the people are sovereign, then they must have a press which never loses sight of its primary mission. The mission is to lay out the issues as fairly as possible so that the people can be informed and engage in democratic decision-making. If this seems oversimplified and naive, it is only because the communication experts, corporate consultants, foundation mavens, and executives of media monopolies have clouded that function.

Pulitzer Prize winner and Ames, Iowa *Daily Tribune* editor Michael Gartner elaborated on that primary mission of the news media before an audience of University of Iowa Journalism School students in 1997. He urged them to take a stand against the civic (or public) journalism philosophy, such as that promoted by the Pew Charitable Trusts, because it compromises their ability to seek the truth.

"News pages are supposed to explain their community, not convene it," emphasized Gartner. "News reporters are supposed to explore issues, not solve them. Newspapers are supposed to expose the wrongs. . . . They're supposed to tell the truth, and God knows that's hard enough to do all by itself."[27] Gartner told the young reporters that they should look to themselves to provide better community coverage—not rely on polls and focus groups funded by outside sources. Gartner added, "They [Pew Charitable Trusts] have bought their way into newsrooms and no one seems to care."[28]

The invasion of foundation operatives, communication consultants, and leadership experts into a number of the nation's newsrooms is evidence of a growing crisis of self-confidence among journalists. Reporters with 15, 20, or 25 years of experience covering the public are suddenly at the feet of consultants who lecture them in the ways of engaging an elusive citizenry. Suddenly, veteran journalists are told that they need help redefining their core professional values and help with connecting to various levels of a multilayered public.

Journalists need to fight back—not simply against the nuisance of newsroom consultants, but against a whole range of noisome meddling that has the profession under siege. Public journalism advocates drone on about the need for proper connections and the need for less concern about the principle of detachment. If there is one place where journalists should show less detachment, it is in the battle to protect their own self-esteem and the integrity of their practice. There are a number of ways to fight back.

Local Journalism Reviews. The first journalism review is often traced to Chicago in the late 1960s, when reporters started a monthly publication to run stories "spiked" or censored by news executives under pressure from forces outside the newsroom. Reviews flourished around the country in the 1970s, but then began to die out. Reporters from different media outlets should cooperate to reestablish local journalism reviews.

Desktop publishing and offset printing have made reviews much easier to establish than they were in the late 1960s. Journalism reviews are a way for reporters to self-police their profession. They can blow the whistle on media companies that treat employees unfairly, engage in unethical journalism practices, or kill stories because of advertising or political pressure. Journalism reviews, though small in circulation, wield power by virtue of exposure. An alarming story in a review often gets picked up by other media for wider dissemination and impact.

Working Conditions. While journalists at Guild newspapers are adequately paid and often have access to levers to improve their working environment, many journalists work in sweatshop environments with wages that are poverty level. These situations should become the target of scrutiny by journalist organizations such as the Society of Professional Journalists (SPJ), the Investigative Reporters and Editors (IRE), and the Guild and Communication Workers of America (CWA). Journalism professors can play a role by researching conditions and publishing guides to the "100 Best" and "100 Worst" news organizations to work for. Company profits, operating expenditures, CEO salaries, and employee remuneration should be examined.

Reining in PR. As news organizations rely increasingly on "info-tainment" pieces, video interview clips, and story material generated by public relations operatives, they have less need for journalists. The journalists are simply there as a conduit to reframe material so the public remains convinced all of it is journalism. Professional journalism organizations should establish strict guidelines on what constitutes acceptable use of public relations materials. Violations of these guidelines should be the subject of academic research papers and journalism review stories.

Reining in Lawyers. "Published and be damned!" used to be the rallying cry of news operations dedicated to the people's right to know. The new proviso is simply, "Don't offend." Now stories are "lawyered" to death, not only to avoid the danger of libel suits, "but also to ward off complaints from powerful people, interest groups, or sensitive collectives."[29] Lawyers always tend to err on the side of extreme caution, and in many instances have robbed the editorial prerogative of editors and reporters.

Professional journalism organizations should establish guidelines on what constitutes the appropriate purview of media attorneys as they scrutinize a story before it goes to press. These organizations should also put pressure on the bar and the courts to sort out the maze of privacy and libel regulation in this country to establish standards that do not inhibit a free press. Efforts in these areas of media litigation should be the subject of academic research papers and journalism review stories.

Reining in Consultants. The entry of foundations and consultants into newsrooms presents a dangerous precedent. Public journalists argue that the intentions of foundations such as Pew and Kettering are benign and should not raise red flags. Perhaps the intentions of the foundations are honorable, but, once the gate is open, who decides what foundation money to fund news projects is acceptable and what money is tainted? What are the consequences if news organizations come to depend on foundation money for special projects? The precedent of news organizations taking subsidies is a dangerous one. A prohibition on such intrusions is the most effective way to guarantee that the wrong decisions won't be made.

Consultants present another dilemma and are a classic example of an infringement on the autonomy of journalists. Consultants can be useful in the age of digitalized news, full color pages, and computer-assisted reporting, but there is a problem when consultants begin tampering with basic values of the profession. The imposition of consultants on newsrooms is too often a top-down phenomenon. News employees should be involved in the decision-making process that brings consultants into the newsroom. Violations of this autonomy should come to the attention of professional journalism organizations and should be the subject of journalism review stories.

Who Is a Journalist? We should never get into the position of licensing journalists in this country. One of the benefits of our First Amendment is that anyone is free to set up a publishing operation to disseminate their take on the world.

On the other hand, the term "journalist" in our own country is thrown about all too freely these days. Sleazy television talk show hosts refer to themselves as journalists. Radio announcers who read the news one minute and then hawk laundry detergent and pasta restaurants call themselves journalists. Television anchors, who haven't researched and written a story in a decade, refer to themselves as journalists. Crackpot extremists who spew a fountain of hate literature are calling themselves journalists.

Much of the public's anger against the behavior of the news media is brought about by characters who have no business calling themselves journalists. Much of public journalism proponent James Fallows' harangue against the traditional news media is inspired by the actions of media celebrities whose credentials as journalists are highly questionable. Fallows favors turning an entire profession upside down based on the actions of a fringe. Professional journalism organizations, journalism reviews, and professors of journalism should be about the task of educating the public about who is a bona fide journalist. Criteria can be established without endangering the free press rights of the street pamphleteer or the dabbler in desktop publishing.

Reaffirming Values. Journalists should not leave the debate about the efficacy of objectivity, balance, fairness, and detachment—traditional journalistic values—to those in the journalism classroom and at the media seminar banquet. Reporters and editors should join the academic roundtables and go on the offensive in answering the critique of public journalism. The dismissal of traditional journalistic values by public journalism supporters should not go unchallenged.

There is much that is wrong with today's journalism, but these maladies have not been brought about because of reporting practices inspired by traditional journalistic values. The most destructive practices often have been brought about by a departure from traditional journalistic values. Many of the evangelists of public journalism may well have good intentions in their quest to reform the traditional practice of journalism. Their desire to connect with the citizenry to revive a faltering democracy may well be a noble and lofty mission. But public journalists are well off the mark on what truly ails journalism, and their remedy is likely to get the profession into deeper trouble. Let us come down from their heights to borrow the simple wisdom of an American pickup truck bumper sticker: "Please, God, Save Us From The Good People!"

NOTES

1. Peter Phillips and Project Censored, *Censored 1997: The News that Didn't Make the News* (New York: Seven Stories Press, 1997), pp. 27–98.

2. Jeff Cohen, and Norman Solomon, *Adventures in Medialand* (Monroe, Maine: Common Courage Press, 1993), p. viii.

3. Ibid.

4. James Fallows, *Breaking the News* (New York: Vintage Books, 1996), p. 246.

5. Davis Merritt, *Public Journalism & Public Life: Why Telling the News Isn't Enough* (Hilldale, New Jersey: Lawrence Erlbaum Associates, 1995), p. 61.

6. Ibid., p. 18.

7. Herbert J. Gans, *Deciding What's News* (New York: Vintage Books, 1980), pp. 78–146.

8. Betty Medsger, *Winds of Change: Challenges Confronting Journalism Education* (Arlington, Virginia: Freedom Forum Press, 1996) p. 141.

9. David L. Protess, et al., *The Journalism of Outrage* (New York: Guilford Press, 1992), p. 30.

10. Ibid., pp. 10–11.

11. Merritt, op. cit., p. 62.

12. Ibid., pp. 61–62.

13. Howard Kurtz, *Media Circus: The Trouble with America's Newspapers* (New York: Times Books, 1993), p. 385.

14. David Remnick, "Scoop," *New Yorker* (January 29, 1996), p. 42.

15. Mort Rosenblum, *Who Stole the News? Why We Can't Keep Up with What Happens in the World.* (New York: John Wiley & Sons, 1993), p. 286.

16. David H. Weaver, and Cleveland G. Wilhoit, *The American Journalist in the 1990s* (Mahwah, New Jersey: Lawrence Erlbaum Associates, 1996), pp. 243–244.

17. Ibid., pp. 244–245.

18. Don Corrigan, "Pay Scales on Newspapers Fail to Keep Pace," *St. Louis Journalism Review* (September, 1990), p. 8.

19. Weaver and Wilhoit, op. cit., pp. 239–240.

20. Calder Pickett, *Voices of the Past* (New York: John Wiley & Sons, 1977), pp. 310–311.

21. Cole Campbell, "Our Republic and Its Press," *St. Louis Post-Dispatch* (May 1,1997), p. 10A.

22. Kurtz, op. cit., p. 387.

23. Medsger, op. cit., p. 1.

24. Ibid., p. 141

25. Ibid., p. 161.

26. Ibid., p. 166.

27. Charlotte Eby, "Gartner Blasts 'Civic Journalism,'" *Iowa Journalist* (Spring, 1997), p. 28.

28. Ibid.

29. Rosenblum, op. cit., p. 7.

APPENDIX
Public Journalism Lexicon

A.

A Whole Journalism: Jay Rosen of the public journalism movement credits Gene Patterson of the *St. Petersburg Times* with the concept of whole journalism. "A whole journalism would not stop at exposing the ills and ailments; it would also focus on creating a healthy public climate. A whole journalism would not equate politics with 'government' and its misdeeds; it would see public problem-solving as the best definition of the political sphere, and it would ask how this sphere could be made to work better."[1]

Action Teams: Public journalism projects often involve a story series assessing the state of a community and its future. The series will point to community problems and may suggest solutions. Ideally, the public will be inspired to organize into action teams to address the various issues raised and to seek solutions. The news media then covers the meetings and deliberations of the action teams.[2]

Advance Information: Reporters are frequently given advance information at meetings, materials such as budgets, agendas, lists of resolutions, and ordinances. This information is not normally given to the audience at government meetings. Public journalists say this practice encourages reporters to look at themselves as insiders in the political process at the expense of citizens.[3]

Adversarial Stance: Adversary journalism is typified by the watchdog role that the press plays in reporting on the rich, the powerful, and those elected to positions of power. Public journalists believe that there is a point where this stance becomes destructive. "There is a sense in which an adversarial posture becomes an ideology that prevents the sensitive interpretation and application of the principles of humaneness, truth telling, justice, freedom/independence, and the stewardship of free expression."[4]

Advocacy Journalism: Reporting that takes a side in an argument or conflict. Advocacy journalism is sometimes traced to the civil rights and Vietnam War coverage of the 1960s and early 1970s, when many alternative newspapers wrote stories that clearly favored civil rights protesters and opposed U.S. policy in Vietnam. Critics of reporting under the public journalism approach contend that it takes positions on community issues rather than striving for objective coverage.

Agora: In ancient Greece, the agora was a marketplace that also served as the location for important conversation and exchange of ideas. According to Davis "Buzz" Merritt, "when presses became free and commonplace, pamphlets, newspapers, magazines and books provided a physically dispersed but common, public and potentially effective agora."[5] Public journalists believe that newspapers should be the community's agora, a sort of public space or meeting place for important conversation about government and public life.

Alternative Framing: Traditional journalism answers the question as to what makes news by using such criteria as conflict, prominence, local impact, and human interest. Public journalists argue that alternative framing involves writing stories that are based on helping a community understand itself better or that helps a community arrive at solutions to its problems. This kind of story framing requires a reporter to forego the traditional journalistic role of dispassionate observer.[6]

B.

Balanced: According to public journalists, traditional reporting has an almost fanatical attachment to the idea that "both sides" must be heard on virtually any story topic. Public journalism practitioner Merritt contends that "balance" too often means giving voice to the extremes—seeking out the viewpoint of A and Z on an issue. "More often than not, 'A' and 'Z' provide a falsely simplistic frame, for many of the other 24 letters would provide nuances reflecting the whole array of opinion."[7]

Balancing: Public journalists say they have a better idea when it comes to achieving balance in stories. Instead of selecting comments from the extremes, such as 'A' and 'Z,' public journalists seek out the views of 'D' and 'J,' 'S,' and 'P.' Public journalists contend that this approach to balancing would bring more rational discussion and possible solutions to polarizing issues such as gun control, abortion, capital punishment, or euthanasia. This approach would also bring more citizens into the process of deliberating on important issues because most citizens are not at the extremes. Framing issues in a more moderate fashion "doesn't mandate dull ambiguity," according to Merritt, but instead "it permits more people to see themselves as included in the discussion."[8]

Bipolar Journalism: One of the major influences on journalism in the West in this century has been the Cold War, which has divided the world into "us" and "them." This has resulted in an "us" and "them" approach as a convenient template for many stories, especially in foreign affairs. Public journalist Ed Fouhy, formerly of the Pew Center for Civic Journalism, argues that the breakdown of the old bipolar world, with the fall of Soviet Communism and the Berlin Wall, should also signal an end to outdated bipolar journalistic approach to news coverage.[9]

C.

Change Agent: Sometimes used interchangeably with the term "civic catalyst." Both a change agent and a civic catalyst can be anything that acts to improve the decision-making process in a community and moves it to find solutions to its problems. Sometimes a new editor with a commitment to public journalism can be brought onto a newspaper as a "change agent" for both the newspaper staff and the local community. Ron Willnow, former deputy managing editor of the *St. Louis Post-Dispatch*, has referred to *Post* editor Cole Campbell as a "change agent." A practitioner of public journalism, Campbell was brought to the *Post* to effect change in the newsroom and in the St. Louis community."[10]

Character Issue: Concern over the character issue crops up at election time and usually focuses on whether a political candidate has problems with philandering or infidelity. Some journalists hold that the issue of infidelity is important because Americans are concerned about family values; also, if a political candidate does not keep a vow made with a spouse, what is the likelihood that the candidate will keep promises made to the American people? Public journalists contend that the press has been obsessed with the character issue, while coverage of real issues is sacrificed.

Civic Capital: "Capital" is classically defined by economists in connection with productivity. Philosophers and practitioners of public journalism have begun to speak about civic capital as something that improves a community and its democratic process. Charity describes civic capital as "anything that improves the productivity of a community—that is, its ability to meet crises, solve problems, live connectedly."[11]

Civic Catalyst: A civic catalyst is anything that acts to improve the decision-making process in a community and moves it to find solutions to its problems. A newspaper that engages in public journalism ideally acts as a civic catalyst in a community. However, civic catalysts might also consist of cultural groups, block clubs, citizen associations, and neighborhood leaders. "Civic Catalyst" is also the title of the newsletter of the Pew Center for Civic Journalism.[12]

Civic Climate: A community's health can be measured by the degree of democratic decision-making that takes place. If citizens are actively conversing with each other and participating in the government process, then it can be said that there is a healthy civic climate. One important gauge of the civic climate of a community is simply the percentage of citizens who vote.

Civic Disintegration: A community is suffering civic disintegration when its citizens are alienated from the political process and when they feel that their participation in the process no longer makes a difference. In a community suffering civic disintegration, citizens feel alienated, powerless, and are unlikely to make the effort to be involved in elective politics. A newspaper can become a civic catalyst in an effort to re-engage citizens and to reverse civic disintegration.

Civic Journalism Interest Group: More than 100 college and university professors, most affiliated with the Association for Education in Journalism and Mass Communication, have become members of this group interested in public journalism. "Some probably see public journalism as a great new tradition, a welcome correction of old practice; others simply as a critical foil for the journalism they've been teaching all along," explains Arthur Charity.[13]

Civic Mapping: In any number of communities, there are locations where conversations are taking place about issues that have not yet surfaced in the body politic. *Colorado Springs Gazette Telegraph* editor Steve Smith contends it is a public journalist's job to seek out those locations and to begin to map them as important sites to track for the community's pulse. Smith attributes the concept to the Harwood Group. "Civic mapping is a process that helps a newspaper staff understand where in a community discussions are taking place on issues to surface in the body politic."[14]

Collaborative Projects: Civic or public journalism projects are often collaborative efforts involving a newspaper, a radio station, and a television station. Public relations agencies and local or national foundations can also be added to the mix. Together they can work toward a common goal of re-invigorating democracy and re-engaging citizens. Public journalist Jay Rosen is fond of citing one of the original projects in Madison, Wisconsin, that involved the daily newspaper, a public relations firm, and televisions stations. Televised forums purportedly showing citizens engaged in deliberative dialogue were a major part of the project, according to Rosen.[15]

Common Ground: Public journalists frequently point out a Times-Mirror poll statistic that shows 71 percent of Americans believe the press gets in the way of solving problems.[16] They argue that the journalists need to show that they are stakeholders in their communities. They should encourage, or even set up, public forums where deliberative dialogue can take place among citizens to settle differences and solve problems. Arthur Charity suggests that journalists study videotapes of John Marks in the "Search for Common Ground" and his techniques for getting adversaries to realize where they have shared interests in the effort to solve problems.[17]

Communitarianism: As a philosophy, communitarianism emphasizes the common interest, as opposed to individualism and classic liberalism. As applied to journalism, John C. Merrill has described it this way, "Journalism should solidify the community, not fractionalize it; absolutist ethics needed for social harmony and cohesion; reluctance to publish stories that might fractionalize society; desire to bring social harmony through 'positive' journalism; de-emphasizing older Enlightenment liberalism and journalistic autonomy."[18]

Community Conversation: Newspapers should give citizens an opportunity to converse with each other through stories and editorial projects. Citizens need to communicate and socialize with each other through the vehicle of their newspapers. "Not just as we socialize at a bake sale," according to Arthur Charity. "But as we'd socialize in the Athenian agora, as fellow citizens sharing ideas."[19]

Community Assets: Underprivileged communities have not fared well in reporting that has employed traditional journalism approaches, according to public journalists. Traditional journalism has given American society a view of these communities as little more than "needy and problematic and deficient neighborhoods populated by needy and problematic and deficient people."[20] Communications professor and public journalism advocate James Ettema argues that journalism should focus on community assets in underprivileged areas to give a more positive rendering of these communities.[21]

Conflict-driven: Public journalists eschew the criterion of conflict as a primary factor for what makes news. They contend that too many stories are driven by conflict. "We need to re-evaluate the usefulness of conflict as the highest coin in the journalistic realm," according to Davis Merritt. "We need to understand balance, not be contrasting polar extremes expressed by absolutists and experts, but as a continuum with myriad points between extremes."[22]

Connectedness: Public journalists have created and embraced this adjective to describe the degree to which citizens are engaged in the life of their communities. Jay Rosen describes this concern in his essay, "Community Connectedness," which he says is in serious decline and results in a concurrent erosion in the news media audience. "At its core is the concern that millions of Americans are somehow withdrawing from public life, at both the local and national levels. Along with this creeping trend toward disengagement has come, of course, the steady decline in newspaper readership."[23]

Connections: Traditional journalists spend too much time worrying about keeping the proper separations, and not enough about making important connections, according to public journalists. For example, traditional journalists worry too much about getting too close to government officials, advertisers, and the chamber of commerce in any given community. As a result, these journalists separate themselves from important aspects of the life of the community. These journalists also arouse resentment, because their distance makes it appear as if they are indifferent, if not hostile, to the life and welfare of the community. These separations also predispose journalists to doing stories "about what is going wrong [rather] that what is going right."[24]

Contrived Indifference: The insistence by traditional journalists on maintaining proper separations and a "culture of toughness" results in a posture of contrived indifference, a posture which alienates the audience for the traditional news media, according to public journalists.[25] When a journalist reports about deep cuts in school programs or massive employee layoffs, without expressing emotion or concern for the well-being of the community, that journalist appears to be uncaring and indifferent. In fact, the indifference is contrived because, as a citizen and member of the community, the journalist does have a stake in seeing the community and public life do well.

Core Values: Traditional journalists often contend that they deal in facts and not in values. Value judgments are to be confined to the editorial page, while the news is to be reported dispassionately on the front page. Public journalists like Davis Merritt insist that traditional journalists are fooling themselves because they are expressing certain core values in the very act of selecting what stories they will write about for front page news. "We are acting out of a set of values: politicians should not steal, companies should not pollute, people should not be exploited."[26] Public journalists would add a number of other core values, including the desirability for public life to go well.

Credibility: Journalists opposed to public journalism argue that the movement's major tenets, which downplay the importance of objectivity and detachment, will destroy the credibility of the press. If reporters are no longer concerned about reporting in an objective manner, their credibility will be lost. Public journalists argue that the credibility of the press is already lost, and detachment is not the answer to rebuilding credibility. "Rather, credibility for journalists, as for any conscientious citizen, arises from other citizens trusting that we and they are broadly aligned in common cause, that both of us share a desire to improve their lot."[27]

Culture of Toughness: Traditional journalists and the newsrooms of the mainstream news media revel in a culture of toughness, according to public journalists. That culture requires reporters to be pushy in *getting* their stories, boorish with reluctant interviewees, and content that an important measure of their success is how much they are hated by story subjects.

Cyberspace Community: Public journalists are ambivalent about the growth in popularity of conversation groups on the internet, the so-called cyberspace community. Some public journalists see these conversations as consistent with public journalism—citizens sharing information without the experts defining what is important and how it should be digested. Other public journalists see the growth of these conversations as another indication of citizen "disconnect"—citizens would rather spend hours at a computer screen than to become involved with neighbors or their communities.

D.

Daily Integration: To paraphrase a popular bumper sticker slogan, "public journalists have to do it daily." Advocates profess that public journalism involves a mindset that must be consciously brought to bear on newsroom life and practice every day. Public journalism should not be episodic or instituted as occasional projects; it requires a broader commitment by a news organization.

Defensible Universalism: Communitarians such as professor and theorist Clifford Christians find much to like in public journalism. Christians makes the case that the public journalism philosophy can and should be adopted on a global scale. He argues for a "defensible universalism," or global core values, that can permeate journalistic efforts in local cultures around the world. In his writings, he gives examples of values, or global notions of a common good, "that can enable civic journalism to operate fruitfully by invigorating community debates in terms of universal human solidarity."[28]

Deliberation Page: Public journalism advocates encourage newspapers to set up a deliberation page, which should not be confused with an op-ed page or a letters page. Letters pages are often filled with rancor from readers on controversial issues or attacks on public figures. A deliberation page encourages discussion which can lead to solutions. Sometimes the newspaper will invite citizens to a roundtable discussion of issues, with the ground rule that participants try to achieve common ground on an issue. The deliberation page might then print a transcript of the discussion or selected quotes.[29]

Deliberative Dialogue: Public journalism seeks to encourage discussion that leads to solutions, rather than to traditional conflict-oriented reportage. Journalists should encourage situations in which people on opposing sides work together to achieve a common ground, rather than working to prove each other wrong. "Deliberation moves us beyond looking out for our own interest to a larger view of the public interest," according to practitioner Cole Campbell.[30]

Deliberative Polling: Traditional methods of polling often ask respondents to answer terse questions with direct answers. There is no room for ambivalency. Furthermore, some polls, such as those legislators use on their constituents, often are designed to elicit particular responses that are strongly biased in one direction or the other. Deliberative polling uses more open-ended questions and gives respondents an opportunity to express themselves in a less restrictive manner.

Deliberative Reporting: Reporters conduct informal, open-minded conversations with citizens and consciously act as the public's representative when meeting with experts, officeholders, and candidates. A reporter's job is subsequently to help citizens assess work that is being done in their behalf in their name. Deliberative reporting might also include a transcript of discussants on a particular issue in a forum in which the reporter acts as a moderator or umpire.

Detachment: Traditional journalism principles value detachment as a way to help ensure fairness. The idea is that journalists should not join business groups or civic organizations, especially if they are going to cover those organizations. Such memberships will hurt a journalist's ability to cover those organization's activities in an impartial manner. Public journalists insist that traditional journalism's emphasis on detachment alienates citizens. Jan Schaeffer of the Pew Center for Civic Journalism quotes a journalist in a 1997 article for *Quill*, a reporter who has grown tired of a passive and detached approach to journalism. "Unless newspapers make people in their communities feel a part of them, as if they have a stake in them, they will disappear. People no longer want to be merely observed. People want to be cared about."[31]

Development Journalism: Development journalism is sometimes associated with the controversies surrounding the 1980 MacBride Report and the New World Information and Communication Order (NWICO). The idea is that underdeveloped countries need a journalism that is less negative, market-driven, and conflict-oriented. Underdeveloped countries need a journalism that leads to harmony and the building of community. Thus, development journalists make much the same criticism of traditional Western journalism as do the advocates of public journalism.

Disconnect: Traditional journalism's obsession with detachment, as a way to help ensure impartiality and fairness, actually creates its own bias, according to public journalists. Public journalists contend that concern over detachment prompts reporters to become aloof and arrogant about the people and communities that they cover. "When caring about a place or circumstance is considered negative, roots cannot be comfortably put down or useful relationships established; familiarity breeds professional discomfort."[32]

Dispassionate Observer: Traditional journalism's emphasis on detachment, on the need to be a neutral observer of events, leads the public to believe that reporters and editors don't care about the life of the community, according to public journalists. Jay Rosen declares, "Journalists should not huddle together in the press box, wondering how the story will come out. They need to rejoin the American experiment. But first they will have to drop the devastating illusion of themselves as bystanders, 'watching the idiots screw it up.' Public journalism begins there."[33]

E.

Egocentric Journalism: On a basic level, egocentric journalism is simply a label given by public journalists to the "know-it-all-journalism" of reporters in mainstream news organizations. Public journalists contend that many of these reporters write to please their own egos—to impress their professional colleagues and to win prizes—rather than to inform the citizenry. From a philosophical perspective, communitarian Clifford Christians notes that public journalism repudiates the "egoistic rationalism which says that individuals make up their own mind based on objective data," and instead assumes the primacy of community and the promotion of values that support a common good.[34]

Elitist Press: Public journalists insist that most of the criticism of their movement comes from the elitist press, which they define as the major news outlets of Washington and New York. "I think the thing that distinguishes them (*The New York Times, The Washington Post, The Wall Street Journal*, etc.) from us is that they have an elite audience," explains public journalist Gil Thelen, former editor of *The State* in Columbia, South Carolina. "*The New York Times* can live with 25 percent penetration in New York City; I can't. In the elite conversation, there can be all of the sanctimoniousness about the extreme separation of church and state [newspaper and community] and an exaggerated kind of independence."[35]

Endangered Readers: Just as biologists and the environmental movement have used the term "endangered species" to emphasize the loss of life forms due to ecological destruction, public journalists speak of readers as endangered because of recent declines in newspaper readership for major dailies. For public journalists, the loss of readers begs the question: What is to be done? "What is to be done. . . . when, in March of this year [1995] only 45 percent of Americans said they read yesterday's newspaper, down 13 percent from one year ago?"[36]

Engage The Citizenry: The word "engage" is a key verb in the public journalism lexicon. Public journalists believe that it is not enough to use a newspaper to inform people, newspapers should prompt people to get involved in their communities and to participate in the democratic process. "What public journalism is fundamentally about is using the power of the press to re-engage people in public life, in the belief that a disengaged, complacent or cynical people cannot make use of what journalism has to offer."[37]

Epiphanies: Many proponents of public journalism talk about a turning point or an "epiphany," an enlightening event that convinced them that it was time to find a different way to do journalism. James Fallows in his book, *Breaking the News*, recounts this transforming experience for Davis "Buzz" Merritt during the 1988 presidential election campaign. Merritt sought a new path after watching his paper carry the predictable campaign stories off the wire service "about the Dukakis campaign's response to the Bush campaign's attacks, about Gary Hart and his girlfriends, about what Willie Horton did or did not do, about what Michael Dukakis would do or would not do if his wife was raped."[38]

Episodic Public Journalism: Public journalism in practice at many news media outlets has been project-oriented, and consequently, episodic in nature. Some public journalism advocates have acknowledged the episodic nature of their media work and are arguing for the development of a public journalism "mindset" that should permeate a newsroom and have influence on everything that is produced by a newsroom.

Episodic Reporting: Traditional or mainstream journalism is almost always episodic. For example, the life story of a school district or a municipality is almost always told meeting by meeting. Public journalists are less bound to meeting coverage and more inclined to report a process or chronicling of issues, with an eye to finding public solutions to problems.

Event-oriented Journalism: Traditional or mainstream journalism has a tendency to react to and to cover events. The grist for the mill of traditional journalism consists of press conferences, court hearings, crime scenes, and city council and school board meetings. The more process-oriented journalism of reporters engaged in public journalism examines issues and tries to provide a whole pattern that illustrates all aspects or a complete chronology of an issue.

F.

Fair-minded Participant: Reporters have put too much emphasis on the value of detachment, which allows them to separate themselves from the consequences of their actions. Reporters should, instead, realize their role in the democratic process of helping various parties in a community arrive at solutions. "What journalists should bring to the arena of public life is knowledge of the rules—how the public has decided a democracy should work—and the ability to provide relevant information and a place for that information to be discussed and turned into democratic consent."[39]

Feeding Frenzy: Public journalists insist that too many reporters in mainstream journalism exhibit the behavior of piranhas or sharks. They are not unlike sharks who have happened upon a wounded animal in the water, and who then proceed to brawl over the prey and to rip it to shreds. These reporters pounce on their own prey and battle each other for every morsel of a story. Examples of such reporting usually involves crimes or sex scandals, such as the O. J. Simpson case or the infidelity of candidates for high office. Such reporting, according to public journalists, has turned off readers and placed the journalism profession in low esteem.

Focus Groups: Focus groups are a more informal method of getting a sense of public opinion than the random survey that may reach out to several hundred, if not several thousand, respondents. Focus groups often involve face-to-face interviewing and questioning of 15 or fewer people who might have been chosen for certain demographics. Focus groups are used most often by marketing experts and advertisers. Focus groups preceded public journalism, but have been adopted as a "public listening" technique by public journalists in an effort to find out what people are thinking about public issues or elective politics.

Fortress Journalism: The egocentric and individualistic reporters and editors in mainstream journalism think that they can "go it alone" in doing what they do. They don't have to cater or be accountable to anybody but their professional ethics. This is a fallacy, according to public journalists. Jay Rosen describes fortress journalism as a journalism, "protected against all entanglements, fighting for truth and justice without need for civic cooperation, or an energized public, a journalism that doesn't need anyone or anything except the First Amendment and the resources that will come from . . . well, from somewhere, this image of the press as standing somehow outside the community it allegedly serves is, in my view, a devastating illusion that offers its proponents nothing but a slow slide into impotence and irrelevance."[40]

Framing: Journalists need to develop new criteria and approaches for what makes news. Traditionally, journalists have focused on conflicts, extremes, the unusual, and the negative. According to public journalist Steve Smith, editor of the *Colorado Springs Gazette Telegraph*, "The process of framing a story civically helps us understand and report in more meaningful ways on how the community interacts with, interrelates to, and potentially solves a pressing community problem."[41] Choosing the frame for a story is the most powerful decision a journalist can make, according to Smith.

Fundamental Shift: For public journalism to be practiced effectively, reporters and editors must do more than simply engage in projects that are inspired by the civic journalism creed. Broad mental shifts must occur, according to Davis Merritt, that move journalists from the limited mission of simply telling the news, to the expanded mission of helping public life go well. "Clearly, it [public journalism] moves beyond current practice because it requires a fundamental shift in thinking. It is not a formula or a set of rules. It is a conviction and resultant attitude about the relationship between journalism and public life."[42]

G.

Ghetto-izing: The practice of public journalism can suffer if it is not adopted as a pervasive attitude in a newsroom, it it is kept at the margins of a newspaper operation. For example, if a newspaper decides to engage in public journalism by simply assigning one reporter a new "public life" beat, that reporter may be "ghetto-ized" and isolated by the rest of the newsroom culture. Bill Theobold, public life reporter for *The Indianapolis Star* and *Indianapolis News* puts himself in this role, "I find myself isolated intellectually because few people in my newsroom know enough about the subject to debate it in a meaningful way. . . . I am left in the odd role of defender of public journalism, even dumb public journalism, and not the role I'd prefer—participant in a reasoned debate about how this philosophy might be applied to our work."[43]

Gotcha' Stories: James Fallows and other journalists who champion public journalism contend that the reporters who cover politics in this country put too much energy into covering the wrong kinds of stories. Instead of concentrating on issues, they concentrate on the horse race aspect of elections and "gotcha' stories."[44] A 'gotcha' story can involve reporters catching a candidate making a statement that contradicts something the candidate said earlier, and focusing on what might simply be an honest gaffe excessively.

H.

High-horse Journalism: According to public journalists, too many newspaper reporters look on ordinary readers with derision, if not contempt. These reporters are interested in writing stories that impress their colleagues in the business, rather than informing readers and finding ways to engage them in the democratic process. They are interested in winning prizes, particularly the Holy Grail of the news business, the Pulitzer Prize. "For too long we have published newspapers aimed at other journalists—talking to ourselves, really, and the insiders we gossip with—and paying scant attention to our readers. . . . Where once newspapers were at the very heart of the national conversation, they now seem remote, arrogant, part of the governing elite."[45]

Horse-race Stuff: This is often defined reporting of political elections that pays more attention to covering who's winning and who's losing, rather than to covering the major issues of concern to citizens. Horse-race stuff is a cardinal sin of mainstream journalism. Former national press corps reporter Stan Cloud confessed in an issue of *Civic Catalyst*, to the horse-race sin, "I have written stories that focused more on campaign tactics than issues. I have interviewed political aides and consultants as if they, and not the voters, should decide the content, if not the very outcome, of an election campaign. I have pretended to know what the country wanted, when in fact I had little or no idea" confessed Cloud. "I am truly sorry and I humbly repent."[46]

Hutchins Commission: The Hutchins Commission on Freedom of the Press was named for the chancellor of the University of Chicago, Robert M. Hutchins, who selected 12 scholars to study news media performance and to make recommendations. The 133-page report issued in 1947 argued that journalists should give more attention to ethics, human values, and their role in democracy and dispense with trivia, negativism and sensationalism. The Hutchins Commission's emphasis on social responsibility aroused the antipathy of many in the news media, but today's public journalists are quite sympathetic to the commission report and can find much to agree with in its recommendations.

I.

Iconoclastic Mentality: Too many journalists, especially those who entered the profession during the Watergate period, are motivated by a desire to bring down public figures and to humble the great, according to public journalism advocates. "The press is often referred to as the fourth branch of government, which means that it should provide the information we need so as to make sense of public problems. But far from making it easier to cope with public problems, the media often make it harder," declares James Fallows. "By choosing to present public life as a contest among scheming political leaders, all of whom the public should view with suspicion, the news media helps bring about that very result."[47]

Intellectual Journey: Many reporters and editors, who are disillusioned with traditional journalism, have tried to conduct public journalism experiments with little success and which have reflected poorly on the new movement. Public journalists contend that this has happened because these well-meaning reporters and editors did not study the tenets of the movement first—they did not take the intellectual journey. That intellectual journey requires a study and an understanding of the paradigm shift that must take place to move from traditional journalism to the new public journalism.

Issue Myopia: Public journalists concede that there are some dangers in their focus on public listening to find out what issues concern citizens, that is, "the citizens' agenda." Important issues in elections, for example, can be missed when there is too much concern with identifying issues through polls, focus groups, and listening projects that can be faulty or can quickly date. Bill Felber, executive editor of the *Manhattan Mercury*, has described such a flaw in a project at the *Mercury*. "If our readers didn't at the outset identify an issue as vital to them, we fluffed it off. In our federal races, this happened with Social Security reform; it happened in one or two instances at the state level as well and caused us to give scant attention to issues I think we probably should have dealt more with."[48]

J.

Journalistic Reflexes: Public journalists contend that reporters in mainstream journalism have conditioned reflexes which cause them to react in predictable ways to what makes news and what constitutes a good story. For example, reporters in traditional journalism are likely to frame stories on controversial issues in the old bipolar fashion, providing two sides with quotes that represent the extremes of those opposing positions. Public journalists also blame attacks by traditional journalists on their new movement and its concepts on an instinctive reaction against anything that seems to challenge such time-honored tenets as objectivity or detachment.

K.

Know-it-all Journalism: The know-it-all journalism of many in the press accounts for their unpopularity with the American public, according to public journalists. That unpopularity is one of the reasons why something "needs to be done." As Jay Rosen declares, "What is to be done when Howard Kurtz of *The Washington Post*, taking note of the 'disconnect' between journalists and the public, describes the news business as an 'incestuous profession,' which has grown increasingly 'self-absorbed,' 'remote' and 'arrogant'?"[49] Stan Cloud, a past national press correspondent and executive director of the Citizens' Election Project, describes know-it-all-journalism in politics as an insiders' game in which journalists employ an arcane language of "spinmeisters," "tracking polls," "soft money," and "media buys" that leaves ordinary citizens out of the loop.[50]

L.

Labeling: Public journalists argue that reporters need to see story subjects as citizens in order to put together a picture of life in which democracy can have an impact. Instead, reporters have too often pushed people into stereotypes or pre-ordained roles. Arthur Charity writes that journalists have a grab bag of labels that they use in approaching someone for an interview. Among the labels: "victims, clients of government programs, dissatisfied customers, racial minorities, party members, and so on."[51]

Leading Civic Indicators: Just as economists use measurements such as the gross national product (GNP) and consumer price index (CPI), public journalists would like to see a measurement that gauges the civic climate of a community. Jay Rosen has suggested that an index of leading civic indicators might include such factors as "citizen participation, coalition building, problem solving, inclusiveness, setting a common agenda, planning the future, etc."[52]

Learned Helplessness: The negativity of mainstream or traditional journalism encourages an attitude of "learned helplessness" among ordinary citizens, according to public journalists. It encourages the feeling that a problem is "so big, so complicated that the viewer or reader is left with a sense that it is beyond the capacity of ordinary men and women."[53]

Lethargic Public Climate: This describes a community in which citizens feel alienated from their political system and feel helpless to effect change. A community such as this lacks a public life. This is a dangerous situation for journalists, according to Rosen, "because when the life of a community no longer matters, neither does journalism."[54]

Libertarian Press Philosophy: According to this journalism philosophy, the emphasis is "on editorial autonomy of the press or the journalist; no prior censorship; wholehearted liberalism, opposed to authoritarian restraints on individual freedom."[55] This philosophy is sometimes contrasted with the social responsibility press philosophy, which holds that the press should engage in restraint or self-censorship when that is in the interests of the common good or the betterment of society. Public journalists and communitarians are generally more sympathetic to a social responsibility philosophy of the press.

M.

Mainstream Journalism: Mainstream journalism or traditional journalism is thought to be at odds with any number of journalism genres of recent years, such as advocacy journalism, new journalism, or public journalism. Mainstream journalism puts a premium on the idea of the reporter as a detached or dispassionate observer, emphasizes reporting that is fair or balanced according to the elusive ideal of objectivity, and subscribes to a formula for news based on traditional criteria of impact, proximity, timeliness, prominence, novelty, and conflict.[56]

Market-driven Journalism: Journalism that places an inordinate emphasis on serving its market segment can easily lose sight of its civic function in the effort to fulfill its commercial function. A newspaper that concentrates on the market segment that it serves will fail in the larger mission of serving and improving the whole community. Davis Merritt holds that public journalism "moves from seeing people as consumers—as readers or non-readers, as bystanders to be informed—to seeing them as a public, as potential actors in arriving at democratic solutions to public problems."[57]

Master Narrative: Journalists who have taken the intellectual journey to understand the public journalism philosophy are especially well prepared to frame stories in a way that will capture the imagination of the public. This is because there is a built-in, master narrative to rely on in every situation. As Jay Rosen professes, "The struggle to come to public judgement is a drama. It is an excellent drama. This is what all other public journalism stories are about. Will the community succeed or fail? Can Dayton, Ohio, come to grips with juvenile violence? We do not know. That's the drama."[58]

Meaningful Participants: The overarching goal of public journalism is to help citizens become effective players in public life—something more than the folks on the sidelines watching the parade go by. Mainstream journalists are content to raise an alarm or to spot an injustice—and their work ends at that point. In public journalism, a reporter's "goal is to treat readers and viewers, not as window dressing and not as passive spectators, but as meaningful participants in important issues, as meaningful as the elites and the experts that journalists so often quote."[59]

Media Intellectual: Newsrooms aren't places to think. Reporters have little time to ponder or question their professional code and the culture of their work environment, which is why it is so important for daily reporters to insist on "networking with those people trying to do this thing called public journalism and paying attention to our intellectual Moseses, like Rosen, who help point to the promised land."[60] Public journalists cite Jay Rosen of New York University and James Carey of Columbia University as two of the best media intellectuals of their movement.

Mobilizing Information: Much of what passes for information in today's news media is irrelevant to today's readers; it gives them no new knowledge that they can act on, according to public journalists. Public journalism, in contrast, gives citizens mobilizing information that empowers them to make decisions that produce solutions.

Mutual Validation Effect: When public journalism projects are collaborative efforts involving a newspaper, a radio station, and a television station, they are more effective and leave a stronger impression with the public. According to public journalists, citizens are impressed when news media outlets cooperate with each other for the common good when they are normally in competition with each other.

N.

Negative Freedom: Public journalism advocates contend that reporters and editors in mainstream journalism look at their relative freedom and their First Amendment privilege in a negative fashion. They look at the First Amendment as a guarantee of freedom from government interference, freedom from censorship by religious authorities, and freedom from threats by public figures who are overly concerned about their reputations or privacy rights. Public journalists think the First Amendment should mean freedom to do positive things, such as encouraging citizen participation in democracy, promoting a substantive political debate, and promoting a healthy civic climate.

Negative-oriented: Traditional journalists often subscribe to a press ethic of "comforting the afflicted and afflicting the comfortable." They place a premium on the watchdog role of sniffing out government malfeasance and political corruption. Public journalists contend that they instinctively favor disaster, failure, and shortcomings as good copy. This penchant for the negative often dominates newspaper headlines, and leaves readers with a sense of hopelessness.

O.

Objectivity: In mainstream journalism, objectivity is the creed and elusive ideal that commands all reporters to strive for fairness and balance in their journalistic accounts. "It has been exalted by leaders of the profession as an essential, if unattainable, ideal," write the authors of the journalism text, *News Reporting & Writing*. "Its [objectivity's] critics, by contrast, have attacked objectivity as, in the phrase of sociologist Gaye Tuchmann, a 'strategic ritual' that conceals a multitude of professional sins while producing superficial and misleading coverage."[61] Public journalists take a dim view of the concept of objectivity and Jay Rosen has referred to it as a "fruitless cliché."[62]

Obtainable Futures: The audience for news is in decline because mainstream journalism gives readers and viewers a sense that the world has become too big and too complex for ordinary citizens to make a difference, according to public journalists. Journalist can turn this situation around by re-invigorating public life with a journalism that empowers ordinary citizens. One way to empower ordinary citizens, according to Jay Rosen, is to produce journalism that shows citizens how to arrive at solutions to problems and how to map out obtainable futures—goals that are reachable for a community.[63]

Outsider Status: There is an obvious hypocrisy involved when traditional journalists reject the observations and criticisms of their profession and its ethics. Public journalists say that hypocrisy comes when traditional journalists reject criticism as coming from academics, policy experts, and ordinary citizens who don't understand the culture, history, and practical requirements of journalism. "Yet much of our own journalistic effort is based in our being 'outside' critics of such institutions as government," noted Davis Merritt. "In that case, we insist that our detachment, or noninvolvement, is precisely what legitimizes our criticism."[64]

P.

Pack Journalism: The concept or idea of pack journalism is sometimes attributed to Timothy Crouse, author of *Boys on the Bus*, who wrote about the political reporters covering the Nixon-McGovern campaigns in the 1972 presidential elections.[65] The term refers to a tendency by reporters to gravitate to the same topics or stories simultaneously, no matter how ephemeral those topics or stories might be as compared to the truly critical issues facing communities and the nation as a whole.

Parachute Journalism: Many advocates of development journalism argue that since reporters for Western news agencies have little real interest or stake in the countries that they cover, their reportage is understandably incomplete, distorted, and exploitative. When a crisis erupts somewhere and attention is deemed necessary, foreign correspondents leave a comfortable world capital and catch a plane to the outpost where trouble is ensuing. The reporter figuratively "parachutes in," spends a few days and files the obligatory dispatches, and then returns to the more civilized base from whence the reporter came. Public journalists make a similar critique of mainstream journalism's coverage of U.S. communities when they refer to the "transience" within the profession.

Paradigm Shift: Sometimes used interchangeably with the concept of fundamental shift, the term is meant to imply the gravity of the change that must take place in a conventional journalist's thinking in order to make the transition to public journalism. For public journalism to be practiced effectively, reporters and editors must do more than simply engage in projects that are inspired by the civic journalism creed. Broad mental shifts must occur, according to Davis Merritt, that move journalists "beyond only describing what 'is going wrong' [in a community] to also describing what 'going right' would be like. By describing realistic possibilities that lie beyond immediate solutions, it informs people of their potential choices for the future."[66]

Participatory Journalism: The term "participatory journalism" precedes public journalism by decades and refers to coverage in which reporters become part of the story. In mainstream journalism, reporters have been discouraged from writing in the first person or becoming part of the story except in unusual circumstances. Those unusual circumstances might involve writing features in the first person about the experience of parachuting with a parachute club or riding with a race car driver. In the new public journalism, participatory journalism is very likely to have an expanded role as journalists are no longer counseled to remain as dispassionate observers in covering most stories.

Political Actors: Ordinary citizens must be brought into the political system to revive our flagging democracy; they must be transformed into political actors. Journalists can play a pivotal role in making this happen, according to public journalists, and they point to a number of their news media projects across the country to show how it can happen. For example, in Seattle, the "Front Page Forum" project of *The Seattle Times* and two public radio stations allowed residents to talk to political candidates and to get answers without the usual "go-betweens" of pundits and expert journalists. The project "used call-in shows, question-and-answer columns, roundtable discussion, and even an unusual candidate debate with five undecided voters as the panel. Their expanded coverage of citizen-identified issues—crime, education, health care—gave people plenty to talk about."[67]

Puff Adder's Nest: This term for the camp of traditional journalists who have reacted negatively to the public journalism philosophy was first coined by author and journalist James Fallows and has become popular with public journalists in describing their critics. Fallows describes the public journalism critics as a "sort of puff adder's nest of modern journalism, where you stick your hand in and the puff adders come out from all corners of the swamp. . . . It has all the earmarks, by the way, of a reflex action, rather than a reasoned counter argument."[68]

Public Agenda: Through the use of questionnaires, focus groups, and public listening, public journalists can determine what issues are on the minds of ordinary citizens, rather than relying on local leaders and political experts to dictate what are the issues and concerns of a community. A newspaper's responsibility is to articulate the public agenda, particularly at election time when political decisions are made.

Public Life: Public life has traditionally been termed as the province of those who become politicians and elected officials. Politicians and elected officials are said to have entered public life. According to public journalists, the news media must scrap this limiting definition of what makes public life. "Public life is everything that pulls people out of their private worlds and puts them in touch with common concerns—everything from nightlife, to bowling leagues to union meetings, to town hall debates. It is also the habits of mind and heart that permit people to understand each other, discuss their views, and get along despite their differences."[69]

Public Life Team: Mainstream journalism gives reporters specific beats such as schools, courts, city hall, police, and the environment, while public journalism sometimes does it differently. Public journalism might reconfigure these reporters into teams to cover problems and to look for solutions. James Fallows notes this technique in his book, *Breaking the News*, when he describes how *The Virginia-Pilot* in Norfolk took reporters and editors off beats and assembled them into a public life team. Fallows writes, "The mission statement for the team was, 'We will revitalize a democracy that has grown sick with disenchantment. We will lead the community to discover itself and act on what it has learned.'"[70]

Public Listening: This reportorial approach involves such techniques as posing open-ended questions to ordinary citizens to provoke detailed responses. It also involves setting up discussion groups with citizens to obtain non-expert opinion on the life of a community. Reporters are advised to engage in public listening to determine what issues are really on the minds of citizens.

Public's Take: Reporters need to rethink and critically consider what it means to listen to a community, according to public journalists. Random man-on-the-street interviews won't do and neither will "rounding up diversity's usual suspects."[71] A good public journalist puts away the Rolodex of usual sources and makes the effort to cross gender, ethnic, race, and age lines to get a full appreciation of the "public's take" on given issues.

Process-oriented Journalism: Process-oriented journalism is the opposite of event-oriented journalism.The fare of traditional journalism consists of a lot of coverage of events.The county board or the city government is covered meeting by meeting. Each meeting story is an entity in itself, with little reference to previous actions at other meetings or with an eye to what is to come. Public journalists are more inclined to report a process or to chronicle the development of issues. They also are not afraid to point to solutions to public issues.

Q.

Quality-Framing Discussions: Journalists need to develop new criteria and approaches for what makes news; however, they cannot achieve this in a vacuum or on their own. Traditionally, journalists have focused on conflicts, extremes, the unusual, and the negative. According to public journalist Steve Smith, editor of the *Colorado Springs Gazette Telegraph*, newsrooms need to have reporters and editors engage in quality framing discussions about how the news is reported. Additional essentials include, "role-playing exercises to frame stories; appropriate staff involvement in the community; programmatic contacts between news staffers and citizens."[72]

R.

Re-engaging the Public: Public journalism advocate Jay Rosen is fond of borrowing a term from communication scholar Michael Schudson, who refers to the journalist's "capacity to include."[73] The most important function of journalism, according to public journalists, is to include the public and thus to re-engage them in public life and the democratic process. For Rosen, journalism has no choice but to include the public and to re-engage the citizenry in public life. "Public journalism is about forming as much as informing a public, for the assumption that the public exists always and for all time is, in fact, a complacent one."[74]

Regenerating Credibility: While mainstream journalists worry about losing credibility if traditional journalism tenets such as objectivity and detachment are jettisoned, public journalists already concede that the news media's credibility with the public has been lost. Public journalists argue that credibility will only be restored when journalists show they care about the community and care about public life going well. "The dilemma is that true credibility with others cannot arise from a person, profession, or institution openly professing not to care, not sharing at least some broad common cause with others."[75]

Reviving Civic Life: Traditional journalists see their job as one of informing the public, while public journalists see their job as re-engaging the public in civic life so that they will want to be informed. Jay Rosen has described "an index of leading civic indicators" for public journalists that can be used to determine the extent of any revival of civic life. Journalists should examine such indicators or measures as "citizen participation, cooperative problem-solving, coalition-building, inclusiveness, setting a common agenda, planning for the future, etc."[76]

S.

Separational Fever: Public journalism advocates accuse traditional journalists of being so obsessed with the professional values of distance, detachment, objectivity, and value-neutrality that it has the appearance of a medical condition. What's worse, it's a medical condition that ordinary citizens loathe and which does nothing to address the question of lost credibility. "We cannot regenerate our credibility if we remain obsessively limited by our 'separational fever,'" declares Davis Merritt. "Rather than worrying about getting the separations right, we could just as easily and with much better effect, worry about getting the connections right."[77]

Social Responsibility: This philosophy is sometimes contrasted with the libertarian press philosophy, which holds that the press should have unlimited freedom and that people have an absolute "right to know." In other words, the press should disseminate all the details of information gathered and let the chips fall where they may. The social responsibility philosophy or view of the press calls for self-restraint or self-censorship when that is in the interests of the common good or the betterment of society. The general welfare of society sometimes has to take precedence over the dissemination of a story that could result in a clear and present danger to domestic tranquility.

Solution-oriented: Traditional journalism is conflict-oriented and a story about divisiveness and rancor is an end in itself. In contrast, public journalists argue that their approach to news is solution-oriented and, consequently, more purposeful. The conflict-oriented emphasis of traditional journalism is the reason why most people feel the press gets in the way of solving community problems, according to public journalists.

Stakeholders: Businesses, civic organizations, churches, schools, government, and ordinary citizens are all stakeholders in a community and its public life. If newspapers are honest with themselves, they will concede that they have a stake in the community and its public life as well. Public journalists insist that newspapers should be candid about how much their futures are bound to their communities.

Strategic Facts: Facts that help a community or a nation "come to public judgement" are strategic, according to public journalists. They should be distinguished from "just plain old, traditionally newsworthy facts." For example, during an election, facts about a politician's family, political consultants, celebrity endorsements, and opinion polls are not strategic in helping citizens make decisions. Facts about the political candidates' positions on immigration, welfare reform, the environment, jobs, and the economy are strategic.[78]

T.

Telling the Narrative: Public journalists insist that their approach to writing stories is much more demanding and intellectually rigorous because they do not restrict themselves to episodic, event reporting. They are engaged in laying out the continuous, unfolding story of the civic life of a community. They are committed to chronicling the ongoing story of a community working through its problems to democratic solutions.

Trained Incapacity: Traditional journalists have so internalized the set of rules that guides their profession—detachment, professional distance, objectivity, value-neutrality—that they seem incapable of going outside the borders or the paradigm that they have created for themselves. For example, as public journalism proponent Davis Merritt observes, "The tradition that says journalists should not deal in the realm of values blinds us to the central fact that other people do. It is another of those 'trained incapacities' that our culture foists on us."[79]

Transience: Public journalists complain that the system for the mainstream news media produces journalists who are trained in a "determined detachment" that sets them apart from the consequences of their work. Journalists "parachute" into disadvantaged communities, report on the latest drive-by shooting or unruly demonstration, then return to the safety of their newsroom to file stories that hopefully will lead to a career advance to a more prestigious work location and newspaper. This transience "chills passions about place and time. The allure of better jobs at larger places [means] that the [journalists have] no lasting stake in the community, and so the problems in the current town need not be resolved, only reported on."[80]

U.

Unorganized Majority: Newspapers and the news media in general give too much of a platform to the organized fringe groups on the extremes of important issues. They catch the attention of reporters precisely because they have articulated positions and often have experience using the media. The majority of people are not so adept at using the media. The majority also tends to be more ambivalent on issues. Public journalists argue that the press needs to give more voice to the ambivalent and unorganized majority, rather than framing issues at the extremes.

V.

Value Neutral: Traditional journalists often contend that they report events dispassionately and deal in facts and not in values. However, values are an increasingly important part of the public debate (witness the frequent use of the term "family values" in the 1990s) over how to interpret issues and to seek solutions to problems. Public journalists contend that mainstream journalism has become suspect with the general citizenry, because of its insistence that it is value neutral. "The people we seek to inform filter virtually everything they learn through their own value systems," argues Davis Merritt. "By reporting and writing as if that does not happen, we create yet another major disconnection between us (and our product) and citizens at large."[81]

Virtual Journalism: Virtual journalism is that news product which is now being creating on what has otherwise been termed "the information highway" or cyberspace. Public journalists argue that if reporters are to cut through all the myriad of fact and fiction in cyberspace, then they will have to adopt the public journalism approach almost by necessity—creating publics for their new electronic products.[82]

Viability of Public Life: Public life can be described as vital and viable when citizens are involved with their communities, when citizens are engaged in public conversation about improving their communities, and when citizens share a hopefulness that they can make a difference in the direction their communities take. The role of journalists, according to the public journalism philosophy, is to see that public life goes well. "The god term of journalism—the be-all and end-all, the term without which the entire enterprise fails to make sense—is the public," declares James Carey. "Insofar as journalism has a client, the client is the public. The press justifies itself in the name of the public: It exists—or so it is regularly said—to inform the public, to serve as the extended eyes and ears of the public, to protect the public's right to know, to serve the public interest."[83]

Voice to Extremes: One of the biggest complaints that public journalism advocates level at traditional journalists is in reference to the issue of giving a voice to extremes. Advocates contend that traditional journalists gravitate to sources who can give good quotes—and good quotes usually come from the fanatics, true-believers, and extremists on either end of the spectrum on an issue. "Journalists keep trying to find people who are at 1 and 9 on a scale of 10, rather than people at 3 and 7 where more people actually are," declares Cole Campbell. "Journalism should say that the people from 3 to 7 are just as newsworthy and quotable as those at either end of the spectrum lobbing bombs toward the middle."[84]

W.

Watchdog Role: One of journalism's primary missions, according to the traditionalist line of thinking, is to keep a watchful eye on the rich, the powerful, and the people at the levers of power. A popular slogan for this approach to journalism is that reporter's job is to "comfort the afflicted and to afflict the comfortable." Public journalism, on the other hand, holds that a reporter "is not merely a watchdog that barked and occasionally bites, but a public policy professional that identifies and fairly assesses the competing values and approaches to complex policy issues."[85]

Watergate Syndrome: Many of today's journalists were inspired by the no-holds-barred muckraking of Bob Woodward and Carl Bernstein, whose investigative work brought down the administration of President Richard M. Nixon. While this bull-dog approach may have been appropriate in tackling the Watergate story, too many journalists bring it to bear on every assignment. Public journalists say this alienates readers and viewers. Watergate also has made journalists famous, and this has had the effect of distancing journalists from the public.[86]

Working Through: The idea of citizens "working through" significant community problems was appropriated by public journalists from Daniel Yankelovitch. The idea is that problems are addressed and solved through a process that takes some time. The first step is to raise consciousness of the problem. "The second step, working through, invariably takes some amount of time for consideration and discussion. It often takes years," explains Davis Merritt. "Compare that reality of how the public decides against how journalists reflect the process back to the public."[87] Public journalists contend that newspapers have an obligation to help communities work through problems by adopting process-oriented coverage of issues.

NOTES

1. Jay Rosen, "Public Journalism as a Democratic Art." Pamphlet adapted from a presentation at the American Press Institute, Reston, Virginia, November 11, 1994, p. 4.

2. Cole Campbell, "Report to the Community: St. Louis 2004," *St. Louis Post-Dispatch* (May 1,1997), p. 10A.

3. Steve Smith, "Developing New Reflexes in Framing Stories," *Civic Catalyst* (April, 1997), p. 4.

4. Edmund Lambeth, *Committed Journalism* (Bloomington, Indiana: Indiana University Press, 1986), p. 99.

5. Davis Merritt, *Public Journalism & Public Life: Why Telling the News Isn't Enough* (Hilldale, New Jersey: Lawrence Erlbaum Associates, 1995), p. 9.

6. Smith, op. cit., p. 4.

7. Merritt, op. cit., p. 20.

8. Davis Merritt, "Missing the Point," *American Journalism Review* (July-August, 1996), p. 31.

9. Remarks made by Ed Fouhy at a seminar panel at the Association for Education in Journalism and Mass Communication (AEJMC), Anaheim, California, August 10, 1996.

10. Remarks made by Ron Willnow, then deputy managing editor of the *St. Louis Post-Dispatch*, at a public journalism panel at the annual public relations/communications workshop sponsored by the United Way, Missouri Botanical Garden in St. Louis, Mo., June 5, 1997.

11. Arthur Charity, *Doing Public Journalism* (New York: Guilford Press, 1995), p. 11.

12. "Civic Catalyst" (October, 1995), published by the Pew Center for Civic Journalism, no author credited, p. 1.

13. Arthur Charity, *Doing Public Journalism, A Teacher's Guide* (New York: Guilford Press, 1995), p. 1.

14. Smith, op. cit., p. 5.

15. Don Corrigan, "Does Public Journalism Serve the Public or Publishers," *St. Louis Journalism Review* (July-August, 1995), p. 9.

16. Ibid., p. 9.

17. Charity, op. cit., p. 24.

18. John Merrill, *Legacy of Wisdom* (Ames, Iowa: Iowa State University Press, 1994), p. 181.

19. Don Corrigan, "Buzzwords of Civic Journalism Appear in Post," *St. Louis Journalism Review* (June, 1997), p. 14.

20. James Ettema, and Limor Peer, "Good News from a Bad Neighborhood: Civic Journalism as a Vocabulary of Community Assets." Paper presented at the annual conference of the International Communication Association (ICA), Chicago, May,1996, p. 5.

21. Ibid., p. 5.

22. Davis Merritt, "The Misconception about Public Journalism," *Editor & Publisher* (July 11, 1995), p. 80.

23. Jay Rosen, "Community Connectedness: Passwords for Public Journalism" (St. Petersburg, Florida: Poynter Institute, 1993), p. 4.

24. Davis Merritt, *Public Journalism & Public Life: Why Telling the News Isn't Enough* (Hilldale, New Jersey: Lawrence Erlbaum Associates, 1995), p. 19.

25. Ibid., pp. 60–61.

26. Ibid., p. 93.

27. Ibid., p. 116.

28. Clifford Christians, "The Common Good in a Global Setting." Paper presented at the AEJMC annual convention, Washington, D.C., August, 1995, p. 2.

29. Charity, op. cit., p. 17.

30. Campbell, op. cit., p. 10A.

31. Jan Schaffer, "The Best or Worst?" *The Quill*, (May, 1997), p. 28.

32. Merritt, *Public Journalism & Public Life*, p. 19.

33. Jay Rosen, *Getting the Connections Right: Public Journalism and the Troubles in the Press* (New York: Twentieth Century Fund Press, 1996), p. 6.

34. Christians, op. cit., p. 2

35. Schaffer, op. cit., p. 26.

36. Jay Rosen, "What Should We Be Doing?" *The IRE Journal* (November-December, 1996), p. 6.

37. Rosen, op. cit., p. 7.

38. James Fallows, *Breaking the News* (New York: Vintage Books, 1996), pp. 248–249.

39. Merritt, *Public Journalism & Public Life*, p. 94.

40. Rosen, op. cit., p. 7.

41. Smith, op. cit., p. 5.

42. Merritt, *Public Journalism & Public Life*, p. 113.

43. Bill Theobold, "Listening to the Public: Ghettoizing the Job," *Civic Catalyst* (April, 1997), p. 9.

44. Jay Rosen, *Getting the Connections Right: Public Journalism and the Troubles in the Press* (New York: The Twentieth Century Fund Press, 1996), p. 6.

45. Howard Kurtz, *Media Circus: The Trouble with America's Newspapers* (New York: Times Books, 1993), pp. 6–7.

46. Stan Cloud, "Confessions of a Sinner," *Civic Catalyst* (April, 1996), p. 3.

47. Fallows, op. cit., p. 7.

48. Bill Felber, "Beware of Issue Myopia," *Civic Catalyst* (January, 1997), p. 4.

49. Jay Rosen, "What Should We Be Doing?" *The IRE Journal* (November-December, 1996), p. 6.

50. Cloud, op. cit., p. 3.

51. Charity, op. cit, p. 4.

52. Rosen, op. cit., p. 8.

53. *Civic Journalism: A Video Study Guide* (Washington, D.C.: Pew Center for Civic Journalism, 1995), pp. 2–3.

54. Rosen, op. cit., pp. 7–8.

55. Merrill, op. cit., p. 184

56. The Missouri Group, *News Reporting and Writing* (New York: St. Martin's Press, 1988), pp. 4–6.

57. Merrill, op. cit., p. 113.

58. Arthur Charity, *Doing Public Journalism* (New York: Guilford Press, 1995), p. 85.

59. "With the People," *Civic Catalyst* (April, 1997), p. 1.

60. Theobold, op. cit., p. 12.

61. The Missouri Group, op. cit., p. 14.

62. Rosen, op. cit., p. 6.

63. Don Corrigan, "Does Public Journalism Serve the Public or Publishers," *St. Louis Journalism Review* (July-August, 1995), p. 9.

64. Merritt, *Public Journalism & Public Life*, pp. 24–25.

65. Timothy Crouse, *Boys on the Bus* (New York: Ballantine, 1976).

66. Merritt, *Public Journalism & Public Life*, p. 113.

67. Staci Kramer, *Civic Journalism: Six Case Studies* (Washington, D.C.: Pew Center for Civic Journalism, 1995), pp. 38–47.

68. James Fallows, "The Puff Adders Nest of Modern Journalism," *Civic Catalyst* (July, 1996), p. 7.

69. Rosen, op. cit., p. 7.

70. James Fallows, *Breaking the News* (New York: Vintage Books, 1996), pp. 257–258.

71. Arthur Charity, *Doing Public Journalism* (New York: Guilford Press, 1995), A Teacher's Guide, p. 4.

72. Smith, op. cit., pp. 4–5.

73. Jay Rosen, "Public Journalism as a Democratic Art." Pamphlet adapted from a presentation at the American Press Institute, Reston, Virginia, November 11, 1994, p. 11.

74. Jay Rosen, "What Should We Be Doing?" *The IRE Journal* (November-December, 1996), p. 7.

75. Merritt, *Public Journalism & Public Life*, p. 117.

76. Rosen, op. cit., p. 8.

77. Merritt, *Public Journalism & Public Life*, p. 18.

78. Arthur Charity, *Doing Public Journalism* (New York: Guilford Press, 1995), p. 72.

79. Merritt, *Public Journalism & Public Life*, p. 95.

80. Merritt, *Public Journalism & Public Life*, pp. 42–43.

81. Merritt, *Public Journalism & Public Life*, pp. 93–95.

82. Merritt, *Public Journalism & Public Life*, p. 110.

83. James Carey, "The Press and the Public Discourse," *Kettering Review* (Winter, 1992), p. 11.

84. Fallows, op. cit., p. 246.

85. Edmund B. Lambeth, "The News Media and Democracy," *Media Studies Journal* (Fall, 1992), pp. 166–167.

86. Merritt, *Public Journalism & Public Life*, p. 47.

87. Merritt, *Public Journalism & Public Life*, p 70.

Bibliography

Aggrawala, Narinder K. "A Third World Perspective on the News." *Freedom at Issue Report*. May-June, 1978.

Altschull, J. H. *Agents of Power: The Media and Public Policy*. White Plains, New York: Longman, 1995.

Anderson, Rob. "The Conversation of Journalism: Communication, Community, and News." In *Mixed News: The Public/Civic/Communitarian Journalism Debate*, edited by Jay Black.

Austin, Lisa, Davis Merritt, and Jay Rosen. *Public Journalism Theory & Practice*. Dayton, Ohio: Kettering, 1997.

Bates, Stephen. *Realigning Journalism with Democracy: The Hutchins Commission, Its Times, and Ours*. Washington, D.C.: The Annenberg Washington Program in Communications Policy Studies of Northwestern University, 1995.

Bishop, Ed. "Doing Journalism to 'Public Journalism.'" *St. Louis Journalism Review*. March, 1997.

Black, Jay, ed. *Mixed News: The Public/Civic/Communitarian Journalism Debate*. Mahwah, New Jersey: Lawrence Erlbaum Associates, 1997.

Bloomquist, David, and Cliff Zukin. *Does Public Journalism Work? The "Campaign Central" Experience*. Washington, D.C.: Pew Center for Civic Journalism Report. May, 1997.

Braestrup, Peter. *Big Story*. New Haven: Yale University Press, 1983.

Browne, Pat, and Robert Browne. *Digging into Popular Culture: Theories and Methodology in Archeology, Anthropology and Other Fields*. Athens, Ohio: Bowling Green State University Press, 1991.

Burek, Deborah, and Martin Connors. *Organized Obsessions*. Detroit: Visible Ink Press, 1992.

Calder Pickett, Calder. *Voices of the Past*. New York: John Wiley & Sons, 1977.

Campbell, Cole. "The Challenge Is to Reclaim Our Moral Authority" from *News Breaks: Can Journalists Fix It?* Washington, D.C.: Pew Center, 1997.

Campbell, Cole. "Our Republic and Its Press." *St. Louis Post-Dispatch*. May 1, 1997.

Carey, James. "The Press and the Public Discourse." *Kettering Review*. Winter, 1992.

Carter, Hodding, III. "1997 Batten Symposium: News Breaks: Can Journalists Fix It." *Civic Catalyst*. Summer, 1997.

Charity, Arthur. *Doing Public Journalism*. New York: Guilford Press, 1995.

Charity, Arthur. *Doing Public Journalism, A Teacher's Guide*. New York: Guilford Press, 1995.

Charity, Arthur. "Reluctant Sea Change." *The Quill*. January/February, 1996.

Christians, Clifford G. "The Common Good in a Global Setting." Paper presented at the AEJMC Convention, Washington, D.C., August, 1995.

Christians, Clifford, Mark Fackler, and John Ferré. *Good News—Social Ethics & the Press*. New York: Oxford University Press, 1993.

Cloud, Stan. "Confessions of a Sinner." *Civic Catalyst*. April, 1996.

Cohen, Jeff, and Norman Solomon. *Adventures in Medialand*. Monroe, Maine: Common Courage Press, 1993.

Coates, K. S., and W. R. Morrison. "Toward a Methodology of Disasters: The Case of the Princess Sophia." From a collection of essays in the book, *Digging into Popular Culture*, by Ray Browne and Pat Browne. Bowling Green, Ohio: Bowling Green State University Press, 1991.

Coleman, Renita. "The Intellectual Antecedents of Public Journalism." Paper presented at a civic journalism interest group session at the AEJMC convention in Anaheim, California, August, 1996.

Corrigan, Don. "Campbell's Gamble: Will Fuzzy Concepts Lead to Sharper Journalism." *St. Louis Journalism Review*. June, 1998.

Corrigan, Don. "Does Public Journalism Serve the Public or Publishers." *St. Louis Journalism Review*. July-August, 1995.

Corrigan, Don. "Pay Scales on Newspapers Fail to Keep Pace." *St. Louis Journalism Review*. September, 1990.

Corrigan, Don. "Public Journalism Opponents and Advocates Not Easily Stereotyped." *St. Louis Journalism Review*. October, 1997.

Corrigan, Don. "Public Journalists Suffer Setback." *St. Louis Journalism Review*. September, 1997.

Corrigan, Don. "St. Louis Native Wins Pulitzer for Racial Study." *St. Louis Journalism Review*. May, 1994.

Crouse, Timothy. *Boys on the Bus*. New York: Ballantine, 1976.

Diamond, Edwin. "Civic Journalism: An Experiment that Didn't Work." *Columbia Journalism Review*. July-August, 1997.

Dinges, John. "Civic Journalism Comes to Buenos Aires." *Civic Catalyst*. July, 1996.

Dionne, E. J., Jr. *Why Americans Hate Politics*. New York: Touchstone, 1991.

Eby, Charlotte. "Gartner Blasts 'Civic Journalism.'" *Iowa Journalist*. Spring, 1997.

Ettema, James, and Limor Peer. "Good News from a Bad Neighborhood: Civic Journalism as a Vocabulary of Community Assets." Paper presented in Chicago at the annual conference of the International Communication Association (ICA), May, 1996.

Etzioni, Amitai. *The Spirit of Community: Rights, Responsibilities, and the Communitarian Agenda*. New York: Crown Publishers, 1993.

Fallows, James. *Breaking the News*. New York: Vintage Books, 1996.

Fallows, James. "The Puff Adders Nest of Modern Journalism." *Civic Catalyst*. July, 1996.

Felber, Bill. "Beware of Issue Myopia." *Civic Catalyst*. January, 1997.

Fishkin, James. *Democracy and Deliberation: New Directions for Democratic Reform.* New Haven, Connecticut: Yale University Press, 1991.

Gans, Herbert J. *Deciding What's News.* New York: Vintage Books, 1980.

Gartner, Michael. "Public Journalism: Seeing through the Gimmicks." *American Editor,* publication of ASNE. Summer, 1997.

Gates, Chris. "The Old vs. a New Model of Journalism, *Civic Catalyst.* Fall, 1997.

Gibbs, Cheryl. *Speaking of Public Journalism.* Dayton, Ohio: Kettering Foundation, 1997.

Grimes, Charlotte. "Whither the Civic Journalism Bandwagon." Position paper presented at S.I. Newhouse School of Communication. Syracuse, New York, 1997.

Hartig, Dennis. "Changing the Personality of Local News Pages." *Civic Catalyst.* Fall, 1997.

Harwood Group, The. *Citizens and Politics: A View from Main Street America.* Dayton, Ohio: Kettering Foundation, 1991.

Harwood Group, The. *Meaningful Chaos: How People Form Relationships with Public Concerns.* Dayton, Ohio: Kettering Foundation, 1991.

Harwood Group, The. *Tapping Civic Life.* Bethesda, Maryland: The Tides Center and The Harwood Group, 1996.

Hoyt, Mike. "Are You Now or Will You Ever Be, A Civic Journalist." *Columbia Journalism Review.* September/October, 1995.

Hume, Janice, et al. "Civic Journalism: The Practitioner's Perspective." Paper presented at the AEJMC Convention. Chicago, August, 1997.

Jamieson, Kathleen Hall. Campaign Mapping Project, a presentation at the International Communication Association (ICA) meeting. Montreal, May, 1997.

Jamieson, Kathleen Hall, and David Birdsell. *Presidential Debates.* New York: Oxford University Press, 1988.

Jennings, Max. "Today's Journalism: An Assessment." *Civic Catalyst.* Fall, 1997.

Jurkowitz, Mark. "From the Citizen Up." *MediaCritic.* Winter, 1996.

Killenberg, George. *Public Affairs Reporting.* New York: St. Martin's Press,1992.

Kramer, Staci. *Civic Journalism: Six Case Studies.* Washington, D.C.: Pew Center for Civic Journalism, 1995.

Kurtz, Howard. *Media Circus: The Trouble with America's Newspapers.* New York: Times Books, 1993.

Ladd, Everett C. *Silent Revolution: The Rebirth of American Civil Life and What It Means for All of Us.* New York: Free Press, 1999.

Lambeth, Ed. *Committed Journalism.* Bloomington, Indiana University Press, 1986.

Lambeth, Edmund B. "The News Media and Democracy." *Media Studies Journal.* Fall, 1992.

Lappé, Francis Moore, and Paul Martin DuBois. *The Quickening of America: Rebuilding Our Nation, Remaking Our Lives.* San Francisco: Josey-Bass, 1994.

Marshall, Alex. "Focusing on the Rotten Barrel." *The IRE Journal* (November-December 1996): pp. 9–10

Mathews, David. *Politics for People: Finding a Responsible Public Voice.* Urbana: University of Illinois Press, 1994.

Medsger, Betty. *Winds of Change: Challenges Confronting Journalism Education.* Arlington, Virginia: Freedom Forum Press, 1996.

Merrill, John. *Legacy of Wisdom.* Ames: Iowa State University, 1994.

Merritt, Davis. "The Misconceptions about Public Journalism." *Editor & Publisher.* July 1, 1995.

Merritt, Davis. "Missing the Point." *American Journalism Review.* July/August 1996.

Merritt, Davis. *Public Journalism & Public Life: Why Telling the News Isn't Enough*. Hilldale, New Jersey: Lawrence Erlbaum Associates, 1995 (Reprinted 1998).

Merritt, Davis, and Jay Rosen. *Imagining Public Journalism: An Editor and Scholar Reflect on the Birth of an Idea*. Bloomington, Indiana: Roy Howard Monograph, 1995.

Meyer, Philip. "Discourse Leading to Solutions." *The IRE Journal*. November-December, 1996.

Missouri Group, The. *News Reporting and Writing*. New York: St. Martin's Press, 1988.

Mudd, Roger. Plenary Session on Broadcast Journalism from remarks made at the annual AEJMC Convention. Washington, D.C., August 1989.

Munson, Eve, and Catherine Warren, ed. *James Carey: A Critical Reader*. Minneapolis: University of Minnesota Press, 1997.

Mustapha, Masmoudi. "The New World Information Order." Document No. 31 submitted to the MacBride Commission. Paris: UNESCO, 1978.

Neuman, W. Russell, Marion R. Just, and Ann N. Crigler, *Common Knowledge: News and the Construction of Political Meaning*. Chicago: University of Chicago Press, 1992.

Newby-Fiebich, Christine. "Issues and Agendas: The Case of Witchita, Kansas Revisited." Paper presented at the AEJMC Convention. Chicago, August, 1997.

Parisi, Peter. "Toward a 'Philosophy of Framing': News Narratives for Public Journalism." *Journalism & Mass Communication Quarterly*. Winter, 1997.

Peterson, Anne. "Peirce Report Offered No Unique Solutions." *St. Louis Journalism Review*. October, 1997.

Pew Center for Civic Journalism. *Civic Journalism: A Video Study Guide*. Washington, D.C., 1995.

Pickett, Calder. *Voices of the Past*. New York: John Wiley & Sons, 1972.

Porter, Cy. *Community Journalism Getting Started*. New York: Radio and Television News Directors Foundation, 1996.

Postman, Neil. *Amusing Ourselves to Death*. New York. Penguin Books, 1985.

Postman, Neil, and Steve Powers. *How to Watch TV News*. New York: Penguin Books, 1992.

Protess, David L., et al. *The Journalism of Outrage*. New York: Guilford Press, 1992.

Putnam, Robert. "Bowling Alone: America's Declining Social Capital." *Journal of Democracy*. January 1995.

Putnam, Robert. *Making Democracy Work: Civic Traditions in Modern Italy*. Princeton, New Jersey: Princeton University Press, 1993.

Remnick, David. "Scoop." *New Yorker*. January 29, 1996.

Rimel Rebecca. "Investing in Risk: Re-engaging the Public." *Civic Catalyst*. July, 1996.

Ritt, Glenn. "Public Journalism Can't Do It All." Pew Center for Civic Journalism Press Release. May 12, 1997.

Ritt, Glenn. "We Need to Do It or They'll Do It Themselves." *Civic Catalyst*. Summer, 1997.

Rosen, Jay. "Community Connectedness: Passwords for Public Journalism." St. Petersburg, Florida: Poynter Institute, 1993.

Rosen, Jay. *Getting the Connections Right: Public Journalism and the Troubles in the Press*. New York: Twentieth Century Fund, 1996.

Rosen, Jay. *Imagining Public Journalism*. Bloomington, Indiana: Indiana University Press, 1995.

Rosen, Jay. "Public Journalism as a Democratic Art." Pamphlet adapted from a presentation at the American Press Institute, Reston, Virginia. November 11, 1994.

Rosen, Jay. "What Should We Be Doing?" *The IRE Journal*. November-December, 1996.

Rosen, Jay, and Davis Merritt. "Imagining Public Journalism: An Editor and Scholar Reflect on the Birth of an Idea." Roy W. Howard Public Lecture. Indiana University, April, 1995.

Rosen, Jay, and Paul Taylor. *The New News vs. the Old News: The Press and Politics in the 1990s.* New York: Twentieth Century Fund, 1992.

Rosenblum, Mort. *Who Stole the News? Why We Can't Keep Up with What Happens in the World.* New York: John Wiley & Sons, 1993.

Ross, Shelley. *Fall from Grace: Sex, Scandal and Corruption in American Politics from 1702 to the Present.* New York: Ballantine Books, 1988.

Sandel, Michael. *Liberalism and the Limits of Justice.* New York: Cambridge University Press, 1982.

Schaffer, Jan. "The Best or Worst?" *The Quill,* May, 1997.

Schaffer, Jan, and Edward Miller. *Civic Journalism: Six Case Studies.* Washington, D.C.: Pew Center for Civic Journalism, 1995.

Shafer, Richard. "Structural Problems and Civic Journalism's Failure to Address External Factors of Community Underdevelopment." *Democratic Communique.* Spring, 1998.

Shepard, Alicia C. "The Change Agents." *American Journalism Review.* May, 1998.

Sherman, Scott. "The Public Defender." *Linguafranca.* April, 1998.

Smith, Steve. "Developing New Reflexes in Framing Stories." *Civic Catalyst.* April, 1997.

Smith, Steve. "Getting Down and Dirty with the Critics." *Civic Catalyst.* January, 1997.

Squires, James D. *Read All About It: The Corporate Takeover of America's Newspapers.* New York: Times Books, 1993.

Stamm, Keith R. *Newspaper Use and Community Ties.* Norwood, New Jersey: Ablex, 1985.

Steele, Robert M. *The Ethics of Civic Journalism: Independence as the Guide.* St. Petersburg, Florida: Poynter Institute Paper. June, 1995.

Stein, M.L. "The Culture of Timidity." *Editor & Publisher.* May, 1997.

Stein, M. L. "Revamping Journalism Education." *Editor & Publisher.* August 28, 1993.

Stone, Chuck. "Heroes and Inspirations: The Making of a Civic Journalist." Honors lecture given to the scholastic journalism division of the AEJMC convention, Chicago, 1997.

Storin, Matthew. "Civic Journalism: Part of the Solution." *Civic Catalyst.* July, 1996.

Strunk, William, Jr., and E. B. White. *The Elements of Style.* New York: The Macmillan Co., 1972.

Thames, Rick. "Covering Politics Civic Journalism Style." *Civic Catalyst.* October, 1995.

Theobold, Bill. "Listening to the Public: Ghettoizing the Job." *Civic Catalyst.* April, 1997.

Twitchell, James B. *Carnival Culture: The Trashing of Taste in America.* New York: Columbia University Press, 1992.

Weaver, David H., and Cleveland G. Wilhoit. *The American Journalist in the 1990s.* Mahwah, New Jersey: Lawrence Erlbaum Associates, 1996.

Wolfe, Allen. *One Nation, After All.* New York: Penguin, 1998.

Yankelovitch, Daniel. *Coming to Public Judgment: Making Democracy Work in a Complex World.* Syracuse: Syracuse University Press, 1991.

Index

About the Author

DON H. CORRIGAN is Professor of Journalism at Webster University in St. Louis and Editor-in-Chief of two weekly newspapers, *Webster-Kirkwood Times* and *South County Times*. He has reported from Washington, D.C., as a writer for investigative columnist Jack Anderson and he has reported for his newspaper group from Russia, Bosnia, Northern Ireland, and other countries. Corrigan has won numerous reporting awards from the Missouri Press Association and the Independent Free Papers of America, has published op-ed pieces in U.S. dailies from coast to coast, and has served on the editorial board of the *St. Louis Journalism Review* for almost two decades.

ISBN 0-275-95781-0

90000>

EAN

9 780275 957810

HARDCOVER BAR CODE